PREPARED CLASSROOM

Ready to Teach, Ready to Learn

Gail Boushey and Allison Behne

Routledge
Taylor & Francis Group
NEW YORK AND LONDON

A Stenhouse Book

Designed cover image: Madeline Boushey Mosbacher

First published 2025
by Routledge
605 Third Avenue, New York, NY 10158

and by Routledge
4 Park Square, Milton Park, Abingdon, Oxon, OX14 4RN

Routledge is an imprint of the Taylor & Francis Group, an informa business

© 2025 Gail Boushey and Allison Behne

The right of Gail Boushey and Allison Behne to be identified as authors of this work has been asserted in accordance with sections 77 and 78 of the Copyright, Designs and Patents Act 1988.

All rights reserved. The purchase of this copyright material confers the right on the purchasing institution to photocopy pages which bear the copyright line at the bottom of the page. No other parts of this book may be reprinted or reproduced or utilised in any form or by any electronic, mechanical, or other means, now known or hereafter invented, including photocopying and recording, or in any information storage or retrieval system, without permission in writing from the publishers.

Trademark notice: Product or corporate names may be trademarks or registered trademarks, and are used only for identification and explanation without intent to infringe.

Credits:
Lesson layout and colors designed by Gina Poirier

ISBN: 9781625314451 (pbk)
ISBN: 9781032682846 (ebk)

DOI: 10.4324/9781032682846

Typeset in ITC Clearface Std and Avenir LT Std
by KnowledgeWorks Global Ltd.

This book is dedicated to all the incredible teachers who navigate the ups and downs of this amazing profession with grit and grace. You tirelessly do what's best for your students, and we see you. We hope this resource helps you build self-regulated learners, so you can keep shining and focus your energy on helping them succeed. Here's to making a difference every single day!

CONTENTS

Where do I even begin? *ix*
Ready... *xi*
Set... *xiii*
GO!!! *xv*

SECTION 1

Welcome! *1*

RELATIONSHIPS	5
ENVIRONMENT	25
DAILY ROUTINES	39
INDEPENDENT LEARNING	51
COLLABORATIVE LEARNING	63
CONFERRING	77
BRIEF AND EFFECTIVE LESSONS	93
PROGRESS MONITORING & ACCOUNTABILITY	103

SECTION 2

LESSONS—How This Will Work *114*

2.1 RELATIONSHIPS *117*

- **R.1** Name Pronunciation *119*
- **R.2** Positive Affirmation *121*
- **R.3** Teach Read-Aloud Behaviors *123*
- **R.4** Turn, Listen, and Talk *125*
- **R.5** Me Too! *127*
- **R.6** Morning Message *129*
- **R.7** True, True, False *131*
- **R.8** Would You Rather? *132*
- **R.9** Exit Slips *135*
- **R.10** I PICK Book Talk *138*
- **R.11** I Wish My Teacher Knew *140*
- **R.12** Planning Template *141*

2.2 ENVIRONMENT 143

- **E.1** Respectful Communication 145
- **E.2** Stress Management 150
- **E.3** S.P.A.C.E. 152
- **E.4** Flexible Seating 155
- **E.5** Gathering Area 156
- **E.6** Word Collector 159
- **E.7** Classroom Tour 161
- **E.8** Introduce What's on the Walls 162
- **E.9** Intro to CAFE Menu 164
- **E.10** Planning Template 165

2.3 DAILY ROUTINES 167

- **DR.1** Quiet Signal 169
- **DR.2** Brain Breaks 171
- **DR.3** Morning Routines 174
- **DR.4** Line Up 176
- **DR.5** Walk in the Hall 178
- **DR.6** Ending the Day 181
- **DR.7** Transitions 184
- **DR.8** Book Shopping 187
- **DR.9** Sharing 189
- **DR.10** Planning Template 190

2.4 INDEPENDENT LEARNING 191

- **IL.1** Ways to Engage with Text 193
- **IL.2** Reading Materials 195
- **IL.3** What's Independent? 197
- **IL.4** I PICK 198
- **IL.5** What's Engagement? 199
- **IL.6** 10 Steps to Independent Learning 201
- **IL.7** Underline and Move On (Um …) 204
- **IL.8** Setting Up a Writing Notebook 206
- **IL.9** What to Write About 208
- **IL.10** Planning Template 209

2.5 COLLABORATIVE LEARNING 211

- **CL.1** Choosing a Partner 213
- **CL.2** Voice Level 215
- **CL.3** Take Turns 217
- **CL.4** Check for Understanding 218
- **CL.5** Think: What's My Purpose? 219
- **CL.6** What To Do When Finished 221
- **CL.7** Planning Template 223

2.6 CONFERRING 225

- **C.1** Engagement Conference 227
- **C.2** Informative Quick Check 229
- **C.3** Planning Template 230

2.7 BRIEF AND EFFECTIVE LESSONS 231

- **BL.1** Brain Break Review 233
- **BL.2** Hook 234
- **BL.3** Active Listening 235
- **BL.4** Planning Template 237

2.8 PROGRESS MONITORING & ACCOUNTABILITY 239

- **PM.1** Goal Setting 241
- **PM.2** Self-Assessment Skills 244
- **PM.3** Understanding Feedback 248
- **PM.4** Planning Template 250

So Now What? *251*

Acknowledgements 256

References 257

Index 263

Where do I even begin?

Have you ever started a new job feeling overwhelmed by unwritten rules, unclear expectations, and a seemingly endless to-do list? If you're a new teacher or teaching a new grade level or in a new building, you're likely nodding your head right now. Unlike many workplaces that offer comprehensive onboarding programs, the transition into a new classroom can feel like diving headfirst into a pool of unknowns.

This book is your life raft.

While there might be an official orientation for your school district, the reality is, setting up a successful classroom goes far beyond a one-day introduction. This book delves into the nitty-gritty of what it truly means to navigate your new professional environment. We'll explore everything from the physical layout of your room to the intricate web of relationships you'll build with students, to the explicit instruction you provide students to communicate expectations.

Forget the sinking feeling of "where do I even begin?" This book equips you with the knowledge and strategies to not only survive the year but to thrive in it. We'll tackle the often-unsaid expectations, from daily routines like lining up and putting materials away to the complexities of lesson planning and assessment. You'll gain insights into evidence-based practices for instruction, relationships, conferring, and more.

Divided into two sections, this book offers a comprehensive guide for both educators and students.

Section 1

This section is all about the teacher. It provides teachers with practical strategies to maximize student engagement. Learn how to create a classroom environment that fosters learning and establishes routines that ensure a smooth and productive year.

Section 2

This section is all about students. It equips the teacher with actionable lessons using the principles of *Prepared Classroom* explored in Section 1 and is designed to communicate expectations and establish routines within the classroom and school. By explicitly teaching these lessons and providing ample practice time, you'll empower your students to acclimate and thrive in their new learning environment.

Consider this book your complete handbook for building a successful and fulfilling school year. Using the practices and lessons in this book, you'll feel confident and have a solid plan to get students ready, and excited to learn. With the practices and lessons in *Prepared Classroom*, students are not just taught productive learning behaviors—these behaviors are woven into their daily learning. Behavior becomes an integrated part of the learning process, not a separate concept.

So, grab a cup of coffee, take a deep breath, and let's dive in!

READY...

Not too long ago, Allison's daughter, Samantha, decided to major in Elementary Education and become a teacher. As she progressed through the program, she shared her learning and experiences with us and we responded with encouragement, questions, and support. She had many opportunities to work in various classrooms with children and would reflect on those moments with us, reminding us of our early days in the classroom. We have many memories from these conversations with Samantha, but one specifically etched a space in both of our minds and, truthfully, became the impetus for this book.

One day during Samantha's last semester before student teaching she shared with us that she felt prepared to teach lessons and work with students; however, she still didn't feel like she was totally ready. She wanted to know how to get kids to know the routines of lining up and walking in the hall and going to the bathroom and all of the day-to-day things they would be doing. She said she asked one of her professors this question and the reply she received was, "Oh! Great question! When you are in the classroom, you will figure out what works for you."

The realization that these fundamental practices lacked explicit guidance in her curriculum surprised Samantha. She wondered aloud, "Is it true? Do teachers really just figure it out as they go? The thought of a room full of eager children on the first day, unaware of what to do, feels daunting." We listened intently, understanding her apprehension, yet also knowing that our experience with Daily 5 (Boushey & Moser, 2014) and CAFE (Boushey & Behne, 2020) had equipped us to offer guidance, and not just the language arts components of Daily 5 and CAFE, but the routines and management and relationship components.

We shared with Samantha the essence of Daily Routines—the cornerstone of classroom management. It's about setting high expectations, maintaining consistency, establishing clear routines, and being explicit with instructions. We emphasized the importance of knowing our expectations, leaving no room for assumptions, and actively teaching and modeling the behaviors we desire from our students. By eliminating guesswork, we create an environment where students can focus on learning and growth.

Samantha is far from alone in her desire to be "ready" for her students. All teachers, new or experienced, want a plan in place so they are ready to teach, and their students are ready to learn.

SET...

Every year, teachers and students come to school with their own unique sets of expectations shaped by their backgrounds. Students bring norms from their cultures, family dynamics, and living conditions, whereas teachers' practices are influenced by all of these and their education, professional experiences, and personal histories. These differences can create a disconnect in the classroom, making it hard for students to adjust and learn effectively. Schools often expect kids to adapt quickly with minimal guidance, which leads to jumping into the curriculum without properly building a classroom community or helping students get comfortable in their new environment.

To improve, schools need a system that blends behavior and learning, respects students' diverse backgrounds, and helps them understand and adapt to school norms. A supportive school environment that values and builds on students' strengths is key to helping them succeed academically and thrive overall.

Imagine a classroom where both teachers and students are perfectly in sync, ready to dive into a day of learning. This is the power of being prepared. The phrase "get set" means to "prepare," and it's the key to creating a dynamic environment where teaching and learning flourish. That's why we've titled this book *Prepared Classroom*. Our mission is simple: to help you create a classroom that's always ready to inspire, engage, and achieve.

This book isn't meant to be read from cover to cover and then passed along to a colleague. While we'd love for you to share it, we think you'll want to hang on to your copy—even write in it, adding your own thoughts and ideas! Use this as your trusted "go-to guide"—something you keep close by, especially at the start of the year, and then revisit whenever you need it. (We made sure the cover is beautiful and calm, like a morning sunrise, so you feel joy when you see it. Clever, huh?) You now have a set of lessons you can refer to every year, so you're not standing in your classroom a few days before school starts wondering, "Where do I begin?"

Here's how we suggest you get ready to use this book:

1. Flip through Section 1. It's organized into eight components of effective, evidence-based teaching, explaining why each is important and offering easy-to-implement practices.

2. Read the core memory section and jot down any memories or thoughts that come to mind (we've even included space for you to write them down!).

3. Highlight any teacher practices you'd like to try.

4. Browse through the lessons in Section 2 and the various resources—make copies of anything you want to use.

And that's it! We know your schedule is full, so we've done the heavy lifting to ensure your plans are ready, letting you focus your energy on your students and your teaching.

GO!!!

If you have made it this far, chances are you are with the majority of teachers who are looking for a way to establish routines and create consistency so that you are able to teach and students are able to learn. We know there is no easy way to do this, and at the same time, there is a way—it takes a little bit of time and patience, but the result is totally worth it.

This isn't a book for passive reading—it's all about active learning. Think of it like those conferences where the presenters actually make you get up and participate. And yeah, we get it, sometimes that makes you groan. But here's the deal—you can't have a prepared classroom without taking action. If you just read this book and note down ideas without implementing them, nothing will change. So, let's get started!

1. If you skipped the previous page (Set …), go back and read it to get prepared.

2. Look at your schedule and decide when you'll teach these lessons. We know this part can be stressful—finding time for "one more thing" in a packed schedule seems impossible. But remember the saying, "If you always do what you've always done, you'll always get what you've always got." You're here because you want to create a classroom of engaged, ready-to-learn students. This requires explicit instruction and effort. Use these lessons at the start of the year to establish norms, throughout the year to review behaviors, and whenever you need to enhance your teaching. They're not meant to be "one more thing" but rather an integral part of your daily teaching and learning process.

3. Make this book your own! Write in the margins, highlight the lessons you want to revisit, and add your own ideas (we've even included blank lesson plans at the end of each section for you). The goal is to have a book that's not just read, but actively used.

4. Got questions or ideas? Reach out! Shoot us an email at GailandAllison@teachdaily.com. We're all ears and excited to collaborate with you. Education is always evolving and staying ahead means staying connected. We're here to support you, and the best way for us to do that is by hearing your thoughts and ideas!

Okay, enough of the "how to." It is time for you to become familiar with the content in this book and get ready to teach, so your students will be ready to learn. Yes, it's that simple.

Section 1

Welcome!

We're thrilled to have you join us on this journey.

Before we dive in let's take a moment to preview what's coming up. The following pages include a roadmap for Section 1.

Each of the eight evidence-based practices we'll explore has its own dedicated section easily identified by its unique color.

Let's get started!

This is where you will find important information about each of the 8 components of Prepared Classroom introduced across Section 1.

WHY? — This section will explain the purpose and reason for the teacher practices and lessons covered in that specific component.

IT'S UNDENIABLE — This book is a resource you will use throughout the year and this section highlights the core reasons for each component included. Here you will find key points that are "undeniable."

A CORE MEMORY — It is easier to relate when there is context and story to go with a concept. Here we will share a core memory specific to that section's central practice. We hope you find them relatable, heartwarming, funny, and even inspiring. We also hope they trigger your own core memories in each area.

TEACHER PRACTICES: What you can do — So often we read professional books that share the *why* and then leave us wondering *how*. In this section we get you started with practical ideas to use right away. Read through them, make notes, look at the additional resources that support the ideas shared, and then go teach!

Evidence-Based Practices to Support

The evidence-based practices that make up Prepared Classroom align with John Hattie's Visible Learning research (Hattie, 2023). The question Hattie built his research around was "Which variables have the greatest impact on student achievement?" He has studied this question for the past 25 years, looking at over 108,000 studies, and 300 million students. **WOW!** He has identified more than 320 factors that influence student achievement and calculated an effect size for each.

The practices listed in this box have an effect size that represent substantial growth. ▶

RECOMMENDED READING — This book is an "easy-to-use" resource that helps to optimize your conditions for teaching and your students' conditions for learning. We focused the energy on the *how*, so rather than fill the pages of each section with an extensive literature review, we instead provide recommended reading to further your learning in this section.

FROM THE FIELD — Teaching is a collaborative profession, and there is so much we can learn from each other! Here you will find some key ideas, advice, and learning shared from other teachers and authors. There are some great ideas included in this section, so you'll want to keep a highlighter handy to make note of things you wish to try!

CHECK-IN: How are you doing? — It is great to learn new things, and sometimes it can seem like a lot. How will you know you are successful with what you are trying to accomplish? This section shares an idea or two for how to "self-assess" how your implementation is going. If you feel successful, great! If you aren't quite there, don't be hard on yourself – go back through the teacher practices and lessons and see what you might try next.

| Impact Statement | This brief statement summarizes the impact the focus component has on teaching and learning to encourage an urgency for integrating what you have learned into your teaching practice. |

LESSONS INCLUDED IN SECTION 2

Here we provide a list of the lessons (specific to the chapter component) that you will find in Section 2 of this book. We know you have a full plate, and so to make it as easy-to-use as possible, we include lessons to help you implement the practices shared in this book. These lessons are meant to bolster your confidence and save you planning time. But they're just a beginning. Understanding that no lesson will fit everyone's needs, we encourage you to adopt them as they are or adapt them and make them your own.

Okay, that's it! Now you know how to read section 1 of this book, so it's time to dive in! Grab a pencil and a highlighter and get ready to make notes as this book becomes your go-to-guide for increasing engagement and helping students be self-regulated learners.

P.S. - We think it sometimes helps to grab a few pieces of chocolate, too. We find it helps us to concentrate. ☺

RELATIONSHIPS

1.1 Relationships

WHY?

As humans we learn best from people we like and respect, who see us, and make us feel like we belong. Enhanced relationships contribute to students' academic success, emotional well-being, and overall development. When relationships are a priority in the classroom, it creates a positive learning environment where students are able to take risks and accept challenges because they feel safe to do so.

IT'S UNDENIABLE

The importance of positive relationships has been proven in every setting in life: family, work, sports, community, and school. A strong, positive relationship with students is crucial to an effective learning environment (Ed Trust and MDRC, 2023). When students feel supported with positive interactions with teachers, they are more likely to engage in learning and have fewer behavioral problems.

Evidence-Based Practices to Support Relationships

- Belonging
- Enjoyment
- Happiness
- Strong class cohesion
- Teacher student relationships

These factors have an effect size that represent substantial growth (Hattie, 2023).

> *Neuroscience helps us understand that the brain releases dopamine during these positive interactions. The student feels good and is motivated to feel that again. This creates a cycle. With this increased motivation students spend more time and attention working on a skill. The teacher gives more praise, sparking the release of more dopamine and the cycle starts all over again.*
>
> —Berger & Strasser, 2015, 4

Meaningful learning requires respect and trust between the teacher and students. Theodore Roosevelt once said, "people don't care how much you know until they know how much you care," and that certainly applies when we talk about the student-teacher relationship. When we build relationships, learning follows. All students are capable and worthy of instruction that meets their needs. Taking time to build trust and demonstrate respect is the foundation upon which all other elements of learning are built (Roehlkepartain et al., 2017).

As academic and professional demands increase relationships can sometimes, unintentionally, take a backseat. However, because relationships are one of the most important factors associated with effective instruction and student success, they must be a priority all year long (Li, Bergin, & Olsen, 2022).

Regardless of the grade level, building effective relationships in the classroom starts even before you receive your class list. It starts with identifying and developing the five fundamental characteristics that are the foundation of all positive relationships:

Kindness. We are intentional and exercise genuine kindness through our words, body language, and feedback. Being compassionate, smiling, listening, and offering assistance when needed all communicate that we care. When students know we care, they open their minds to what we have to say (Jones & Bouffard, 2012).

Honesty. Students know they can count on us to say what we mean. Being upfront and clear removes the guesswork for students and lets them focus their energy on the expectations at hand (Cornelius-White, 2007).

Dependability. Students know we are going to do what we say when we say we will do it. Reliability builds trust and communicates respect (Hafen, Hamre, & Pianta, 2012).

Acceptance. We communicate the belief that all students are capable and worthy. One way we do this is by providing opportunities for all students to develop their skills as independent learners. Being open to ideas and accepting of student differences increases comfort for risk-taking and builds community (Rimm-Kaufman & Hulleman, 2015).

Perspective. When we practice empathy and put ourselves in our students' shoes, we better understand them as individuals. This perspective informs our conversations, lessons, and day-to-day interactions by making them more meaningful (Eisenberg, Spinrad, & Knafo-Noam, 2015).

Reflect

> *Think of a teacher in your life who was kind, honest, dependable, accepting, and empathic. What kind of relationship did you have with this teacher? What was the classroom environment like? How well did you perform academically in that class?*

Likely you're thinking, yes, this is who I am, I believe these and live these practices. To that we say, wonderful, and include high-impact strategies and activities in the upcoming Teacher Practices section to support and enhance your ongoing work in building relationships with your students.

A CORE MEMORY FROM GAIL

During a class discussion when I was in high school, I jumped up and sat on a table. Moments later the legs of the table broke and crashed to the floor, with me toppling down with it. In shock, eyes wide, I saw my teacher, Mrs. Bartelson, come running. In that split second, I thought … *I am in big trouble, I broke the table. Why was I sitting on the table? Wasn't that a rule—Don't sit on tables?* Mrs. Bartelson reached her hand down to mine and said, "Oh Gail, are you ok?" I nodded and waited for the lecture to start. She said, "I am so sorry that happened to you, accidents happen and that totally was an accident."

What? She didn't yell and she wasn't angry. She was empathetic and understanding. My life changed that day. So much so it's now a core memory. Until that moment, any "accident" I experienced was first looked at as "Whose fault was it?" It was on that day that I learned a new definition for the word "accident," that it truly was something you didn't mean to do, but just happened. And, I experienced something profound, an emotional safety net. Mrs. Bartelson was there for me, she saved me from embarrassment and offered me safety, understanding, and love.

Do you have an example from your life to prove that a relationship grounded in safety, understanding, and love makes a difference?

This Makes Me Think Of

TEACHER PRACTICES: What you can do

Beginning of the Year

BE CONFIDENT

You may spend more time with your students this year than they will spend with their families. Building trust with your students and their families is paramount for creating a positive supportive learning environment. One way to do that is by exuding confidence and we give you permission to do that!

Here is how: every time you see a caregiver, say hello, smile, call them by name, ask them how they are, and say something positive that you noticed about their child. These small, mighty acts will build trust and connection with caregivers and ultimately, they will feel more confident in your ability to be their child's teacher.

SEND A WELCOME NOTE AND/OR PICTURE

If you are lucky enough to know who your students are a few days before the first day of school, consider sending a postcard or letter welcoming them to school. This can be as simple as a photo of you waving, with a smile, that simply says, WELCOME! SEE YOU SOON! with the date and time of the first day of school, and signing it with, Your Teacher. A wave and a smile are universal, making this inclusive to all families regardless of the language spoken in the home. And think how special this will be when your student gets mail addressed to them from their teacher. It just might become a permanent fixture on their refrigerator. (See page 16.)

SCHOOL WELCOME

Having a designated time to meet students and their families before school starts allows them to become familiar with their school home. This time is as much for the caregivers and you, as it is for the students. Those who attend become familiar with their school and classroom environment, and get to know you, their teacher. This especially helps with those who are new to the school or those who are nervous about the first day. You may also wish to invite students to bring their supplies and while they are there have them select books from the classroom library to fill their book box. There are many great ideas to make this time a success!

The checklist located on page 17 includes some helpful suggestions, and there are two we highlight with importance:

1. Take a photo of the child and those who attend with them. Post these photos around your room. Add names to help you learn and remember each family.

2. Obtain a way to communicate with your students' caregivers. A sign-up sheet for email and phone number is a great idea. You may also wish to ask if they are okay to receive text messages.

LEARN THEIR NAMES

Learn every student's name by the end of the first day and help students learn classmates' names by the end of the first week. And that's not all! Make it a goal to also learn every caregiver's name by the end of the first few weeks. How?

- For you, it begins before school starts by building class lists, adding caregivers' names to the list, making name tags, and then throughout the first day using those lists to help you put the name to the face. Practice saying their names with each interaction. And make sure you are saying their names correctly. (See Lesson R.1 in Section 2 on page 119.)

- To help students learn the names of their classmates, play name games and encourage students to address each other by their names.

- Caregivers' names may take a bit more time, ask students to help you, call on students and say student names and their caregivers' names. Take pictures and post the pictures throughout the room with student and caregivers' names, this provides a constant reminder and a way to check yourself so you can reach that goal.

ALL ABOUT ME

This is a fun way to get to know your students. Learn their birthday, age, their favorites, what they like to do, and more! You may send this to students before school, give it to them at a school welcome event, or have them fill it out the first few days. (See the All About Me template on page 19.)

We suggest posting completed forms around the classroom so students can learn about each other, and even keeping this information in your conferring notebook (see below) so that the information is readily available when needed.

MAKE A PHONE CALL

Take the time to call students before school starts. This takes extra time and patience but almost always proves to be worth it. It not only helps build relationships with students, but it helps build relationships with parents, too. Chat briefly with the child and if you wish, ask them to bring a favorite book from home they want to share in the first week of school.

If students' home language is different than yours, you may find it helpful to use a video conference platform with the translation caption feature, a translation app, or enlist the help of a community translator.

During the Year

SHARE THEIR SMILE

A teacher's demeanor, including the act of smiling, can significantly impact the learning environment and student engagement throughout the school year. It can make students from all backgrounds feel more comfortable and accepted. Authenticity is key. Genuine smiles are more effective in creating a positive classroom environment than forced ones. And, while the teacher's smile is important, so are the students'! Get the whole class involved! Take a close-up photo of each child's smile and yours too, and post them in the classroom!

SHOWCASE STUDENT WORK

When designing your room at the beginning of the year, leave a lot of open space for student work to be posted after they arrive. The classroom belongs to students, and therefore their work should be showcased. Help to make their effort noticed and special. While some pieces such as a self-portrait or family picture may remain all year, others will be taken down and replaced frequently to highlight work throughout the year.

The goal is to build community, show respect, and honor all students as valuable members of the learning community.

SHOWER THEM WITH KINDNESS

Write a note and leave it on a desk, send it in the mail, place it in their book box, or email their families. These notes don't have to be expansive or artistic, just a quick reminder that the students are special. A few sincere words can be more impactful than anything elaborate. (See Way to Go template page 22.)

TALK AND CONNECT

Engage students in conversation about their life interests. What did they do the night or weekend before? Do they have siblings, pets, or favorite hobbies? What can you learn and discuss that is unique to them? Show genuine interest through eye contact, body language, and thoughtful responses. Write these snippets of information down in your conferring notebook throughout the year. (See Get to Know You Conferring Form on page 20.)

INVITATION TO LUNCH

Gather a small group of three to five students and have lunch together. Engage everyone in sharing, listening, and learning about each other. Students enjoy it and so will you! Set yourself a goal to have lunch with every student a few times throughout the year. (See invitation on page 21.)

BE RELATABLE—BRING YOUR EXPERIENCES INTO CLASS

Let students get to know you. Through modeled writing, morning messages, conversations, and instructional examples, share your experiences and life with students. The more students feel they know you, the more comfortable they feel to share about themselves. When you share about your weekend or evening or family or pets or interests, they realize you are human and that maybe you don't actually eat, live, and breathe school!! And even if they still think you live there, being relatable can only enhance relationships and learning.

GIVE THEM AN OPPORTUNITY TO SHINE

Tap into their strengths, talents, and interests to set them up for success. For example, do you have a student who has beautiful handwriting? Ask them to write something for you that goes on display. Have a student who knows a lot about dinosaurs? Ask for their help or expertise when you study that unit in science or read a book on that subject. You will learn so much about students through the All About Me activity (page 19) and you can use this to spotlight them. There are so many ways to build confidence and community through words of encouragement and an opportunity to shine.

BE AVAILABLE—OPEN YOUR DOOR

Before, during, and after school, let students know you are there for them and your door is open. Provide various ways for them to reach out to you (through notes, conversation, or whatever is needed). Being accessible builds trust and rapport.

CONFER: A CONVERSATION

Take time as often as possible to confer with students. Whether it's a brief conference about student engagement, an informative quick check about their understanding of current learning, or a goal-oriented conference to provide instruction and practice toward a learning goal, individual conferences promote reflection, enhance communication, clarify expectations, and provide a place for individualized support. For curricular coherence and accountability, keep track of student learning and next steps in a conferring notebook. (See Get to Know You Conferring Form, page 20.)

MEET STUDENTS AT THE DOOR

Set a positive tone each day by meeting your students at the door with a warm hello and a friendly smile. Greeting learners at the door is a personal and immediate way to acknowledge each student individually and helps to establish a connection between the teacher and their students from the moment they enter the classroom. This also helps to promote a sense of routine and structure, which can be reassuring for students. It's a meaningful gesture that can have a lasting impact on building a positive classroom culture and fostering strong student-teacher relationships.

This is such a great start to any day, why not end the day the same? Stand at the door and wish them well or tell them something you enjoyed or learned from them that day. Talk about building relationships and showing students how much you care and can't wait to see them tomorrow. (See page 24.)

RECOMMENDED READING

Classroom Management Matters: The Social-Emotional Learning Approach Children Deserve by Gianna Cassetta and Brook Sawyer (2015).

Classroom 180: A Framework for Creating, Sustaining, and Assessing the Trauma-Informed Classroom by Heather Forbes (2020).

Good to Great Teaching: Focusing on the Literacy Work that Matters by Mary Howard (2012).

Heart!: Fully Forming Your Professional Life as a Teacher and Leader by Timothy Kanold (2017).

Kids These Days: A Game Plan for (Re)connecting with Those We Teach, Lead, & Love by Jody Carrington (2019).

The Art of Gathering: How We Meet and Why It Matters by Priya Parker (2018).

The Invisible Classroom: Relationships, Neuroscience & Mindfulness in School by Kirke Olson (2014).

What Great Teachers Do Differently: Nineteen Things that Matter Most by Todd Whitaker (2020).

FROM THE FIELD

Have amnesia. Students are human and therefore they are not perfect. Just like us! They will make mistakes, just like we do. And, we know it is no fun to have someone constantly remind you of your mistakes or lose faith in you because of a poor choice or bad moment in time. So instead of having that moment replay in your mind when you interact with that student, have amnesia. Forget about it and believe in the fact that they can and will do better next time.

—Brittany Daniel, North Carolina

Culture first, learning second, leads to higher achievement.

—Dr. John Hattie, Professor and Educational Researcher, (Jan. 30, 2024)

....

Relationship is about knowing students well, building trust, and listening to and responding to their needs. It must include learning about the individual realities that students bring into the classroom with them. Understand the cultural differences among students and you and what it means when building a positive classroom culture. As questions, be open to change, and don't assume that your way is the right way. Know your students. Talk to them about what they need and adjust accordingly. Most importantly, create the conditions you need to be responsive to all students.

—Berger & Strasser, 2015, 2

....

Give them the benefit of the doubt. Students want to do good. They do not enter school with the desire to get in trouble or to have a bad day. So, regardless of how yesterday went, give them the benefit of the doubt today. In fact, regardless of how the last 15 minutes went, take a breath and give them the benefit of the doubt in the next 15 minutes. And, if something happens where they don't follow expectations, don't assume it was purposeful. Sometimes it can seem they don't care and often this attitude is a way to deflect their emotions from what has happened. Treat each student as you would want to be treated, or you would want someone to treat your child, and give them the benefit of the doubt.

—Jessica Hellberg, Iowa

CHECK-IN: How are you doing?

Can you list five details about each of your students? By details we don't mean hair color or reading level, we are talking about pieces of information or interests they have outside of school. Qualities you can only learn about a person you've spent time with. Take time to list your students and five things you know about them. You can learn a lot through the practices listed above. Don't have five yet? Set a goal and get back to work!

Impact Statement

The teacher-student relationship is a crucial factor in the teaching and learning process. Positive relationships can foster a supportive and conducive learning environment, enhance motivation and engagement, and contribute to students' overall well-being and academic success. Building and nurturing these relationships is essential for effective teaching and learning.

RELATIONSHIP BUILDING

Lessons Included in Section 2

There are many activities and lessons you can do to not only get to know your students at the beginning of the year, but to continue to build and grow relationships throughout the year. The lessons in Section 2 provide a springboard of ideas. Use them as they are or adjust to fit the group of students in front of you. Remember to use these throughout the year. Relationships evolve and as we nourish them, they only grow stronger. As always, we encourage you to add more of your own lessons to this list using the blank template located on page 141.

- R.1   Name Pronunciation
- R.2   Positive Affirmation
- R.3   Teach Read-Aloud Behaviors
- R.4   Turn, Listen, and Talk
- R.5   Me Too!
- R.6   Morning Message
- R.7   True, True, False
- R.8   Would You Rather
- R.9   Exit Slips
- R.10   I PICK Book Talk
- R.11   I Wish My Teacher Knew
- R.12   Planning Template

 # Hello

HELLO!

Dear _____,
I am so excited you are in my class this year!
We are going to learn so much and have a lot of fun!
Enjoy your last few days of summer break.
I can't wait to see you!

♥ Your Teacher,

HELLO!

Dear _____,
I am so excited you are in my class this year!
We are going to learn so much and have a lot of fun!
Enjoy your last few days of summer break. I can't wait to see you!

♥ Your Teacher,

School Welcome Checklist

Welcome to your classroom! I'm so glad you're here! Please use this checklist to guide you through the room. You can complete them in any order.

- [ ] Say hello to your teacher! I am so excited to meet you!
- [ ] Find your name in different places around the room.
- [ ] Have your caregiver provide their phone and email on the sign-up sheet
- [ ] Find your book box. Select five books from the classroom library for your book box.
- [ ] Put any supplies you brought in their designated spots (There are signs around the room.)
- [ ] If you see other students in here, introduce yourself! They might be your new classmate.
- [ ] Write your favorite song on our class playlist chart. I will use these to make a playlist for our class.
- [ ] Walk around the school to find the gym, music room, lunch room, library and playground.

If you have any questions, be sure to ask me!

Phone & Email Sign-up

STUDENT NAME	CAREGIVER NAME	PHONE NUMBER	EMAIL	CIRCLE PREFERRED COMMUNICATION METHOD
				Phone Email
				Phone Email
				Phone Email
				Phone Email
				Phone Email
				Phone Email
				Phone Email
				Phone Email

All About Me!

ALL ABOUT ME!

NAME: _____

AGE: _____ **BIRTHDAY:** _____

MY FAVORITES:

FOOD: _____
COLOR: _____
MOVIE: _____
SONG: _____
ANIMAL: _____
SUBJECT: _____
BOOK: _____

ONE THING I WANT OTHERS TO KNOW ABOUT ME IS . . .

WHEN I GROW UP I WANT TO BE . . .

MY FAVORITE THING TO DO IS . . .

Get to Know You Conferring Form

Student Name

Siblings–How Many? Names and ages?

Pets

Who lives in their home

Favorite things to do when not in school

What they like about school

What they like about home

Other information

You're Invited

Join me for lunch in our classroom on

_____

I can't wait to enjoy lunch with you and a few other friends from our class!

♥ Love,

Join me for lunch in our classroom on

_____

I can't wait to enjoy lunch with you and a few other friends from our class!

♥ Love,

Way to Go

I noticed you . . .

Conference Notes

NAME	
STRENGTHS	
GOAL & STRATEGY	

📅	TOUCH POINT	OBSERVATIONS & INSTRUCTIONS	NEXT STEPS

Ways to Say Hello

ENVIRONMENT

1.2 Environment

WHY?

A positive and supportive environment sets the stage for meaningful learning experiences. Students are more likely to be engaged, motivated, and attentive in a classroom that is welcoming and supportive. A supportive and inclusive environment helps students feel valued, accepted, and encouraged to express themselves and take risks.

IT'S UNDENIABLE

All aspects of the classroom environment come together to create a supportive learning space that meets the needs of all students (Evanshen & Faulk, 2019). When considering the environment of a classroom, it's essential to think about more than just the physical layout. Environment is the physical, visual, and emotional space in which teaching and learning happens (Smith, Johnson, & Thompson, 2023).

Evidence-Based Practices to Support Environment

- Belonging
- Self-regulation strategies
- Happiness
- Strong class cohesion
- Teacher-student relationships
- Concept mapping

These factors have an effect size that represent substantial growth (Hattie, 2023).

The physical space of a classroom plays a fundamental role in shaping the overall learning environment. A well-designed physical space is essential for improving the flow of activities, ensuring comfort, and promoting effective communication (Brown, Jones, & Smith, 2023). Flexible seating arrangements, well-defined learning spaces, and sufficient space for movement contribute to a classroom that is conducive to learning. The organization of desks, the placement of teaching aids, and the accessibility of learning resources all influence the dynamics of the learning space. Additionally, a thoughtfully arranged physical environment accommodates diverse learning styles and needs, creating an inclusive atmosphere where every student can engage with the curriculum in a meaningful way (van den Berg, Segers, & Cillessen, 2016).

Visual space in a classroom is equally important, as it contributes to the creation of an engaging and stimulating learning environment. Visual elements such as displays, charts, and content menus serve as tools to reinforce key concepts, provide visual cues, and offer reference points for students. These visual aids not only support learning but also contribute to a visually appealing atmosphere that inspires curiosity and creativity (Johnson, Smith, & Williams, 2022). Visual space is also an avenue for showcasing student work, celebrating achievements, and promoting a sense of pride and accomplishment. By carefully curating visual elements, educators can enhance the aesthetic appeal of the classroom, making it a welcoming and vibrant space for both teaching and learning (O'Donnell Wicklund Pigozzi and Peterson Inc, VS Furniture, & Bruce Mau Design, 2010). The emotional space within a classroom is a crucial aspect that strongly influences the overall well-being and success of students. Emotional space refers to the climate of the classroom, including the relationships between students and teachers, as well as the emotional tone set by the learning environment (Lester & Cross, 2015). A positive emotional space is characterized by trust, respect, and a sense of belonging. Teachers play a pivotal role in creating this atmosphere by encouraging a supportive and inclusive classroom culture. Emotional space is also impacted by the consideration given to students' social and emotional needs. By recognizing and validating the diverse emotions of students, educators contribute to an environment where emotional well-being is prioritized, allowing students to thrive academically and personally (Smith et al., 2019).

The physical, visual, and emotional aspects of the classroom are interconnected components that collectively shape an effective learning environment.

> **Reflect**
>
> *Consider your classroom environment in the three areas mentioned above–physical, visual, and emotional. What works well? What areas have room for improvement. Write down three ideas from the teacher practices section, or from your further reading that you can work to improve this year.*

A CORE MEMORY FROM ALLISON

When I think back to my elementary school classrooms, I recall desks neatly aligned in rows, the teacher's desk prominently positioned at the front, a dedicated table for reading groups tucked away in one corner, a chalkboard showing signs of use, and shelves at the back filled with a mix of games and books. Despite occasional premade posters and a classroom job bulletin board, the overall ambiance felt stark and somewhat cold, lacking in vibrant colors or cozy elements. One distinct memory from my first-grade classroom was a large wooden chair with a green vinyl seat, known among my peers and me as "the green chair," reserved for students whose behavior was less than desirable. I can still hear the teacher say, "Go sit in the chair until you can follow directions."

Reflecting on those early classroom environments, I realize that while they didn't cause any lasting harm, they were devoid of the warmth and creativity that could have enhanced the learning experience. It's interesting to imagine how different it might have felt if there had been colorful rugs, a cozy library nook with cushions, and more flexible seating options instead of the imposing "green chair." These elements could have transformed the atmosphere, making it more inviting and conducive to learning and collaboration.

What do you remember from your elementary days? Think about the walls, seating, available materials, and overall emotional feel of the classrooms you were a student in. You may find that your memories mirror mine, or maybe they are completely the opposite. Regardless, we can learn a lot from reflecting on our experiences. As you reflect on the learning environments you were a part of, what would you keep the same, and what would you do differently?

This Makes Me Think Of

TEACHER PRACTICES:
What you can do

Physical Space

LIGHTING

We must be deliberate in the lighting of our classroom and prioritize student comfort. Fluorescent lights are common, but they can blink, buzz, and affect students' circadian rhythms. Look to increase natural lighting if you can. Where possible, reduce or eliminate fluorescent lighting by using fluorescent light covers, bringing in outside lighting sources that are code approved (table lamps, task lights, or floor lamps), or even being selective in how many overhead lights we turn on.

SOUND

The acoustics in a room make a difference in a learner's ability to focus and absorb what's being said. A carpeted room can eliminate echo and minimize noise. When it isn't possible to have a carpeted room, we add rugs and other textures to absorb the sound and keep noise to a minimum. When students are working independently, it can help to have light instrumental music playing in the background.

SCENT

Ideally, our learning space will have a clean or neutral smell. When it's occupied by 25–30 bodies, we sometimes have to do a little work to neutralize the scent. We are aware that essential oils, diffusers, and room sprays can trigger allergies in some people, so we don't overcompensate with artificial smells. The goal is to be aware of and reduce any strong smell that could negatively affect the learning environment. Sometimes this can be done by opening a window or turning on a fan; other times it may take a deep cleaning or a light room deodorizer.

TEMPERATURE

Being too hot or too cold can make a person miserable and distracts from learning. Work to establish a comfortable temperature that is consistent year-round so students know what to expect and can dress accordingly. (And let's be real … we would all love to have an air conditioner and heater that work!)

GATHERING SPACE

A gathering place is an open space large enough for the whole class to gather while sitting on the floor. It often includes a chart rack and whiteboard, class-created anchor charts, an interactive smart board, and other teaching materials. Sitting in a group provides students with an opportunity to turn, listen, and talk, enhancing engagement and giving each student an opportunity to express their thinking. In addition, being able to move from their independent workspace to the gathering place provides a needed brain and body break. The gathering space may be identified by a rug or sit spots or simply an open area in which children come together.

CALMING CORNER

A calming corner in a classroom is a designated area that provides students with a quiet and peaceful space to regulate their emotions, self-soothe, and manage stress or anxiety. It's designed with sensory experiences and relaxation tools that help students calm down and refocus when they are feeling overwhelmed or dysregulated. A calming corner typically includes items such as soft cushions or beanbags, calming music or nature sounds, sensory tools like stress balls or fidget toys, and visual aids such as calming posters or breathing exercises. When creating this area remember the purpose, to empower students to navigate moments of being overwhelmed or emotional dysregulation and find strategies to help them return to learning.

CLASSROOM LIBRARY

A well-stocked classroom library provides students with easy access to a variety of books, building a love for reading and promoting literacy development. It creates an inviting space where students can explore different genres, cultures, and perspectives, enhancing their understanding of the world. A well-curated classroom library supports differentiated instruction by offering materials that cater to diverse reading abilities and interests, helping every student find books that resonate with them. By encouraging independent reading, the classroom library also helps build critical thinking skills, vocabulary, and overall academic achievement. If you're looking for ideas to build a classroom library, see page 38.

FLEXIBLE SEATING

Comfort plays a role in being able to stay focused and engaged. With a few shifts in our thinking, we can provide a variety of places and positions in which students can work so they discover several options where they can be successful. Possible options include sitting on the floor, sitting up against a wall, standing at a table, using an exercise ball chair, folding chairs, saucer chair, bucket seats, cushions, padded crates, wobble cushions, towels, and more. By providing students with choices on where to sit, we can transform our classroom into a space that fosters student agency, comfort and, ultimately, academic success.

Visual Space

WALLS

The design of classroom walls impacts the visual accessibility of information. Clear, well-organized displays and visual aids that are intentionally designed become a visual reminder of key learning all students can access. Displays include anchor charts that visually represent key concepts, interactive displays like pocket charts, and student work showcasing achievement and inspiring ongoing learning. When adding displays to your classroom, ask yourself: does this display reflect students' diverse cultures and add value by helping them process information and engage in learning?

STUDENT WORK

Showcasing student work in the classroom is a powerful strategy to foster a positive, motivating, and inclusive learning environment. You may create a designated space for students to display their own self-selected work they wish to share, or you may have a space where you change out all class work routinely. Displaying student work helps to build confidence, celebrate achievements, engage learners, and provide the recognition they appreciate.

MAKE LEARNING VISIBLE

Displaying learning concepts in an organized way with concept mapping helps with memory retention, active learning, and learning transfer. Learning becomes visible in the classroom environment through use of anchor charts, sound walls, word collectors, and content menus such as CAFE (page 35).

Emotional Space

RELATIONSHIP

The teacher-student relationship contributes to a supportive atmosphere where students feel comfortable seeking help, sharing their ideas, and expressing their thoughts. Similarly, positive peer relationships enhance collaboration, teamwork, and the overall social dynamics of the classroom. Strong relationships within the classroom not only enrich the academic experience but also contribute to the social and emotional well-being of students, creating a holistic and conducive learning environment.

CHOICE

Student choice empowers learners, fosters autonomy, and enhances engagement. When students make choices about their learning experiences, they become active participants in their education. This autonomy instills a sense of ownership and responsibility, leading to increased motivation and a deeper connection to the learning process. Student choice can be provided in topic selection, seating options, goal setting, peer collaboration, authentic application, book picks, and more. The key is to provide limited options that align with their educational goals.

STRESS LEVELS

Reducing stress levels in the classroom creates a more relaxed and supportive atmosphere, allowing students to feel emotionally safe and comfortable. This positive emotional space promotes a sense of well-being, reduces anxiety, and encourages students to engage more effectively in learning activities. By prioritizing stress reduction strategies, educators can cultivate a conducive environment for emotional growth, resilience, and positive interactions among students. (See page 36.)

BODY LANGUAGE

Body language is a form of nonverbal communication that helps us understand others. It includes gestures, facial expressions, and posture. When interacting with others, it's important to be aware of our body language as well as those we are engaging with, as it provides valuable insights into emotions and intentions. By paying attention to body language cues and improving our own nonverbal communication skills, we create a more positive classroom atmosphere.

TONE OF VOICE/LANGUAGE WE USE

A warm, supportive tone, and positive word choice create a welcoming and inclusive environment that encourages student participation, fosters trust, and promotes a sense of belonging. Conversely, a harsh or negative tone, along with insensitive word choices, can create tension, erode trust, and hinder effective communication within the classroom. (See page 37.)

RECOMMENDED READING

Choice Words: How Our Language Affects Children's Learning by Peter Johnston (2024).

Classroom Design for Student Agency by Lynsey Burkins and Franki Sibberson (2023).

Room to Learn: Elementary Classrooms Designed for Interactive Explorations by Pam Evanshen and Janet Faulk (2019).

The Third Teacher: 79 Ways You Can Use Design to Transform Teaching & Learning by O'Donnell Wicklund Pigozzi and Peterson Architects Inc, VS Furniture, & Bruce Mau Design (2010).

Through a Child's Eyes: How Classroom Design Inspires Learning and Wonder by Sandra Duncan, Jody Martin, & Sally Haughey (2018).

FROM THE FIELD

The moment I step in your classroom I know what your beliefs are in teaching and learning. Does your classroom environment reflect your beliefs?

—Margaret Mooney, New Zealand

A well-organized classroom can make all the difference for some students in their ability to function. A classroom that has a strong sense of order can be powerful enough to help students feel a sense of calm. It truly is possible that this may be enough to be considered a trauma-informed classroom. Indeed, an external environment of order and strength has the power to override a student's internal environment of chaos and confusion.

— Heather T. Forbes, *LCSW, Classroom 180,* 2020, 66

The physical space we live in impacts our emotional well-being and overall comfort.... In fact, our immediate environment influences how well we learn, feel part of a community, take risks and thrive—or not. While there are so many factors in our lives we have little or no control, we can take steps—even small ones—to organize and enhance our workplace and living spaces in a manner that improves the quality of our lives. Being flexible and open to such change is not easy, but it is possible.

— Regie Routman, *The Heart Centered Teacher,* 2024, 92

CHECK-IN:
How are you doing?

Physical Assessment:

- Are your seating arrangements flexible and adaptable to different learning needs and activities?
- Is your classroom well-lit, with natural light, if possible, to create a conducive learning environment?
- Are there comfortable seating options, ergonomic furniture, and appropriate temperature controls to support student comfort and engagement?

Visual Assessment:

- Are the walls visually stimulating, representative of the children in your class, and educational, with relevant displays and student work?
- Look around your classroom and visually assess the functionality of the layout. Are there clear pathways, accessible materials, and designated areas for different activities that make it favorable to learning?
- Are there visual distractions or clutter that could be minimized to create a more focused environment?

Emotional Assessment:

- Do students feel safe, respected, and valued in the classroom environment?
- Are there opportunities for positive social interactions, collaborative learning, and peer support?
- Do students have a voice and opportunities for choice and autonomy in their learning experiences?

Additionally, you can gather feedback from students through surveys, class discussions, or one-on-one conversations to gain insights into their perceptions of the classroom environment. Ask students about what they like and dislike about their classroom setup, what improvements they would suggest, and how they feel when they walk in the room. Their input can provide valuable perspectives and ideas for enhancing the visual, physical, and emotional aspects of the classroom environment.

Impact Statement

A purposeful learning environment is essential in schools. It has the power to shape and transform students' academic, social, and emotional development. It enhances engagement, increases motivation, fosters relationships, and has a lasting positive impact.

ENVIRONMENT

Lessons Included in Section 2

There are many activities and lessons you can do to grow and maintain a purposeful learning environment throughout the year. The lessons provided in Section 2 provide a springboard of ideas. Use them as they are or adjust them to fit the group of students in front of you. We must continually nurture the environment in which we teach and students learn, therefore we use (and revisit) these lessons as needed during the year. As always, we encourage you to add more of your own lessons to this list using the blank template located on page 165.

    E.1   Respectful Communication

    E.2   Stress Management

    E.3   S.P.A.C.E.

    E.4   Flexible Seating

    E.5   Gathering Area

    E.6   Word Collector

    E.7   Classroom Tour

    E.8   Introduce What's on the Walls

    E.9   Intro to CAFE Menu

    E.10 Planning Template

 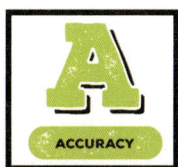  

I understand what I read	I can read the words	I can read accurately, with expression, and at a rate that matches the text	I know, find, and use interesting words

Stress Reduction

Stress can adversely affect the ability to make decisions, solve problems, and set goals. It impairs students' and teachers' abilities to process information accurately and clearly, and it compromises the memory system. Consider the following strategies to create an environment that is safe and nurturing so the brain can relax, let go of any stress, and turn its attention to teaching and learning.

STRATEGY	CONSIDER
Deepen positive relationships	The brain feels safest and relaxed when we are connected to others we trust who will treat us well. Make building positive relationships in the classroom and workplace a priority. Revisit to the relationship section and review ways to deepen positive relationships with all your students.
Create a sense of safety and reduce stress	Visually display a daily schedule that includes specific events and times. Review the schedule as a morning ritual.
Minimize worry	Use visual aids such as anchor charts, "to do" lists, schedules, and directions so students know what is needed to do to be successful. These aids provide support and guidance, so students are able to focus on their learning.
Use calm signals when getting student attention	Consider using a wind chime, a meditation chime, or some type of pleasing sound that is calming when signaling attention. Loud clapping can startle students and may cause more stress. Students will respond to non-verbal cues and signals as well, like your hand raised, your finger over your lips as if you were saying "shhhh," or starting each transition by whispering the word "class."
Release stress	Build in breaks, that are simple actions that you can return too. You may stand and stretch, take deep breaths, sing a song, go for a walk around the playground, play a lively song and/or have a dance party.
Reduce cognitive load	Keep lesson length to less than ten minutes by chunking the information into fewer items being taught, resulting in fewer items to remember per lesson.
Increase focus and regulation	Play music during work time and then gradually add it throughout the day. Our relationship with music is personal, the best way to figure out what works for your students is to simply try things out. Pay attention to how students behave in the presence of different music. And talk with your students about why music is on and ask them to help choose the music that helps them the most.
Keep students regulated	Dr. Jody Carrington (2019) stated in her book, *Kids These Days*, you cannot chew and swallow when your lid is flipped or when you are unregulated. In times of stress, taking a drink of water can help a person stay regulated. Keep hydrated and have students grab that water bottle, and you grab yours as well.
Provide sensory focus that promotes a sense of calm and well-being	Provide a "Calming Box" of tools containing sensory items. Take time to teach students what tools are in the box, how to use them and when to access them along with how to put them back. Tools may include noise reducing head phones, a stuffed animal, pillow, weighted blanket, putty, fidget, small action figure, small bag of Legos, or I Spy books.
Use tools	Drawing or doodling can help some students shift attention away from anxious thoughts. Teach students when and how to doodle or draw during class, and why it can be a strategy to use for focus and calm. And most important, by recognizing the potential benefits of this strategy, you create a supportive atmosphere that encourages artistic expression as a means of promoting focus and well-being.

The Tone We Use

Our tone of voice plays a vital role in conveying meaning and impacts the way students interpret our words. How we speak affects the overall classroom atmosphere.

Here are 5 examples of how our tone of voice influences the perception of the messages in the classroom.

WHAT MIGHT BE SAID	WHEN THE TONE IS SUPPORTIVE, COLLABORATIVE AND ENGAGING . . .	WHEN THE TONE IS FRUSTRATED, DISMISSIVE, INDIGNANT . . .
"Let's finish the work"	may indicate a desire to assist the student in completing their task, emphasizing cooperation and understanding.	may imply impatience or irritation, potentially discouraging the student and hindering their progress.
"Attention please"	captures the student's interest, encouraging active listening and involvement in the lesson.	may evoke a sense of strictness and demand compliance, potentially creating a tense and oppressive classroom environment.
"Let's try that again"	conveys encouragement, emphasizing the importance of resilience and growth in the face of challenges.	may undermine the student's confidence, implying their efforts were insufficient and may discourage them from further attempts.
"Please help each other"	invites students to actively participate, fostering a sense of teamwork and shared responsibility.	may imply insincerity, or a lack of genuine care and support.
"I can't believe you did that"	expresses excitement for what the student completed.	expresses anger or frustration and implies that the person's actions were unacceptable.

Building a Classroom Library

Book Drive:
A school book drive is a fantastic way to gather books and expand classroom libraries, providing students with a broader range of reading materials. By donating new and gently used books, the community can help create enriching literary environments that foster a love for reading.

Book Orders:
Many school trade-book publishers offer bonus points based on classroom order quantities. When your students place orders, be sure to investigate how to use the points to get more books. If your classroom order is small, team up with other teachers, and split the bonus points with participating colleagues.

Bookroom:
If your school has sets of books or guided reading packs that are not being used, divvy up the books to be distributed to individual classrooms. Explore some of the science and/or social studies kits that may no longer be in use. Sometimes, they include sets of books that can be broken apart and distributed to classrooms. You may also look for single copies of magazines that can be added to your classroom library.

Flea Markets/Garage Sales/Moving Sales:
Be on the lookout for children's books during these types of sales. Enlist your relatives' help so that they can look in their neighborhoods, too. Let your family and friends know that you are always appreciative of children's books or magazines that they might otherwise discard.

In Honor Of:
Often families, volunteers, and staff members want to remember special events such as an addition to the family, a birthday, a graduation, or a retirement by donating a book. You can discuss this option during a school literacy night. Display bookplates that would-be donors can place in the book to identify the honoree.

Internet Resources:
Donors Choose is a free service where teachers can post a classroom need that they would like to have funded. Interested donors can contribute to funding the request for books and/or other classroom materials.

Library Book Sales:
Check out your public library website, and put the date of the next library used-book sale on your calendar. There are bound to be several inexpensive books, both fiction and nonfiction, that you can add to your classroom library collection.

Newsletter/Class Website Reminders:
As you keep families informed about their children's learning via your class newsletter and/or website, include a "Coming Soon" section that describes upcoming themes and topics. Ask if they have any related books or magazines that they could donate to help students build background knowledge on future topics.

School Book Fair:
Explore hosting a school book fair. Book vendors often offer specials or buy-one/get-one-free book deals that can be used to expand your classroom library.

Thrift Stores:
Shop at local thrift shops for additions to your classroom library. Let the manager know that you are a teacher, and ask to be informed if any larger-scale donations of children's books come into the store.

Wish List:
Post lists of books or genres that you would like to have for your class in your newsletter, on your classroom door, or on your class website. Generous parents, volunteers, or visitors might be able to supply a few.

DAILY ROUTINES

1.3 Daily Routines

WHY?

Teaching daily routines to students is important because it helps establish structure, consistency, and predictability in their day-to-day activities, which can reduce anxiety, improve time management skills, and promote a sense of security and well-being. By learning and practicing routines, students develop valuable organizational habits that support their academic success and overall development.

IT'S UNDENIABLE

Establishing daily routines in the classroom plays a crucial role in supporting students' academic and socioemotional development. Research consistently highlights the positive impact of structured routines on student outcomes, including improved behavior, increased engagement, and enhanced learning experiences (Argyropulo-Palmer, 2022).

> **Evidence-Based Practices to Support Daily Routines**
> - Explicit teaching strategies
> - Self-regulation strategies
> - Direct instruction
> - Success criteria
> - Concept mapping
>
> *These factors have an effect size that represent substantial growth (Hattie, 2023).*

Daily routines provide students with a sense of predictability and consistency, which can significantly reduce anxiety and stress levels. According to a study by Durlak and colleagues (2010), routines create a stable and secure environment that helps students feel safe and confident, leading to better emotional regulation and overall well-being. When students know what to expect each day, they are better equipped to manage transitions between activities, stay focused on tasks, and adapt to changes more effectively.

In addition, research conducted by Jones and Jones (2017) emphasized the significant impact of daily routines on classroom management and student engagement. Well-established routines create a structured environment that helps teachers manage transitions between activities, minimize disruptions, and optimize instructional time. This structured approach not only reduces behavior issues but also fosters a positive classroom atmosphere conducive to learning. Students benefit from the predictability and consistency of routines, leading to increased engagement, participation, and focus on learning tasks.

A study by Robinson and Patall (2013) highlighted the positive correlation between daily routines and academic performance. Consistent routines support students in developing organizational skills, time management strategies, and self-regulation abilities. These essential skills contribute to improved academic outcomes by enhancing students' ability to stay on task, complete assignments efficiently, and manage their learning effectively. Routines create a supportive learning environment that promotes student success, academic achievement, and overall well-being.

Consistent routines establish clear expectations and boundaries, reducing disruptions and conflicts among students. Research by Rimm-Kaufman and Pianta (2000) emphasized the importance of routines in promoting positive behavior and classroom management. This structured environment fosters a sense of responsibility and accountability, encouraging students to take ownership of their actions and participate actively in classroom activities. Routines support the development of self-regulation skills, such as time management and organization, which are essential for academic success (Cambourne, 2020).

Daily routines contribute to improved learning outcomes by optimizing instructional time and facilitating smoother transitions between lessons. According to a meta-analysis by Wang, Haertel, and Walberg (1990), well-established routines help teachers maximize instructional efficiency and minimize disruptions, leading to increased time-on-task and enhanced learning engagement. This structured approach allows teachers to focus on delivering high-quality instruction and providing meaningful learning experiences, ultimately benefiting student achievement and academic progress. Research by Lerner et al. (2019) underscores the importance of daily routines in the classroom as a key factor in promoting students' emotional well-being, positive behavior, and academic success.

By creating a structured and predictable environment, routines support students' development of essential skills, foster a sense of security and responsibility, and optimize learning opportunities for improved educational outcomes (Crouch & Cambourne, 2020).

Reflect ▶ *Take a moment to consider. What daily routines are your students involved in regularly? How were the expectations regarding these routines conveyed to them? Compile a list of daily routines that would be advantageous for your class to adopt and practice.*

A CORE MEMORY FROM GAIL AND ALLISON

Throughout our numerous discussions about school, we've noticed clear contrasts in our encounters with students, staff, school administrators, curriculum, and school standards. Despite these variations, we've also discovered numerous commonalities, one of which we believe resonates with all educators, regardless of years of experience or geographical location. What common thread do you believe unites all of us as teachers across diverse backgrounds and experiences?

If you said student behavior challenges, or some form of that answer, you are correct. As we shared our experiences we found that we had both spent an exorbitant amount of time managing student behavior. We sent letters home, had class marble jars, worked to have the class earn letters that would spell words in exchange for a class party, tried tickets for prizes, and more. And when this didn't work, we switched to something like the "flip a card" behavior system, because of course if rewards didn't work, consequences had to (or so we thought). In fact, we are confident you are thinking of some to add to this list right now, maybe even some that you are currently using, that we would quickly say, "Oh yes! We remember that, too!"

You know what else we remember? We remember being exhausted and broke. Exhaustion hit from trying something, having it work for a few weeks, and then having to regroup to try something new. It was a constant creative balancing act. Instead of using our energy for designing dynamic lessons, we were using it to get kids to behave. Not to mention the monetary expense of some of these practices—food and prizes and more food and more prizes. Do you find yourself nodding in agreement? Most of us do.

So, if rewards or consequences aren't the answer, what is? It might seem all too simple, and truly you may almost laugh at what we have found to work, but after time and exhaustion and expense caused us to almost turn from the profession we loved, we went back to the basics. We know that kids want to do well. No matter how much we think this may happen, our students don't wake up in the morning and think, "How can I upset my teacher and get in trouble today?" So, if that isn't their goal, then why do some of them behave the way they do?

Here is what we know. Regardless of class size, all our students come from different families and different backgrounds and of course, live with different sets of norms and expectations. We can't expect these children to all come together on the first day of school and know what is expected. It just doesn't work like that ... so we teach them. We explicitly explain every behavior we wish to see. We model the behavior, and then we give students a chance to practice and reflect and set a goal. We do this a lot at the beginning of the year, and then we continue to sprinkle it throughout the year as needed. If we notice a behavior that isn't productive, we teach replacement behaviors we want to see, so that everyone has a chance to be successful.

Teaching desired behaviors was the cornerstone of the Daily 5 Literacy Structure, and when the result was increased engagement and productivity, we knew we could spread that outcome throughout our day. And we did. We used the 10 Steps located on page 49 to teach almost everything! And that is where this section on Daily Routines was born. We took the lessons that became a natural part of our teaching over time and wrote them down, because when we have them written as a plan, they become a concrete plan we use not by chance, but on purpose. Use these lessons as is or adjust to meet your needs and expectations. Then, add more lessons as needed. There are days it may seem redundant, but that is what consistency looks like. And when students learn routines and become successful and consistent in their behaviors, they no longer spend their time trying to figure out what to do, and instead spend their time engaged in learning.

This Makes Me Think Of

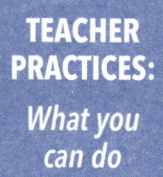

TEACHER PRACTICES: *What you can do*

What Routines to Teach

Consider the overall goals and objectives of your classroom. It's essential to prioritize routines that promote a positive learning environment, support student well-being, enhance academic engagement, and facilitate effective classroom management. Consider routines such as entering the room, lining up, walking in the hall, recess and lunchroom behaviors, end-of-day routines, transition time, turn and talk, being an active listener, sitting in the gathering area, going to the library, and more. Additionally, you may involve students in the process by seeking their input and feedback on routines that would benefit them the most.

Routines to Consider Teaching

Getting Explicit

Clearly communicate the expectations regarding behavior, academic tasks, and classroom procedures. This includes providing specific instructions, modeling expected behaviors, and using visual aids or written guidelines to reinforce understanding. Additionally, use verbal reminders and consistent feedback to help students internalize and meet these expectations consistently. It's important to never assume, and to teach every little detail. Think: What are their hands, eyes, and mouth doing? What does it sound like? What does it feel like? Communicate this to students.

State in Positive, not Negative

When stating expectations in the positive, focus on describing the desired behavior or outcome rather than what you don't want to see. For example, instead of saying "Don't interrupt when others are speaking," state the expectation positively as "Wait for your turn to speak and listen attentively when others are sharing." This approach helps students understand the desired behavior more clearly and encourages them to actively engage in meeting those expectations.

Make Learning Visible

Making learning visible when teaching expectations helps to provide concrete examples and models for students to follow. By demonstrating expected behaviors and showcasing successful examples, abstract concepts are made more tangible and understandable for students. Additionally, this helps create a shared understanding of expectations among students, leading to greater consistency and attention to classroom norms. Learning daily routines can be made visible through modeling, pictures, and practice.

10 Steps to Teaching and Learning Independence

These are the steps we use to teach students how to be independent at just about anything. Originating with The Daily 5 Literacy Framework, the 10 Steps for Teaching and Learning Independence has expanded to math, science, social studies, and even with daily routines such as learning to walk down the hall. Simply follow the steps for whatever you'd like students to do independently. (See Page 49.)

Classroom Routines That Really Work for Pre-K and Kindergarten by Jill Norris (2006).

Routines for Reasoning: Fostering the Mathematical Practices in All Students by Grace Kelemanik, Amy Lucenta, and Susan Janssen Creighton (2016).

The Daily 5: Fostering Literacy Independence in the Elementary Grades by Gail Boushey and Joan Moser (2014).

The First Days of School: How to Be an Effective Teacher by Harry K. Wong and Rosemary T. Wong (2009).

The First Six Weeks of School by Paula Denton and Roxann Kriete (2000).

The Morning Meeting Book by Roxann Kriete and Carol Davis (2014).

FROM THE FIELD

I have students start their day with a 'To Do List' to help them focus and feel successful. They complete tasks like handing in work, sharpening pencils, and organizing their bins. This routine gives them a sense of accomplishment and independence. The list also helps students who need more structure stay on track. Everyone feels prepared for the day's learning after completing their list and enjoying some quiet reading time in their first moments of the school day.

—Sara Benes, Wisconsin

Greet each child every morning! Welcome them with a smile, a high five, a handshake, or positive words about something you notice about them. Be happy and enthusiastic and USE THEIR NAME when you greet them! For example, in a cheerful voice say, "Good morning, Mary! I like your new shoes. We are going to have a great day today!" Research shows student scores go up just from the simple act of a greeting with a name. It shows the students you see them and they are important to you. It can also set the tone for the day as well as the added bonus of giving you the opportunity for a quick check in with each student.

—Julie Halborg, Illinois

Daily routines are vital to the success of your classroom management. In the beginning of the year, it may seem like your expectations for these routines are daunting but stick with it! Don't give up! Use the 21/90 rule: It takes 21 days to create a habit and 90 days to create a lifestyle. The modeling of these daily routines is imperative! Students must see and practice the routine to be able to meet the expectations. Your students will learn these routines and feel so much success when they are able to independently complete them. Bonus Tip: I have also found that if a daily routine needs a little amendment, it helps to frame it as a collaborative decision. Student input fosters ownership and a positive learning environment.

—Jessica Latta, New York

Start your year strong by explicitly teaching routines with anchor charts. Model them clearly, then practice, practice, practice! Just like 'practice makes perfect,' consistent practice helps routines become second nature. For example, need to teach students what restroom breaks look like during independent learning? Teach students to sign out, leave a pass, and quietly return. This frees you to help other students and gives them bathroom freedom without interrupting the flow.

—Sherie Hammonds, Arkansas

Some of the best activities I have incorporated when introducing independent and collaborative learning are with music and art! Here's how:

1. *Draw it Out: Create colorful scenes depicting both independent activities (like reading quietly) and collaborative activities (like working with a partner). Let the students watch you draw to build excitement!*

Prepared Classroom

2. Sing It!: Compose rhymes or short songs for the expectations of each type of learning (e.g., for Independent Learning the expectations are Work the whole time, Work quietly, Stay in one spot, Get started Right Away, Persevere, and Ignore Distractions. Sing each of these behaviors to the tune of "Frère Jacques" or a catchy tune for easy memorization.) The students love it!

3. Act It Out!: Have students dramatize good and not-so-good scenarios for both independent and collaborative learning while singing the expectations. This reinforces the expectations in a fun way.

—Michelle Jenkins, Michigan

CHECK-IN: *How are you doing?*

1. **Reflect:** Take time to reflect on your teaching practices related to daily routines. Ask yourself questions such as:
   - Are the routines clearly communicated and consistently reinforced?
   - Are students following the routines effectively and independently?
   - Are there any challenges or areas for improvement in how the routines are taught or implemented?
   - Are the routines contributing to a positive and productive classroom environment?

2. **Observation:** Observe how students are engaging with the daily routines. Look for signs of understanding, independence, and attention to the routines. Take note of any areas where students may need additional support, practice, or clarification.

3. **Review and Adjust:** Based on your and your students' self-reflection and observations, make adjustments and improvements to your teaching of daily routines as needed. Continuously monitor and evaluate the effectiveness of the routines to ensure they are meeting the intended goals and benefiting students' learning experiences.

Impact Statement

Teaching daily routines fosters student independence, organization, and time management skills, leading to a structured and conducive learning environment that promotes academic engagement and success. Daily routines support students in developing self-regulation abilities and maintaining consistency in their learning habits, contributing to improved focus, productivity, and overall academic achievement.

DAILY ROUTINE
Lessons Included in Section 2

There are many activities and lessons you can do to communicate daily routines and expectations to students. The lessons provided in Section 2 include a springboard of ideas. Use them as they are or adjust to fit the group of students in front of you. Remember to return to these throughout the year as needed, continually revisiting expectations to create a learning environment that produces independent and capable learners. As always, we encourage you to add more of your own lessons to this list using the blank template located on page 190.

DR.1   Quiet Signal

DR.2   Brain Breaks

DR.3   Morning Routine

DR.4   Line Up

DR.5   Walk in the Hall

DR.6   Ending the Day

DR.7   Transitions

DR.8   Book Shopping

DR.9   Sharing

DR.10 Planning Template

10 STEPS
to Teaching and Learning Independence

1 Identify what is to be taught

2 Set a purpose: Create a sense of urgency

3 Record desired behaviors on I-chart

4 Model most-desirable behaviors

5 Model least-desirable behaviors, then desirable *(same student)*

6 Students check in; teacher places students around the room

7 Practice and build stamina

8 Stay out of the way; when necessary, confer and set behavior goals

9 Use a quiet signal—come back to group

10 Group check-in—"How did it go?" Graph stamina

INDEPENDENT LEARNING

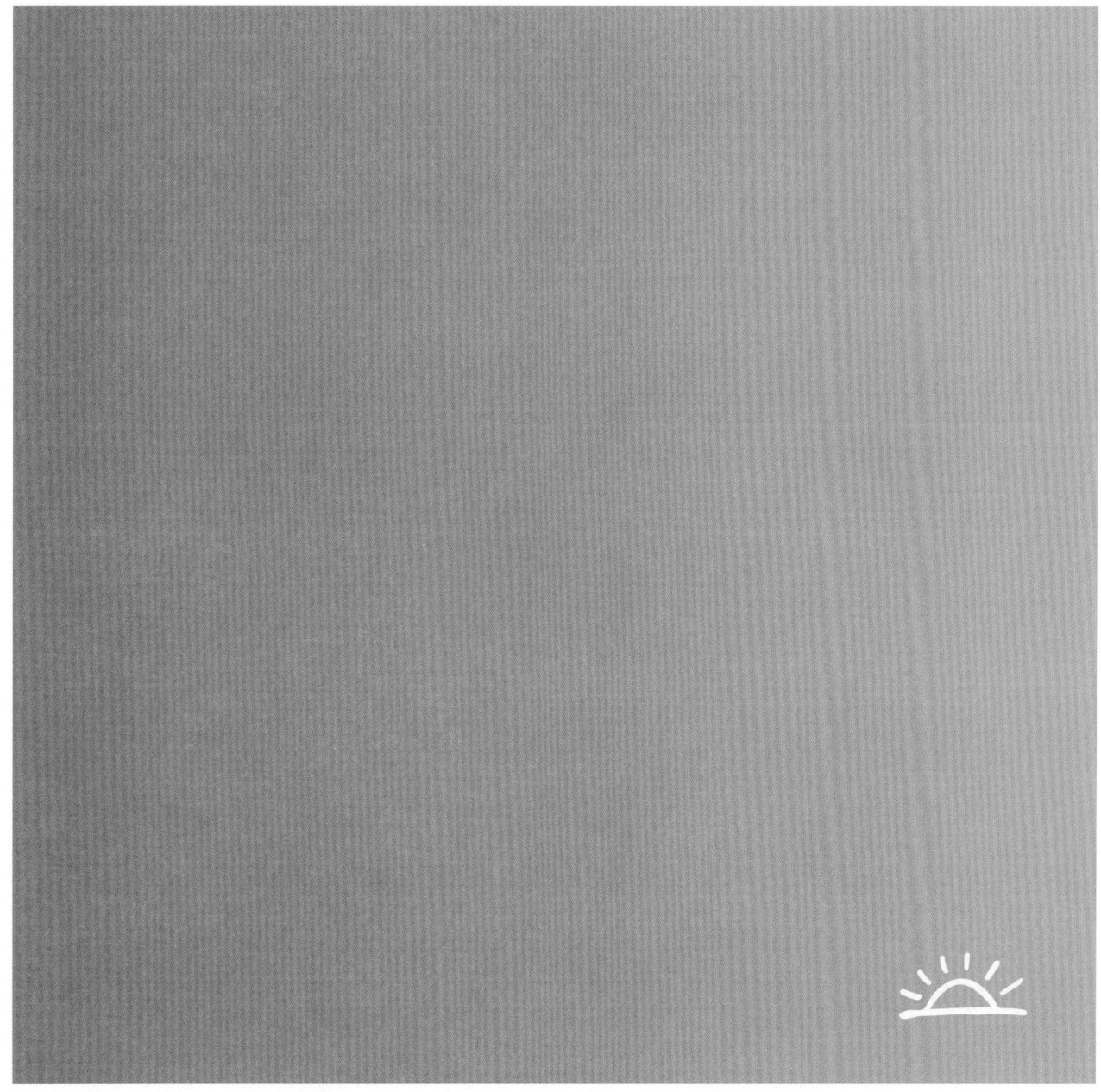

1.4 Independent Learning

WHY?

Teaching students to work independently with support from the teacher (as needed) allows them to develop autonomy and problem-solving skills while still having access to valuable teacher assistance when faced with challenges. It promotes critical thinking skills, problem-solving abilities, and self-discipline, which are beneficial in the present, and also in preparing them for future academic and real-world challenges.

IT'S UNDENIABLE

As teachers, our overarching goal is to facilitate meaningful learning experiences that empower students to reach their full potential academically, socially, and emotionally. This entails more than just delivering new content; it involves offering opportunities for students to engage with, comprehend, and apply their learning in real-world contexts. To achieve this goal, we employ various instructional strategies such as explicit instruction, modeling, guided practice, and facilitating both independent and collaborative learning experiences. We help students develop their metacognitive skills, which allows them to be more expert-like in their thinking and more effective and efficient in their learning (Stanton, Sebesta, & Dunlosky, 2021). It isn't enough for students to do well with our guidance, but to truly succeed, they need to be able to apply their learning independently.

Many studies in education have emphasized the importance of teaching students to work independently, with teacher support as needed. For example, a study by Zimmerman and Kitsantas (2014) highlighted the role of self-regulated learning in enhancing student outcomes. They found that students who were able to work independently and regulate their learning process effectively showed higher levels of academic achievement and motivation. This suggests that teaching students to work independently, while providing targeted support, when necessary, can contribute to their overall success in school.

In another study, Vansteenkiste, Ryan, and Soenens (2020) examined the role of autonomy-supportive teaching practices in promoting students' intrinsic motivation and self-regulation. The study demonstrated that teachers who adopt autonomy-supportive

---

Evidence-Based Practices to Support Independent Learning

- Exposure to reading
- Differentiation
- Spaced vs. mass practice
- Clear goal intentions
- Teacher clarity
- Response to intervention
- Deliberate practice
- Effort management
- Persistence, Engagement
- Direct instruction
- Success criteria

These factors have an effect size that represent substantial growth (Hattie, 2023).

strategies, such as providing meaningful choices and acknowledging students' perspectives, contribute significantly to students' ability to work independently and engage in learning with a sense of autonomy and purpose. These findings reinforce the notion that teaching students to work independently within a supportive environment is essential for increasing academic success and lifelong learning skills.

Furthermore, a study by Zimmerman and Moylan (2009) highlighted the importance of providing explicit instruction and guidance on self-regulation skills while also creating a supportive classroom environment that encourages autonomy and self-directed learning. It emphasizes the role of teachers in scaffolding students' development of self-regulated learning skills, gradually shifting responsibility to students as they gain competence.

Teaching self-regulated skills of independence fosters lifelong learning habits and enhances students' ability to transfer knowledge and skills to new situations. Research by Hmelo-Silver (2004) on transfer of learning emphasized that students who possess self-regulated learning skills are better equipped to apply their knowledge and problem-solving strategies in real-world contexts, leading to deeper understanding and more meaningful learning experiences. Overall, teaching self-regulated skills of independence not only enhances immediate learning outcomes but also equips students with valuable skills for lifelong learning and success.

> **Reflect** ▶ *What risk-free opportunities do your students have to think about, apply, and ask questions about new learning?*

A CORE MEMORY FROM GAIL

As a second grader, I vividly remember my quiet and orderly classroom, where desks were in rows all facing forward, while we all worked individually and independently.

This image of my classmates and I being quiet, orderly, engaged, and independent stayed with me as I began my teaching career. I never gave it much thought that a class that I was teaching would be anything but orderly. Because here is the thing.... I didn't remember a teacher teaching our class "how" to work quietly or independently. Nor did I learn how to teach students to be independent in any of my college courses.

So, you can imagine what a shock it was to me when I walked into my own classroom and my students weren't automatically quiet and independent. I couldn't figure out where exactly I went wrong. I even found myself blaming the students, saying, "I must have gotten 'that' class again this year."

I was desperate to figure out what was missing in my students' journey toward independence. I did a ton of research, talked to people, and tried different things, and then it hit me—the problem wasn't the kids; it was me. I didn't know how to teach them to be independent and so I didn't.

With my Special Education Degree, I learned about this powerful technique called task analysis. It helped me break down the specific behaviors my students needed to learn to be independent. And that's how the 10 Steps for Teaching and Learning Independence was born. It's been a game changer. Now, we teach students "how" to be independent in everything school related. It's amazing to see how it's transforming their engagement and learning. They're really thriving in this new environment where independence is taught, practiced, and built in every aspect of school life.

This Makes Me Think Of

TEACHER PRACTICES:
What you can do

Peer Book Review

Peer reviews (see page 59) can be completed independently when students finish a book. They provide authentic recommendations and insights from peers, which are relatable and engaging. This creates a sense of curiosity and excitement about the books being reviewed. Peer reviews can be posted in a specific area of the classroom or even placed inside the cover of the recommended book.

Reading Response

During independent work time, one option for students to share their learning is through a Reading Response Journal, or a Reading Response Form (see page 61). If using a journal, students record their initial response to reading after reading a specific portion of text. Journal entries can be a free write of thoughts or can be directed around student goals. If using a form, students simply respond to the questions on the form, which gives them an opportunity to reflect while providing the teacher with information to help guide instruction.

SECTION 1 — Independent Learning

Reading Log

In order for reading logs to work, there must be a purpose and students must understand the purpose. Students can use them to keep track of minutes read, chapters read, or books read. For example, the log on page 60 could be used for just about any goal students want to set. When they meet the criteria, they color in one lightbulb. Then, when you confer with students you can use their reading log to help direct the conversation. If Henry has colored in three lightbulbs on his chapter log, you might ask him what book he is reading and talk about what happened in the three chapters he has read. Or, when conferring with Chantel, you might see she has colored in two lightbulbs, which means she has completed two picture books, and you talk about the books she read and what she thought of them. With older students, it's beneficial to keep it simple and authentic. A small notebook where students simply keep track of the the title, author, date, and one statement about the book is effective and can be used throughout their lifetime.

RECOMMENDED READING

The Motivated Student: Unlocking the Enthusiasm for Learning by Bob Sullo (2009).

Teach Like a Champion 2.0: 62 Techniques That Put Students on the Path to College by Doug Lemov (2015).

Empower: What Happens When Students Own Their Learning by John Spencer and A.J. Juliani (2017).

Teaching Students to Drive Their Learning: A Playbook on Engagement and Self-Regulation, K-12 by Douglas Fisher, Nancy Frey, Sarah Ortega, and John Hattie (2020).

Envoy: Your Personal Guide to Classroom Management by Michael Grinder (2007).

FROM THE FIELD

Providing time for independent work is like giving students the canvas to paint their understanding. It's in these moments that they connect the dots, experiment with new concepts, and truly internalize their learning. Imagine a math class where students tackle problems on their own, applying the methods they've learned, and then discuss their approaches with peers. This fosters a deeper comprehension and confidence in their abilities. Independent work isn't just about practice; it's about empowering students to own their learning journey.

—Lance Jones, Texas

As a 1st Grade teacher, I wanted independent learners in the classroom. The 10 Steps to Independence was my road map. Through the consistency provided in the 10 Steps, my 1st graders were able to name their goal, strategy, and choice each round. It honored their voice, empowered their learning, and created accountability. Now as a Curriculum Director, I see the impact from a different lens. I see how the process for independence also fosters inclusion, elements of Universal Design, and motivated learners.

—Carrie Fiel, California

Don't throw students into the independent learning without teaching them how! Scaffold their success by providing clear instructions, modeling tasks, and offering choices with varying difficulty. Gradually decrease support as they gain confidence, and watch your independent learners grow.

—Janet Scott, Washington

Very early in my career, I had the pleasure of working on the same grade level team as Gail Boushey. I can remember walking into her classroom one afternoon and being profoundly aware of how independent her students were compared to my own. They were spread out into different spaces and places, working on different learning tasks based on their individual goals or learning target, helping each other, and highly engaged. I asked so many questions and took fierce notes as Gail talked about knowing each student, trusting them, providing choices in their practice, and using the data collected that day to inform the next. It was all about setting students up to be INDEPENDENT…what a profound and liberating concept! I had a new vision of student agency, self-awareness, and connection that took root in my beliefs and practice as a teacher and continues to inspire and guide me now as a veteran principal.

—Anne Plenkovich, Arizona

CHECK-IN: *How are you doing?*

Using the behaviors from the Independent Learning anchor chart (see page 203), create a checklist or rubric that outlines your criteria for successful independent work. Include categories such as get started right away, work the whole time, stay in one spot, ignore distractions, work quietly, and persevere. You may also wish to include self-monitoring, problem solving, and sharing/collaboration (if applicable).

During independent learning sessions, observe students and monitor their progress using the checklist you create. Note behaviors and actions that align with successful independent learning, as well as areas where students may need improvement.

In addition, have students engage in reflective journaling or conversation where they evaluate their own independent learning skills based on the criteria in your checklist. Encourage them to identify strengths and areas for growth.

Use both your reflection and the students' reflections to set goals for enhancing independent learning skills. Keep track of progress over time and adjust as needed. If there is a commonality among student goals, it can be beneficial to revisit the behavior or expectation as a class.

Impact Statement

Providing dedicated time for independent learning allows students to practice and apply what they have learned, leading to deeper understanding and long-term retention of knowledge.

INDEPENDENT LEARNING

Lessons Included in Section 2

There are many activities and lessons that help teach students to be productive and engaged during independent learning time. The lessons provided in Section 2 provide a springboard of ideas. Use them as they are or adjust them to fit the group of students in front of you. Remember to use these throughout the year. Find out more about routines for launching independent learning on page 71. And, as always, we encourage you to add more of your own lessons to this list using the blank template located on page 209.

IL.1 Ways to Engage with Text

IL.2 Reading Materials

IL.3 What's Independent?

IL.4 I PICK

IL.5 What's Engagement?

IL.6 10 Steps to Independent Learning

IL.7 Underline and Move On (Um . . .)

IL.8 Setting Up a Writing Notebook

IL.9 What to Write About

IL.10 Planning Template

My Book Review

Title:

Author:

Rating: ☆ ☆ ☆ ☆ ☆

Did not like — Liked a lot

♥ **My favorite part of the book is . . .**

_____
_____
_____
_____

If I could ask the author a question, it would be . . .

_____
_____
_____
_____

One of my classmates would like this book.   YES!   NO!   MAYBE?

READING is always a good idea!

Color in a lightbulb for each _____ _____ .

START:
END:

Woohoo! Way to go!

_____'s Reading Response

Book Title:

Author:

Genre?   **Fiction**   **Non-Fiction**

Book/Chapter Summary:

COLLABORATIVE LEARNING

1.5 Collaborative Learning

WHY?

Teaching children to work collaboratively helps them develop essential social skills such as communication, teamwork, and conflict resolution, which are crucial for their overall development. Collaborative work gives students an opportunity to learn from one another, benefiting from diverse perspectives and strengths, and enhancing their problem-solving abilities. Together, students can effectively navigate challenges, build confidence in their cooperative skills, and create a positive learning environment where everyone can succeed.

IT'S UNDENIABLE

Collaboration allows students to engage more deeply with the material they're learning (Hess, 2018). When students work together, they actively participate in their learning journey by discussing ideas, solving problems, and learning from each other's perspectives. This active involvement not only enhances their understanding of the subject matter but also creates a sense of community within the classroom (Kagan, 2009).

Collaborative learning promotes essential life skills such as teamwork, communication, and leadership. These skills are invaluable in both academic and real-world settings. It cultivates a supportive learning community that enhances motivation and engagement, further aiding retention and transfer. When students feel connected to their peers and supported in their learning journey, they are more motivated to participate actively and persist through challenges. Vygotsky's (1978) social development theory highlighted the importance of social interactions in cognitive development, suggesting that learning is inherently a social process. By working collaboratively, students build a network of peer support that encourages continuous learning and application of knowledge, leading to more enduring and transferable learning outcomes.

By engaging students in active, meaningful interactions, collaborative learning improves their ability to retain information and transfer their knowledge to new contexts. When students work together to solve problems or discuss concepts, they are more likely to process and internalize the material deeply. According to research by

Evidence-Based Practices to Support Collaborative Learning

- Exposure to reading
- Differentiation
- Spaced vs. mass practice
- Clear goal intentions
- Teacher clarity
- Response to intervention
- Deliberate practice
- Effort management
- Persistence, Engagement
- Direct instruction
- Success criteria
- Transfer strategies

These factors have an effect size that represent substantial growth (Hattie, 2023).

Johnson and Johnson (1999), students engaged in collaborative learning exhibit higher levels of retention and understanding compared with those who learn individually. This is because the social interaction inherent in collaborative activities requires students to explain their thinking, justify their reasoning, and address misunderstandings, all of which reinforce their learning and have a powerful effect on student relationships (Barron & Kinney, 2021).

In addition, collaborative learning can lead to higher academic achievement. Over 1200 studies have demonstrated that cooperative learning methods enhance students' time-on-task and intrinsic motivation to learn. Collaboration also improves students' interpersonal relationships and their expectations for success (Johnson & Johnson, 2009).

Finally, collaborative learning helps students transfer their learning to new situations by fostering critical thinking and problem-solving skills. As students collaborate, they encounter diverse perspectives and strategies, which broadens their cognitive toolkit. A study by Slavin (2014) found that collaborative learning environments encourage students to apply their knowledge in novel ways, improving their ability to generalize and transfer skills across different subjects and real-world scenarios. This adaptability is crucial for students' success beyond the classroom, as it prepares them to tackle complex problems in various contexts.

Reflect

How effectively do your students collaborate and support each other during group activities, and what strategies might you implement to enhance their cooperative learning experiences in the future?

A CORE MEMORY FROM ALLISON

Collaborative learning brings mixed feelings to the forefront for many. My mind goes directly to fifth grade when we were assigned a group project to share our learning from a social studies unit we had just completed on the three branches of government. Placed in a small group with a few classmates, we had to determine who would do what parts of the assignment and how we would bring it all together. As is typical, the group was a mix of students who were very concerned with every detail and students who truly didn't have a care in the world. Similarly, there were a few who completed work in a timely manner with full effort, and a few who were unconcerned with deadlines or the finished product. Some were outspoken, others reserved, and with very different family dynamics, working together outside of school hours wasn't an option. This scenario is pretty common in the collaborative learning setting; however, my fifth-grade example came so clearly because I received a low grade and our group was encouraged to resubmit the assignment. We were even given the "opportunity" to stay in at recess until it was complete and met the standard requirements. This was a first for me and created a distaste for collaborative learning and group projects.

Fast forward to my first years of teaching when I knew the benefit of collaborative learning and worked to incorporate it in my classroom. Aware of my previous experiences, and not wanting my students to experience group work in the same way, it became a goal to create groups that provided every opportunity for students to be successful. When collaborative learning is purposeful and properly planned, taught, and managed, it works.

This Makes Me Think Of

TEACHER PRACTICES:
What you can do

Jigsaw Activity

Form small groups of three to four students. Assign each student a different section of the overall topic, article to read, or concept to discuss. Each student will focus on a different aspect of the topic.

1. Each participant works alone to understand their bit of information.

2. Students from different groups who have the same section meet and work together to understand the material, answer questions, and prepare to teach their section to their original group.

3. Students return to their original group and take turns teaching their section of the topic to their peers. Each student shares their learning and ensures that the entire group learns about the full topic through each of their explanations.

4. After each student has a chance to teach about their topic, the group engages in a discussion to synthesize and discuss their understanding.

SECTION 1 — Collaborative Learning

Think-Pair-Share

This strategy is a powerful tool to encourage student engagement and deepen understanding.

1. Students listen as the teacher poses a thought-provoking question or problem to the class.
2. Students think individually about their response, allowing them to formulate their ideas independently.
3. They pair up with a classmate to discuss their thoughts and responses.
4. Partners share their conclusions with the whole class.

Collaborative Story Writing

This activity not only enhances writing skills but also teaches students how to cooperate, respect each other's contributions, and combine their strengths to create a cohesive and imaginative story.

1. Divide students into small groups of two to four and provide them with a story prompt to spark their imagination.
2. Each group works together to brainstorm ideas and outline their story, deciding on characters, setting, and plot.
3. Students take turns writing different parts of the story, passing it along to their group members to continue the narrative. This rotation makes it so each student contributes their unique voice and ideas to the story.
4. Once the story is complete, the group collaborates on editing and refining their work.
5. Students share with the class.

RECOMMENDED READING

A Teacher's Guide to Flexible Grouping and Collaborative Learning: Form, Manage, Assess, and Differentiate in Groups by Dina Brulles and Karen Brown (2018).

Better Learning Through Structured Teaching: A Framework for the Gradual Release of Responsibility by Doug Fisher and Nancy Frey (2021).

Kagan Cooperative Learning by Spencer Kagan (2009).

Learning to Collaborate, Collaborating to Learn: Engaging Students in the Classroom and Online by Janet Salmons (2019).

FROM THE FIELD

If collaboration is challenging for students, don't ditch it, structure it. Teach partner selection, communication skills, how to ask for help, and turn-taking. Structured collaboration builds teamwork – a win for all!

—Steve Boolos, Washington

When I want students to collaborate. I give them each a role to ensure responsibility, accountability, and equitable learning. Some of these rules include the timekeeper, the recorder, the note taker, the facilitator, and the material manager. As with any teaching practice, modeling and practicing these roles is crucial for success. Be patient and the results will be worth it.

—Tara Brooks, Iowa

Think-pair-share is a great way to get everyone participating, but sometimes those initial 'think' moments can be a struggle. Here's a tip I've found helpful: provide a graphic organizer or sentence starter. Students fresh out of a group lesson or teacher directed assignment might need a little nudge to get their independent thinking started. Offering a graphic organizer with key questions or prompts, or even just a simple sentence starter like 'I think this means …' can give them a springboard to jump from. Once they've had a chance to grapple with the idea individually, the 'pair' and 'share' stages flow much more smoothly. They come to the discussion table with some initial thoughts, ready to bounce ideas off their partner and learn from other perspectives.

—Rachel Mosbacher, Arizona

CHECK-IN: How are you doing?

Using the behaviors from the Collaborative Learning anchor chart (see page 76), create a checklist or rubric that outlines your criteria for successful collaborative learning. Include categories such as get started right away, work the whole time, stay in one spot, ignore distractions, work quietly, and persevere. You may also wish to include self-monitoring, problem solving, and sharing/collaboration.

During collaborative learning sessions, observe students and monitor their progress using the checklist you create. Note behaviors and actions that align with successful collaborative learning, as well as areas where students may need improvement.

In addition, have students engage in reflective journaling or conversation where they evaluate their own collaborative learning skills based on the criteria in your checklist. Encourage them to identify strengths and areas for growth.

Use both your reflection and the students' reflections to set goals for enhancing collaborative learning skills. Keep track of progress over time and adjust as needed. If you notice a commonality among student goals, it can be beneficial to revisit the behavior or expectation as a class.

Impact Statement

Collaborative learning in the classroom significantly enhances students' engagement with the material, promoting deeper understanding and retention of concepts. It helps develop essential social skills, such as communication, teamwork, and problem solving, which are crucial for students' future success.

COLLABORATIVE LEARNING
Lessons Included in Section 2

There are many activities and lessons that help create and sustain collaborative learning throughout the year. The lessons provided in Section 2 provide a springboard of ideas. Use them as they are or adjust to fit the group of students in front of you. Remember to use these throughout the year. Find out more about routines for launching collaborative learning on page 71. And, as always, we encourage you to add more of your own lessons to this list using the blank template located on page 223.

CL.1 Choosing a Partner

CL.2 Voice Level

CL.3 Take Turns

CL.4 Check for Understanding

CL.5 Think: What's My Purpose?

CL.6 What To Do When Finished

CL.7 Planning Template

Launching Independent and Collaborative Learning (with Support)

Independent and collaborative learning takes place throughout the day in each subject when students practice the lessons and concepts taught by transferring the coordinating skills to their own work.

Teaching students to work independently and collaboratively in their learning is established in three phases. We have included launching briefs for both Independent Learning (page 75) and Collaborative Learning (page 76) to guide you as you introduce these to your class. Each launching brief is a one-page document that includes the essential steps to a successful launch. The three phases included in each launching brief include the following:

Phase 1: Foundation Lessons

Phase 2: Teacher-Directed Independent/Collaborative Learning

Phase 3: Student-Directed Independent/Collaborative Learning

FOUNDATION LESSONS

Foundation lessons are short bursts of instruction that teach students the necessary behaviors to successfully learn and engage in what they are working on. These are prerequisite lessons that set students up to build understanding and include skills to successfully engage in the learning.

The foundation lessons specific to getting Independent and Collaborative Learning up and going in your class are listed on the Launching Briefs found on pages 75–76, and you'll find the lessons themselves in Section 2 of this book. Each foundation lesson on the launching briefs were determined essential by asking and answering this question, "What do students need to know and be able to do to be successful with Independent and Collaborative Learning?" Of course, you'll want to add any other lesson you think will help prepare your students for successful engagement when working independently or collaboratively.

The foundation lessons for Independent Learning include but aren't limited to: What's Independent? (page 197), What's Engagement? (page 199) as well as instruction around managing reading materials (page 195), choosing a good-fit S.P.A.C.E. to work (page 152), thinking about the purpose for learning (page 219), and planning what to do when finished with an activity (page 221).

The foundation lessons for Collaborative Learning include the foundation lessons for Independent Learning but layer in four additional lessons: Choosing a Partner (page 213), Check for Understanding (page 218), Voice Level (page 215), and Take Turns (page 217).

10 STEPS TO TEACHING AND LEARNING INDEPENDENCE

These are the steps we use to teach students how to be independent at just about anything. In addition to daily routines, they are used in literacy, math, science, and to teach any subject or behavior where students benefit from knowing and displaying consistent expectations. When teaching students to engage in learning independently and collaboratively, we first teach the foundation lessons, and then use the 10 Steps to Teaching and Learning Independence to teach the behaviors needed to be successful in Independent Learning, Collaborative Learning, or any task at hand. (See page 49.)

TEACHER-DIRECTED WORK

Teacher-directed work refers to the instructional activities or tasks assigned by the teacher for students to complete under the guidance of the teacher or independently. This can include assignments, projects, worksheets, or any other tasks that are designed to reinforce and apply the concepts taught during teacher-directed instruction.

By structuring the learning experience and directing students' attention to key concepts, teacher-directed work helps reinforce specific concepts, clarify misunderstandings, address misconceptions, and ensure that students acquire a solid foundation of knowledge and skills essential for academic success.

Teacher-directed work takes place in the whole group setting and can then move to independent or collaborative learning time. It's often considered the "must-do" part of work that students complete before selecting their option for student-directed work or the "may-do" part of work.

STUDENT-DIRECTED WORK

Student-directed work refers to the student taking an active role in directing their own learning, making choices, setting goals, and managing their progress independently or collaboratively with peers. It's during this time that students decide to engage in learning through reading, writing, listening, speaking, viewing, visually representing, or a combination of these (see the section "Authentic Application").

Student-directed work takes place during independent and collaborative work time. It's often considered the "may-do" part of work that students engage in after completing any teacher-directed or "must-do" work. Student-directed work includes read to self, work on writing, and listen to reading, along with any other authentic application they choose to engage in.

CHOICE

When possible, allowing students choice helps to empower them to take ownership of their learning, building intrinsic motivation and engagement. When completing teacher-directed work, it can still be possible to provide students the freedom to choose the topics, tasks, or methods they prefer to complete the work at hand. During student-directed work, the ability to choose means learners are more likely to stay focused, demonstrate initiative, and invest effort in their work. This personalized approach promotes a sense of autonomy and responsibility, leading to deeper learning experiences and increased enthusiasm for independent and collaborative learning.

The key is to provide choices that all lead to the desired goals and outcomes. This choice may be as minor as whether work is completed in a notebook or on designated paper, or written with pen or pencil, or it may be as large as what topic, or modality students wish to use to highlight their learning.

ACCOUNTABILITY

During student independent and collaborative learning, accountability involves setting clear expectations, providing guidance and support as needed, and assessing student progress and outcomes. Teachers may use strategies such as engagement conferences (page 227), informative quick-checks (page 229), progress monitoring tools, and conferring with feedback (page 105) to ensure students stay on track and meet learning goals. This practice promotes student responsibility and autonomy while ensuring they receive necessary support and guidance for success in independent and collaborative learning.

INCREASE INTRINSIC MOTIVATION

While rewards can provide short-term motivation and reinforcement in learning, it's essential to consider the potential impact on intrinsic motivation, autonomy, and long-term engagement. Opportunities for intrinsic satisfaction are key to promoting sustained engagement and motivation in independent and collaborative learning.

Increasing intrinsic motivation in students involves a multifaceted approach that encompasses various factors such as feedback, attention, encouraging words, goals, and purpose.

> Feedback—Providing constructive and specific feedback that focuses on effort, progress, and improvement rather than solely on outcomes or grades can enhance students' intrinsic motivation by fostering a growth mindset and a sense of competence.
>
> Individualized Attention—Demonstrating genuine interest in their learning journey, and actively listening to their ideas and perspectives can help create a supportive and engaging learning environment that fuels intrinsic motivation.
>
> Encouraging Words—Using positive and encouraging words, affirmations, and encouragement can boost students' confidence, self-esteem, and belief in their abilities, further strengthening their intrinsic motivation to succeed.
>
> Goals/Purpose—Setting meaningful and challenging goals that align with students' interests, values, and aspirations can also stimulate intrinsic motivation by providing a sense of purpose, direction, and satisfaction in their learning endeavors.

Building intrinsic motivation in students involves a holistic approach that considers their individual needs, strengths, and aspirations while fostering a positive and supportive learning environment that values effort, growth, and personal fulfillment.

AUTHENTIC APPLICATION

As students take on new skills, look for ways to incorporate authentic application during independent and collaborative learning:

> Reading: Students read from a variety of self-selected, good-fit texts such as books, articles, poems, or digital resources. This is done independently or with a partner. Encourage them to apply the strategies that were taught.
>
> Writing: Students write daily on a variety of self-selected topics. They may also use writing prompts or complete required writing tasks. Their writing may be in the form of journal entries, essays, narratives, persuasive writing, or creative pieces. Encourage them to use writing strategies, revise and edit their work, and express their ideas clearly and cohesively.
>
> Speaking: Create opportunities for students to engage in speaking tasks, such as delivering oral presentations, participating in debates, conducting interviews, or sharing reflections orally. Encourage active listening skills, effective communication, and articulation of thoughts and ideas.
>
> Listening: Provide audio resources or recordings for students to listen to, such as podcasts, speeches, interviews, or audio books. Encourage active listening skills, comprehension, note-taking, turn and talk, and reflection on the content heard.

Viewing: Incorporate visual materials or media for students to view, such as videos, documentaries, infographics, or multimedia presentations. Encourage critical viewing skills, interpretation of visual information, analysis of media messages, and synthesis of visual and textual information.

Visually Representing: Assign tasks that require students to visually represent their ideas or concepts, such as creating mind maps, diagrams, charts, posters, or digital presentations. Encourage creativity, organization of information, visual literacy, and effective use of visual elements to convey meaning.

INTEGRATING CURRICULUM INTO INDEPENDENT AND COLLABORATIVE LEARNING

All of this involves aligning learning objectives, activities, and assessments with the broader curriculum goals and standards you cover throughout the year. Both teacher-directed and student-directed work tasks directly relate to and reinforce concepts, skills, and content covered in the curriculum or that align with individual student goals. This can include assigning research projects, inquiry-based tasks, problem-solving activities, or creative projects that require students to apply and extend their learning independently and/or collaboratively.

INDEPENDENT LEARNING
Launching Brief

➡ PHASE 1: FOUNDATION LESSONS

Teach these lessons before launching Independent Learning:
- What is independent (all by yourself)
- What is engagement (engaged, not engaged, actively disengaged)
- Material management (book boxes/notebook/computer/device)
- Choosing a good-fit S.P.A.C.E. to work
- Think: What is my purpose?

➡ PHASE 2: INDEPENDENT LEARNING (TEACHER-DIRECTED)

Use the 10 Steps to Teaching and Learning Independence to launch Independent Learning:

1. Identify what is to be taught: Independent Learning
2. Set a purpose: Create a sense of urgency
3. Identify the behaviors of Independent Learning on I-chart
4. Model most-desirable behaviors
5. Model least-desirable behaviors, then most-desirable behaviors (same student)
6. Students check-in and state their purpose
7. Students practice sustained effort and engagement
8. Monitor student engagement-informative quick checks and behavior conferences
9. Use a quiet signal-come back to group
10. Self-reflection: "How did you do?"

SAMPLE I-CHART

Fun! *Learn More*
Respectful to Others

Independent Learning

Students	Teacher
Get started right away	Work with students
Stay in one spot	
Work the whole time	
Work quietly	
Ignore distractions	
Persevere	

➡ PHASE 3: INDEPENDENT LEARNING (STUDENT-DIRECTED)*

Teach the following lessons one at a time so students know what to do when they complete the teacher directed work.

Independent Reading Lessons
- 3 ways to engage with a text (receptive)
- I PICK

Independent Writing Lessons
- Underline and move on
- What to write about
- Ways to engage when writing (expressive)

Technology Lessons
- Material management

*optional

COLLABORATIVE LEARNING
Launching Brief

➡ PHASE 1: FOUNDATION LESSONS

Teach these lesson before launching Collaborative Learning:
- Choose a partner (optional)
- Choosing a good fit S.P.A.C.E. to work
- What is collaborative engagement?
  - Check for understanding
  - Listen and talk
  - Voice level and tone (respectful)
  - Coaching or time?
- Material management (book boxes, notebook, computer/device)
- Think: What is my purpose?

➡ PHASE 2: COLLABORATIVE LEARNING (TEACHER-DIRECTED)

Use the 10 Steps to Teaching and Learning Independence to launch Collaborative Learning:

1. Identify what is to be taught: Collaborative Learning
2. Set a purpose: Create a sense of urgency
3. Identify the behaviors of Collaborative Learning on I-chart
4. Model most-desirable behaviors
5. Model least-desirable behaviors, then most-desirable behaviors (same student)
6. Students check-in and state their intention
7. Students practice sustained effort and engagement
8. Monitor student engagement-informative quick checks and behavior conferences
9. Use a quiet signal- come back to group
10. Self-Reflection: "How did you do?"

SAMPLE I-CHART

Fun! Respectful to Others Learn More

Collaborative Work

Students	Teacher
Get started right away	Work with students
Stay in one spot	
Work the whole time	
Work quietly	
Ignore distractions	
Persevere	

➡ PHASE 2: COLLABORATIVE LEARNING (STUDENT-DIRECTED)*

Read to Someone Lessons
- Who goes first
- What to read
- Take turns
- Check for understanding

Write with someone Lessons
- What to write

*optional

CONFERRING

1.6 Conferring

WHY?

Conferring gives teachers an opportunity to provide personalized feedback and support, addressing each student's unique learning needs and challenges. This one-on-one interaction helps build strong teacher-student relationships, building a supportive and trusting classroom environment. It also enables teachers to identify and address any misconceptions or difficulties early on, ensuring students stay on track with their learning. Regular conferences empower students to take an active role in their learning, promoting self-reflection and encouraging a growth mindset.

Evidence-Based Practices to Support Conferring

- Strategy monitoring
- Feedback: Reinforcement and cues
- Help seeking
- Response to intervention
- Formative evaluation
- Success criteria

These factors have an effect size that represent substantial growth (Hattie, 2023).

IT'S UNDENIABLE

Research has consistently highlighted the benefits of conferring, particularly in enhancing student learning and engagement. Anderson (2000) described conferring as a powerful tool for differentiation, allowing teachers to tailor their instruction to meet the individual needs of students, addressing specific skills and challenges in real time. This personalized approach not only helps in identifying students' strengths and areas for improvement but also fosters a more supportive and student-centered learning environment. "Conferring allows teachers to meet students where they are, providing individualized support that fosters academic growth and cultivates a deeper connection to the learning material" (Serravallo, 2015, 67).

One of the primary advantages of conferring is its role in promoting active learning and student agency. According to Berger (2003), conferring encourages students to take ownership of their learning by setting goals, reflecting on their progress, and identifying strategies to overcome challenges. This process helps students to become self-regulated learners, a key factor in academic success. "Conferring with students empowers them to articulate their learning goals, reflect on their progress, and take charge of their educational outcomes, thereby fostering a strong sense of agency" (Anderson, 2000, 89).

In addition, the practice of conferring creates stronger teacher-student relationships, which are crucial for creating a supportive and engaging learning environment. Research by Pianta, Hamre, and Allen (2012) highlighted the importance of these relationships, emphasizing that positive interactions between teachers and students significantly boost student engagement and motivation. When students feel understood and valued during conferring sessions, they are more likely to invest in their learning and participate actively in classroom activities.

Zwiers and Crawford (2020) highlighted that conferring is integral in promoting culturally responsive teaching practices. By engaging in one-on-one discussions, teachers can better understand the diverse cultural backgrounds of their students, allowing them to tailor instruction that is inclusive and relevant. This approach not only enhances academic achievement but also helps to bridge cultural gaps, fostering a more inclusive classroom environment. Furthermore, Zwiers and Crawford argued that these personalized interactions help to validate students' identities and experiences, contributing to their overall sense of belonging and motivation to learn. "Conferring transforms the traditional teacher-student dynamic into a partnership where personalized dialogue drives deeper understanding and empowers students to take ownership of their learning journey" (Zwiers & Crawford, 2020, 123).

Moreover, research by Henderson and Corry (2021) demonstrated the positive impact of conferring on students' metacognitive skills. In their study, they found that regular conferring sessions helped students to become more aware of their own learning processes, enabling them to set more effective goals and develop strategies for self-improvement. This metacognitive awareness is crucial for lifelong learning, as it empowers students to take control of their educational journeys. Additionally, Henderson and Corry noted that conferring provides an opportunity for formative assessment, where teachers can gather real-time data on student understanding and adjust their teaching methods accordingly. This dynamic and responsive approach to instruction has been shown to significantly improve student outcomes, making conferring an essential practice in modern classrooms.

In conclusion, the practice of conferring in the classroom promotes personalized learning, student engagement, and academic growth. By fostering meaningful teacher-student interactions, conferring helps students develop a sense of agency and ownership over their learning. Embracing this approach can lead to a more inclusive, responsive, and effective learning environment that benefits all students.

> **Reflect** ▶ *How effectively am I using our conferring sessions to address individual student needs and promote their academic and personal growth, and what specific changes can I make to enhance these interactions?*

A CORE MEMORY FROM GAIL

Back in my days of teaching third grade, when I had first started dabbling in conferring and the conferring notebook, I noticed one of my students, who was usually happy and engaged, had become increasingly withdrawn and the effort in her work was slipping. Concerned, I decided to have a one-on-one conference with her during their independent learning time. I invited this student to sit with me at a back table, away from the noise of the classroom, and gently asked how she was feeling about school and her work.

She hesitated at first but then slowly began to open up. She revealed that her grandmother was living with them and she was very sick. The whole family was sad and she felt overwhelmed and distracted. I listened intently, offering empathy and understanding, and assured her that it was okay to feel upset and that her feelings were valid. We talked about strategies to help manage stress, like a morning check in with me, taking a library break when needed.

Over the next few weeks, I continued to check in with this student regularly and I noticed a significant change: she started to smile more, participate in class discussions again, and her overall engagement improved. One day, she handed in a writing assignment she had completed and at the bottom of the essay she had written, "Thank you for listening to me."

That simple yet profound conference, along with the follow-up conversations, are something I will never forget. I witnessed firsthand the power of personalized attention and genuine care. And although conferences are often based on academic needs, I also know that sometimes what students need goes beyond academic support. They need someone who listens and understands them.

As I share this core memory, I think of all I have learned from conferring and want to share seven secrets I've discovered. Well, I guess they aren't so secret anymore … but that's a good thing!

1. **Take the time to truly assess your students**: Listen to them, ask questions, and understand their strengths and areas for growth. While computers can assist, nothing can replace the teacher's role in this process.

2. **Write it down**: We can't rely on memory alone. That's why a conferring notebook is invaluable. We've done the work to find what works best, and you can choose whether to write it or type it. The choice is yours!

3. **Start, don't wait**: Building the habit of conferring is like developing a new muscle. Begin small, with just one or two students each day, and gradually increase the number. The key is to start and keep going.

4. **It's a gift**: Conferring isn't just beneficial for your students, but also for yourself. You deserve to set aside dedicated time each day to work individually with students, fostering relationships, celebrating accomplishments, and planning for their progress.

5. **Consider the other students**: Before effective conferring can happen, it's important to ensure that the rest of your students are engaged and working independently. This book will guide you in creating an environment where students can thrive without constant supervision.

6. **Conferring is a conversation**: Remember, conferring is more than just checking off a to-do list. It's a time for meaningful conversations, where you talk, listen, discuss, plan, and celebrate together with your students.

7. **It's fun!**: Embrace the joy of conferring! Enjoy the personal connections you make with your students, the insights you gain from their perspectives, and the progress you witness firsthand. Conferring can be an exciting and rewarding experience for both you and your students.

This Makes Me Think Of

TEACHER PRACTICES: *What you can do*

Conferring Notebook

Each time you confer with a student, open your notebook and know the plan for your time together. The goal is to waste no time. Have everything you need right in front of you so you can pick up where you left off, seamlessly. Listen and then take notes. Record what you observe, how and what you teach, and the next steps. Set goals and make an appointment that holds both the student and you accountable. The amount of information for each student grows as the year goes on, creating a more complete picture of them as a learner and helping to determine what they need to keep moving forward.

The conferring notebook contains specific forms.

- Conference Notes (for individual students for any subject)—page 88
- Group Conference Notes (for any subject)—page 89
- Keeping Track Sheet—page 90
- Calendar (blank for any month)—page 91

You can choose to use these forms to create your own physical copy of the conferring notebook, or if an online version meets your needs, visit www.conferringnotebook.com. Both work wonderfully, and the one advantage of the online notebook is the curricular coherence it provides between all educators that work with a child.

WHAT TO WRITE DOWN

It can be easy to want to write everything we see and hear, but there isn't enough room on the page or time during the conference to get it all down. Instead, it's important that we stick to the main points that will affect our teaching and student learning moving forward.

When conferring with a student, write down the specific areas where the student excels and any strengths they demonstrate. Note any challenges or misconceptions the student has, along with strategies or suggestions provided to address these issues. Finally, document the goals set during the conference and any follow-up actions to monitor the student's progress.

In the left-hand column of the conferring sheet write what you notice during the conference:

What book are they reading? What page are they on? Do they use their strategy goal when they are reading? Does anything else stand out that needs to be noted?	

In the right-hand column of the conferring sheet, write two points of action for your next conference.

	What are two things they can do between now and then?

Here's an example:

TOUCH POINT	OBSERVATIONS + INSTRUCTION	NEXT STEPS
Explicitly Explain Model Think Aloud Guide/Prompt Offer Advice Feedback	Flat Stanley, p.39 Using - ing and - est endings Stuck on a few words (disguise, bandanna) Able to understand what is happening.	Continue to look for word parts Write down difficult words on sticky note

Learning Goals vs. Performance Goals

Learning goals and performance goals are two distinct types of goals that serve different purposes. **Learning goals** guide students in understanding what they need to achieve in terms of acquiring knowledge, developing skills, and deepening understanding. This clarity helps students set meaningful goals, engage in self-directed learning, and take ownership of their learning process. **Performance goals** provide specific benchmarks or outcomes that students aim to achieve, such as demonstrating mastery of skills or meeting standards of performance. These goals motivate students to strive for excellence, monitor their progress, and take responsibility for demonstrating their learning outcomes independently. Together, learning goals and performance goals create a structured framework that supports students in working autonomously, making informed decisions, and achieving success.

Examples ▶

> **Learning Goal (Math):** Students will understand and apply multiplication concepts to solve real-world problems accurately.
>
> **Performance Goal (Math):** Students will achieve an 80% or higher score on the multiplication skills assessment.
>
> **Learning Goal (Language Arts):** Students will demonstrate comprehension and critical thinking skills by analyzing and interpreting complex texts.
>
> **Performance Goal (Language Arts):** Students will write a persuasive essay that effectively supports a claim with relevant evidence and logical reasoning.

Tangible Learning Aids

Tangible learning aids, such as charts and menus posted on the wall or placed in a personal folder, are invaluable for students working independently. They provide clear, accessible references that can guide their learning process. These tools help students stay organized, understand expectations, and follow step-by-step procedures without immediate teacher intervention. By having visual aids readily available, students can quickly recall information, reinforce their understanding of concepts, and apply them effectively in their work. This builds self-reliance, boosts confidence, and enhances their ability to solve problems independently. Examples of learning aids include anchor charts, the CAFE menu, sound walls, and word collectors.

Engagement Conference

Typically, conferences are based on academic goals and strategies. However, if students struggle with focusing or staying on task, those behaviors also need attention for them to make desired progress. Engagement conferences help students who could benefit from more direction on specific behaviors of engagement. Using the continuum of engagement (page 200) and the desired behaviors of engagement we have a brief conversation and set an engagement goal. Examples of engagement goals include: I will work the whole time, I will work quietly, I will get started right away, I will ignore distractions, I will check for understanding, and I will stay in one spot. See lesson C.1 page 221.

Informative Quick Check

Informative quick checks are very brief. They are a quick check in to see what a child is reading, writing, or working on and give a quick indicator of pace or engagement with their learning. Start these once you have completed any necessary engagement conferences and have a few extra minutes. Then, as the year goes on, do these two or three times a week to check in when you have a few extra minutes.

During a quick check, ask a few brief questions to help with accountability and to inform future instruction. Write this information on the child's conferring sheet. Examples of quick check questions include: What book are you reading? What page are you on? Who are the main characters? What strategy has helped you the most today? Please explain your thinking on this math problem. What is something new you learned when studying _____ in science? (See page 229.)

RECOMMENDED READING

Conferring: The Keystone of Reader's Workshop by Patrick Allen (2009).

Step Into Student Goal Setting: A Path to Growth, Motivation, and Agency by Chase Nordengren (2022).

The Cafe Book: Engaging All Students in Daily Literacy Assessment and Instruction by Gail Boushey and Allison Behne (2020).

Ruthless Equity: Disrupt the Status Quo and Ensure Learning for All Students by Ken Williams (2022).

Teaching for Racial Equity: Becoming Interculturally Competent in the Classroom by Tonya Perry, Steven Zemelman, and Katy Smith (2022).

The Heart-Centered Teacher by Regie Routman (2024).

FROM THE FIELD

Starting the school year with conferring sessions during the first 10 days is crucial for understanding your students as readers. This practice helps you promptly support each unique reader, ensuring no time is wasted.

As students take their beginning-of-year tests (iReady) to gather baseline data, I walked around, sat with each child, and conferred with them. Recording snippets of our conversations, I learned about their learning styles, book preferences, and reading engagement levels. This information allowed me to form small groups based on strengths and weaknesses, gather necessary materials, and adjust my plans for the coming weeks.

Each conference was unique. Supporting students who were already reading fluently, posed a challenge as I sought ways to further their growth. Conversely, I was excited to learn about those who were initially playful but highly enthusiastic about their reading. I found joy in watching my students read with passion. Conferring truly is powerful!

—Victora Cabreza, North Carolina

Our chats with people who care about us are often our most cherished moments. Meaningful conversations with each student builds relationships, creating deep connections and motivation. When we confer with students, it's like putting our arm around them and saying, 'Hey, let's figure out this reading thing together,' whether it's reading, writing, math, or any important skill. From that first conversation, a partnership is built, and as partners, engagement and growth multiply, fostering a love for lifelong learning.

Take the time to get comfy and chat about the most important things they do each day—becoming readers, writers, and problem solvers. They may not remember every lesson, but they'll remember how it felt when their teacher took the time to listen and confer with them.

—Tara Wilson, California

Conferring is a powerful teaching tool that helps build deeper relationships with students. A few years ago, I had the chance to teach Basic Human Rights. At first, I thought teaching topics like democracy, the constitution, and human rights would be difficult, but I decided to use conferring in my class, even at the collegiate level.

Everyone was surprised at how interested they became in the subject. The conferring technique made the lessons engaging and allowed me to connect with the students on a deeper level. Students who never liked reading began to enjoy it. This activity also improved their vocabulary and speaking skills. A small change in my teaching method had a lasting, positive impact on the students.

—Dr. Anjum Qureshi, India

CHECK-IN: *How are you doing?*

1. **Keeping Track:** Review the keeping track page of your conferring notebook to see who you have met with frequently and if there are any children who need to be met with more often.

2. **Touchpoints:** Regularly review students' progress based on the goals set during conferences and the touchpoints (page 108) given after each meeting. Compare their growth and performance over time to evaluate how well your conferring practices are supporting their learning.

3. **Seek Feedback from Students:** Ask students for their feedback on the conferring sessions. Inquire about what they find helpful, what they would like more of, and how the conferences can be more beneficial for their learning. Use this feedback to adjust and enhance your practices.

Impact Statement

Conferring with students provides personalized guidance, supporting each student with their unique challenges, and helping them reach their full potential. Conferring enhances academic growth, empowers students to take an active role in their learning, and helps students feel valued and supported in their learning.

CONFERRING
Lessons Included in Section 2

The following are lessons for two different types of conferences that build an effective conferring routine. These lessons can be found in Section 2 of this book, and work to provide a springboard of ideas. Use them as they are or adjust them to fit the students in front of you. As always, we encourage you to add more of your own lessons to this list using the blank template located on page 230.

C.1   Engagement Conference

C.2   Informative Quick Check

C.3   Planning Template

Conferring Notes

NAME	
STRENGTHS	
GOAL + STRATEGY	

COGNITIVE PROCESSES
- Remember
- Understand
- Apply
- Analyze
- Evaluate
- Create

📅	TOUCH POINT	OBSERVATIONS + INSTRUCTION	NEXT STEPS
	Explicitly Explain Model Think Aloud Guide/Prompt Offer Advice Feedback		
	Explicitly Explain Model Think Aloud Guide/Prompt Offer Advice Feedback		
	Explicitly Explain Model Think Aloud Guide/Prompt Offer Advice Feedback		
	Explicitly Explain Model Think Aloud Guide/Prompt Offer Advice Feedback		
	Explicitly Explain Model Think Aloud Guide/Prompt Offer Advice Feedback		

Group Conferring Notes

COGNITIVE PROCESSES
- Remember
- Understand
- Apply
- Analyze
- Evaluate
- Create

GROUP NAME

GOAL + STRATEGY

📅	STUDENTS	TOUCH POINTS	OBSERVATIONS + INSTRUCTION	NEXT STEPS
Explicitly Explain Model Think Aloud Guide/Prompt Offer Advice Feedback				
Explicitly Explain Model Think Aloud Guide/Prompt Offer Advice Feedback				
Explicitly Explain Model Think Aloud Guide/Prompt Offer Advice Feedback				
Explicitly Explain Model Think Aloud Guide/Prompt Offer Advice Feedback				

Copyright material from Gail Boushey and Allison Behne (2025), *Prepared Classroom*, Stenhouse

Keeping Track

STUDENTS	DATES

SUNDAY	MONDAY	TUESDAY	WEDNESDAY	THURSDAY	FRIDAY	SATURDAY

BRIEF AND EFFECTIVE LESSONS

1.7 Brief and Effective Lessons

WHY?

Teaching brief and effective lessons captures students' attention and helps them remain engaged without feeling overwhelmed. These concise lessons utilize targeted instruction on specific skills or concepts, maximizing learning efficiency and retention. Brief and effective lessons save time for independent and collaborative practice and application of the teaching points and build deeper understanding.

IT'S UNDENIABLE

Research in the field of education has consistently shown the benefits of teaching lessons that are brain compatible in time, emphasizing the importance of brevity and focus. Medina (2014) and Sousa (2011) highlighted the importance of cognitive load management in learning. Cognitive load refers to the amount of mental effort required to process information, and when cognitive load exceeds a certain threshold, learning can be impaired. Sweller's cognitive load theory (1988) suggested that breaking down information into smaller, meaningful segments reduces cognitive overload and facilitates learning. By designing lessons that are concise and targeted, educators present information in manageable chunks, allowing students to process and retain information more effectively. This helps to optimize learning outcomes and support students' cognitive processes, leading to improved retention and transfer of knowledge.

Brief and focused lessons align with principles of effective instructional design, such as the use of chunking and spaced repetition. Studies by Hattie (2009) and Kirschner et al. (2006) emphasized the benefits of chunking information and presenting it in a structured, manageable format. Chunking involves organizing information into smaller, meaningful units, which allows students to process and remember information more effectively. By breaking down content into digestible chunks and avoiding overwhelming students with excessive information, educators optimize learning outcomes and support students' cognitive processes.

In addition, research in cognitive psychology and educational neuroscience supports the idea that the human brain has limited capacity for processing information. Studies by Cowan (2001) and Baddeley (2012) emphasized the concept of working memory limitations, which suggest that individuals can only hold a limited amount of information in their conscious awareness at any given time. When students are overwhelmed with excessive content or information overload, their working memory becomes strained, hindering their ability to absorb and retain knowledge effectively.

Evidence-Based Practices to Support Brief & Effective Lessons

- Differentiation
- Spaced vs. mass practice
- Teacher clarity
- Direct instruction
- Clear goal intentions
- Response to intervention
- Concept mapping
- Success criteria

These factors have an effect size that represent substantial growth (Hattie, 2023).

Brain research also highlights the importance of novelty and variety in learning experiences. Jensen (2008) and Willis (2006) highlighted that brief and focused lessons incorporate elements of novelty, such as interactive activities, multimedia presentations, and real-world applications. This variety stimulates different areas of the brain, enhancing engagement and promoting deeper learning. By structuring lessons to include brief but varied activities, educators create a dynamic learning environment that caters to diverse learning styles and maximizes students' cognitive engagement.

Furthermore, the concept of "primacy and recency" in memory formation supports the practice of teaching brief and focused lessons. Ebbinghaus' forgetting curve (1964) suggested that learners are more likely to remember information presented at the beginning (primacy effect) and end (recency effect) of a learning session. Brief lessons capitalize on these memory principles by front-loading important concepts and reinforcing key points toward the end, optimizing students' retention and recall of essential information.

Research indicates that brain-compatible teaching practices that prioritize brief and focused lessons align well with the demands of our world now. According to Davis and Chan (2015), the rapid pace of contemporary life and the prevalence of digital technology have led to a noticeable decrease in attention spans. This shift necessitates that educators adapt their teaching methods to maintain student engagement and optimize learning outcomes.

Brief and focused lessons align with the brain's natural attention span and cognitive processing capabilities. By preventing cognitive overload and maintaining student engagement, these lessons enhance retention and understanding of the material. Additionally, they cater to the demands of the modern world, where attention spans are decreasing, and the ability to process information efficiently is essential.

> **Reflect** ▶ *How can I use the research on lesson length to make lessons more engaging and help students remember what they learn?*

A CORE MEMORY FROM ALLISON

Years ago, when I first implemented Daily 5 and CAFE in my classroom, I struggled with the idea of brief focus lessons. I listened to Gail talk about brain research and its implications for the classroom. I remember her saying, many times, "If your lessons go too long, you are likely trying to teach too much." Although it all made sense, I was still confident that my lessons were effective. Gail recommended I record a lesson or two, and then watch them to observe student behaviors. I did this soon after she suggested it, and what I saw was astonishing.

At the time, I was teaching kindergarten (five- and six-year-olds). While watching the video, I noticed student behaviors start to decline at about the five-minute mark, and by the time the lesson hit eight minutes, I was basically teaching to the four students who were still focused on me. How could this be? I know when I was teaching this lesson, it couldn't have been this obvious! But the videos don't lie. My lessons weren't as effective as I thought they were.

This was the turning point for me. I started to become very aware of student behaviors and signals showing they were "done." I realized I needed to adjust my teaching to meet their needs. I was spending five minutes of each lesson accessing prior knowledge, and by the time I got to the new learning material, my students were done. I had to find a way to adapt my lessons so they would fit the definition of a brief focus lesson.

I am pleased to say that although it didn't happen overnight, it did happen. I changed my teaching style, and the result was shortened focus lessons that were explicit and effective.

If you struggle to keep your focus lessons brief, I encourage you to record a lesson, take the time to watch the video, and reflect on your teaching and student engagement in the lesson. It may not happen overnight, but you will find that if you continue to reflect on your teaching and adjust as needed, it will impact the effectiveness of your focus lessons.

This Makes Me Think Of

TEACHER PRACTICES: *What you can do*

Lesson Length

The average age of the children we teach equals the average number of minutes they can maintain attention during direct instruction. In other words, AGE = TIME.

In his book *Brain Rules: 12 Principles for Surviving and Thriving at Work, Home, and School*, Dr. John Medina (2014) discussed the fact that the brain has a stubborn timing pattern of ten. After about ten minutes of direct instruction, the brain must shift to refocus. We cannot ignore the implications of this. Regardless of our students' ages, when our lessons run longer than ten minutes, our instructional time is less effective because our students aren't able to take in as much information as we'd like.

One to Two Learning Targets

When lessons go too long, we're probably trying to teach too much. And, because we have so much information to teach our students, we often try to cram multiple teaching points into one lesson. However, what this does is increase the time of the lesson, and it makes it so the learner has more than one focus to remember. When planning for a lesson, it's important to consider the number of teaching points. If it looks like the lesson will need more than ten minutes, divide that single lesson into more than one. This increases the students' chance for success and there's a much better chance that the content will stick.

Brain Break vs. Hook

Brain breaks significantly improve students' focus and productivity by allowing students to recharge and return to tasks with renewed energy and concentration. These short, physical or mental breaks also enhance overall classroom behavior and engagement, leading to a more effective learning environment.

When a few more minutes are needed to complete a lesson, it's beneficial to incorporate a brain break. And, when this "break" falls in the middle of a lesson, it's called a "hook." In an interview with Dr. John Medina, he shared that when you want a learner to continue to gain new information and have reached the optimal lesson length, it's important to provide a "brain break" that allows students to process what they have already learned. He recommends this "brain break" be a "hook" that relates to the lesson and allows students an emotional, kinesthetic, or cognitive shift of some sort. If the lesson is going to continue, the "break" must relate to the content being taught.

A "hook" helps to hook students' brains and relates to their learning. For example, a personal story about the content that ties in emotion, a fun fact to interest them, or a turn and talk about the content are all "hooks." They are still considered brain breaks, but instead of just being an action or song to get students moving, it's a hook that relates to the content.

So, when is the time to use brain breaks that don't provide a hook? Traditional brain breaks are used any time students are in the same area or expected to engage for longer than the age = time rule, but the content may not relate. For example, if you finish sharing at the end of the literacy block and move to the first focus lesson of your math block, you may wish to insert a brain break, and a hook isn't needed.

In the same way age-appropriate lesson lengths allow students to maintain focus, effective transitions recharge learners before they re-engage their concentration.

Four Stages of a Brief Lesson

To keep lesson length down and to help with consistency of the lessons we teach, we use a four-stage lesson plan that is basic yet effective. We use this plan for all lessons, in all subject areas. The four stages are the following:

STAGE 1: UNDERSTAND

The first stage is crucial because it involves observation and planning based on students' current knowledge and needs, rather than following a predetermined curriculum sequence. This step ensures that instructional decisions are tailored to help students progress effectively. By using formal and informal observations, we can determine the most appropriate strategies, settings, and practices to support student learning. For whole-group instruction, this involves aligning with grade-level standards, whereas for small group or individual conferences, it involves more personalized planning based on specific observations made during student interactions.

STAGE 2: PREPARE

This stage involves three interconnected steps: engaging students by making a connection, identifying the teaching point, and sharing the success criteria. This stage is distinct from traditional frameworks because it explicitly communicates to students what they are learning, why it's important, and how they will know they have succeeded. By the end of the lesson, students should be able to clearly articulate what they have learned.

STAGE 3: TEACH

This is where explicit instruction takes place. After planning and preparing students for their learning, this stage involves delivering the lesson and providing time for practice. Teachers have various instructional options, such as explaining, thinking aloud, modeling, guiding, offering suggestions, and giving feedback. Multiple instructional practices are often used within a single teaching session to reinforce concepts in diverse ways, recognizing that students learn differently.

STAGE 4: SUPPORT

The last section of the lesson plan provides space for possible considerations or pivots to help students understand and retain information. A template of the lesson is found on page 237.

SETTING (WHOLE GROUP/SMALL GROUP/INDIVIDUAL)

Purposeful instruction doesn't just consist of a set number of whole-group, small-group, and conferring lessons, or, for that matter, a scripted program. When we teach based on setting, rather than focusing our efforts on teaching the students in front of us, we are in essence "doing" instruction rather than teaching children based on their actual needs. We need to know our students, their strengths, and their needs before we can design a path to move them forward. Therefore, the lesson framework is the same in whole-group, small-group, and individual instruction because as we have learned, good teaching is good teaching, and the lesson framework sets the stage for teaching brief, explicit lessons that engage students, and that is good teaching.

RECOMMENDED READING

Brain Rules: 12 Principles for Surviving and Thriving at Work, Home, and School by John Medina (2014).

Explaining Reading: A Resource for Explicit Teaching of the Common Core Standards by Gerald Duffy (2014).

Advancing Formative Assessment in Every Classroom: A Guide for Instructional Leaders by Connie M. Moss and Susan Brookhart (2019).

FROM THE FIELD

Less is often more! Keep lessons focused and concise to boost student engagement. Think 'laser focus'—cover key points clearly, then let students practice or explore. They'll retain more and stay energized for the whole lesson!

—Elena Maksymova, Kazakhstan

To ensure smooth and efficient transitions to the gathering area for a whole group lesson, establish a consistent routine. Start by having a clear signal, like ringing a chime, to indicate it's time to move. Teach and practice this routine with your students until it becomes a habit. Encourage them to move quietly and quickly. Consider assigning specific spots or a seating arrangement to minimize settling time. Reducing transition time helps save time for instruction and focus.

—Alex Myers, Australia

Incorporate a variety of teaching methods—such as quick demonstrations, interactive questions, and brief student activities—to maintain interest and reinforce learning. Remember, it's better to have a concise, focused lesson that students can easily absorb than to overload them with too much information at once. Summarize key points at the end to reinforce learning and transition smoothly to the next activity.

—Þorbjörg Halldórsdóttir, Iceland

CHECK-IN: How are you doing?

A good self-check or reflection tool to determine whether lessons are brief and effective might include the following questions:

1. Clarity of Objectives:
   - Did I clearly define the lesson objectives and communicate them to my students?
   - Were the objectives specific and focused on key concepts?

2. Engagement and Interaction:
   - Did I incorporate active learning strategies to engage students?
   - Did I use a variety of instructional practices (e.g., modeling, think-alouds, guided practice) to cater to different learning styles?

3. Pacing and Timing:
   - Did I keep the lesson within the planned time frame?
   - Was the pacing appropriate, ensuring all students had time to understand and practice the new material?

4. Assessment and Feedback:
   - Did I include formative assessments to check for understanding throughout the lesson?
   - Was I able to provide immediate and constructive feedback to students?
5. Student Understanding:
   - At the end of the lesson, could students articulate what they learned and why it was important?
   - Did I observe signs of student engagement and comprehension during the lesson?

Using this self-check regularly can help teachers refine their approach to delivering brief and effective focus lessons so they meet their students' learning needs efficiently and effectively.

Impact Statement

Teaching brief, brain-compatible lessons is essential because they align with cognitive load theory, maximizing student retention and engagement by optimizing information processing. Shorter lessons allow for focused, impactful learning experiences that respect students' attention spans and promote deep understanding.

BRIEF AND EFFECTIVE LESSON

Lessons included in Section 2

There are many ways to align instruction with brain-compatible learning. The lessons provided in Section 2 provide a springboard of ideas to get you started. Use them as they are or adjust them to fit the group of students in front of you. As always, we encourage you to add more of your own lessons to this list using the blank template located on page 237.

BL.1 Brain Break Review

BL.2 Hook

BL.3 Active Listening

BL.4 Planning Template

Brief Focus Lesson

UNDERSTAND (Why?)
Why   **Materials**
PREPARE (Students)
TEACH (Explicitly)
SUPPORT (Pivots)

PROGRESS MONITORING & ACCOUNTABILITY

1.8 Progress Monitoring & Accountability

WHY?

Progress monitoring and accountability are an essential part of making sure that learning goals are being met. It also helps to identify areas where students may need additional support. Regularly tracking progress keeps students motivated and focused. With consistent progress monitoring and accountability, teachers can provide timely feedback, guiding students toward continuous improvement and deeper understanding.

IT'S UNDENIABLE

Progress monitoring and accountability are critical components of effective teaching and learning. These practices ensure that students receive timely feedback and that instructional strategies are adjusted to meet individual learning needs.

Research consistently shows that progress monitoring leads to significant improvements in student outcomes. Fuchs and Fuchs (2006) found that regular progress monitoring helps identify learning gaps early, allowing for targeted interventions that boost academic performance. A systematic review by Stecker, Lembke, and Foegen (2008) emphasized that data-driven decision making, facilitated by progress monitoring, is crucial for tailoring instruction to meet the diverse needs of students, thereby enhancing learning outcomes. When students understand their progress, they are more motivated and engaged, which further supports academic success.

Progress monitoring provides educators with valuable data that informs instructional practices. Fisher and Frey (2021) highlighted that frequent and systematic progress monitoring allows teachers to make informed decisions about instructional strategies, ensuring that each student's learning needs are successfully addressed. Effective use of student achievement data isn't just about knowing where they are but also about using that information to make decisions that will move them forward in their learning journey, leading to improved engagement and achievement (Hamilton et al., 2009).

Evidence-Based Practices to Support
Progress Monitoring & Accountability

- Deliberate practice
- Effort management
- Persistence, engagement
- Direct instruction
- Success criteria
- Differentiation
- Strategy monitoring
- Help seeking
- Formative evaluation
- Clear goal intentions
- Feedback: Reinforcement and cues
- Response to intervention

These factors have an effect size that represent substantial growth (Hattie, 2023).

The role of progress monitoring in fostering student self-efficacy and ownership of learning is well-documented. Schunk and Zimmerman (2007) asserted that when students track their progress, they develop a stronger belief in their abilities, which enhances their motivation to learn. Moss and Brookhart (2019) argued that formative assessment, a key component of progress monitoring, involves continuous feedback that helps students understand their learning journey. By setting clear learning targets and success criteria, learners are able to take an active role in their education, leading to greater self-efficacy and improved learning outcomes. In addition, Dueck (2021) emphasized the need for student involvement in the assessment process. He argued that students be given opportunities to self-report their progress and that educators create deliberate spaces for meaningful self-evaluation. Students gain more control and agency over their learning by being actively involved.

Progress monitoring and accountability are essential for enhancing student learning and instructional effectiveness. Effective data use in the classroom transforms information into actionable knowledge, empowering educators to make informed decisions that positively impact student learning outcomes (Wayman et al., 2012). By providing timely feedback and data-driven insights, these practices create a responsive and adaptive learning environment. However, successful implementation requires adequate resources, professional development, and a supportive approach to accountability. As research continues to evolve, it's crucial for educators to stay informed and adopt best practices that promote student success.

> **Reflect** ▶ *How effectively am I using progress monitoring strategies to track student growth and adjust instructional practices accordingly? What steps can I take to ensure that students are actively engaged in their own learning and take ownership of their progress?*

A CORE MEMORY FROM GAIL AND ALLISON

When we started talking about our experiences with assessment, we realized that even though 2000 miles separate us, there was a common thread running through our stories. Both of us felt the weight of expectations for our students to excel in assessments that were administered three times a year. The pressure was obvious, and the time constraints only added to the stress as we juggled teaching responsibilities alongside test preparation.

Ironically, the data collected from these assessments, which played a pivotal role in determining student proficiency and our effectiveness as teachers, often ended up gathering dust in file cabinets until the next assessment cycle. It was a cycle of anticipation, administration, and then neglect. There was little to no opportunity to glean insights from these assessments that would inform daily instruction or provide timely interventions for struggling students.

It was in each of our next steps that our core memories around progress monitoring and accountability were formed. For Gail, this happened as she changed her perspective around district required assessments. Since they must be given, she was determined to make the most of them and gain any information she could that would help her. She designated time after each assessment period to look at data and make notes that would help. This, partnered with a deep dive into the practice of conferring and keeping track of student information, changed her practice and student outcomes. Each interaction she had with a student became yet one more piece of information to inform her next steps of instruction. Brief conferences or small group lessons, whole-group interactions, goal-setting conferences, and each conversation became a way to learn more about each student.

Allison's core memory came as a result of Gail's work with conferring. It was when Gail shared the many strategies she had implemented to monitor student progress and hold students accountable for their learning that Allison's perspective shifted. Inspired by Gail's dedication and the positive impact it had on her students, Allison decided to integrate similar practices into her own classroom.

Sometimes it takes a change in perspective, and other times it takes collaboration with a colleague. Regardless, each teacher has a similar, yet unique journey, to finding their way through progress monitoring and accountability. We are always on the journey because we are always looking for ways to be more effective and impactful educators.

Progress monitoring and accountability aren't just tasks on a checklist but essential components of effective teaching and learning. There is a transformative power of ongoing assessment and personalized support. It's important to celebrate small victories, adjust instructional strategies based on student needs, and create a sense of ownership and responsibility among students. When this happens, the once daunting cycle of assessments and neglect transforms into a cycle of growth, reflection, and meaningful learning experiences.

This Makes Me Think Of

TEACHER PRACTICES: *What you can do*

Set Clear Learning Objectives

Establish clear, measurable learning goals for students. This supports both teachers' and students' understanding of what's expected and provides a basis for assessing progress. See learning goals and performance goals (page 241).

Use Formative Assessments

Formative assessment is an ongoing, interactive process that involves gathering evidence of student learning during instruction to inform and adjust teaching strategies, enhance student understanding, and promote academic growth. Incorporate regular formative assessments to gather ongoing feedback about student learning. This can include quizzes, polls, exit tickets (page 135), observations, think-pair-share, and informal checks for understanding

Regularly Review Data

Analyze assessment data regularly to identify trends, strengths, and areas for improvement. Use this data to inform instructional decisions and to provide targeted support where needed.

Feedback

Offer students timely and constructive feedback on their performance. Feedback should be specific, actionable, and focused on guiding students toward improvement. For example, "I noticed_____, and as a result_____."

Communicate with Caregivers

Keep parents and guardians informed about their child's progress. Regular communication can help build a partnership that supports student learning.

Keep Track of Student Information

Keep a record of student progress. This documentation can help track growth over time and is useful for reporting purposes and for planning future instruction. (See page 90.)

Foster Self-Efficacy

Encouraging students to reflect on their own learning and set personal goals empowers them to take ownership of their educational journey, thereby enhancing their self-efficacy.

Touchpoints

Touchpoints enable us to evaluate the effectiveness of our instruction, and they help us monitor student progress. Every time we touch base with a student, whether in a small group or in a one-on-one conference, we take notes about what we noticed, the instruction we provided, and what the student's next steps might be. We stay focused on the child's goal and strategy to keep the conference brief and to maintain curricular coherence. Touchpoints are used to evaluate and determine how a child is progressing in learning and using an assigned strategy.

- 4 = exceeding standard
- 3 = meeting standard
- 2 = approaching standard
- 1 = below standard

When a child has received two or three 3s or 4s in a row, they show us they have competently added the strategy to their repertoire and are ready to layer on a new skill or strategy. A check mark and date in the touchpoint box on the conferring form or strategy-group page signals the end of the daily teaching and coaching support for that strategy. Though we phase out direct instruction, we continue to monitor periodically.

We value touchpoints because of how easily they allow us to monitor student understanding and application of the strategies taught.

Pivots

Using touchpoints as a tool to guide us, we pivot our instruction as needed. If after three teaching attempts a student has only touchpoints of 1s or 2s, we look at our instruction and change something. This might involve reteaching concepts, offering additional practice, or providing enrichment activities to those who would benefit. When looking for instructional pivots, consider:

- books and materials being used (fiction, nonfiction, good-fit books?),
- instructional setting (one-on-one or small group),
- the form of instruction (modeling, think-aloud, explicit instruction),
- student's reading behaviors (from the I-chart), and
- strategy and goal (asking whether this is the best strategy/goal for this child at this time).

RECOMMENDED READING

Accountability in Action: A Blueprint for Learning Organizations by Douglas B. Reeves (2004).

Advancing Formative Assessment in Every Classroom: A Guide for Instructional Leaders by Connie M. Moss and Susan M. Brookhart (2019).

Cultivating Genius: An Equity Framework for Culturally and Historically Responsive Literacy by Gholdy Muhammad (2020).

Embedded Formative Assessment (Strategies for Classroom Formative Assessment That Drives Student Engagement and Learning) (New Art and Science of Teaching) by Dylan Wiliam (2017).

Redefining Student Accountability: A Proactive Approach to Teaching Behavior Outside the Gradebook (Your Guide to Improving Student Learning by Teaching and Nurturing Positive Student Behavior) by Tom Schimmer (2017).

Student Assessment: Better Evidence, Better Decisions, Better Learning by Dylan Wiliam, Douglas Fisher, Nancy Frey (2024).

Using Data to Focus Instructional Improvement by Cheryl James-Ward, Douglas Fisher, Nancy Frey, and Diane Lapp (2016).

FROM THE FIELD

This year, my teaching role shifted from Kindergarten teacher to Reading Resource teacher, focusing on Tier 2 and Tier 3 Phonics interventions for striving readers. I served around 42 students, each needing weekly or biweekly progress monitoring. Initially, the data collection was overwhelming. I first tried assessing one student per day after their 30-minute session, but this approach failed. Then, I attempted to assess during students' fine arts rotations by pulling them from their beloved lessons, but that didn't work either.

Finally, I devised a plan to teach a review lesson on Fridays. During this time, students could choose to read decodable books or play decodable word games while I pulled individuals to gather data. This strategy succeeded! The students enjoyed the change of pace, and I was able to collect the necessary data to assess our interventions' effectiveness. Perseverance was key, as I had no predecessor in this role to seek advice from. I just had to keep trying until I found a solution that worked for both my students and me.

—Jennifer Haylett, Florida

Keep everyone in the loop: Ensure there are no surprises for parents, principals, or your team. Getting caught off guard by unexpected student performance is never fun or productive. Have regular conversations with parents throughout the year to build trust and keep them informed. Also, after a busy day, simplify your reflection process by sorting student work into three piles: at level, above level, and needs more practice. This makes it easier for you to process and plan. Focus on how to support the students who need more practice. Use this information to plan your next steps, discuss with parents, and provide additional support as needed.

—Emily Kaye, Canada

Students love to see their progress week after week. By creating a data notebook for each student, they can track their own scores and monitor their progress, holding themselves more accountable for their learning. Since implementing this, I've seen test scores drastically improve!

—McKenzie Bakken, South Dakota

CHECK-IN: How are you doing?

Want to know if you are effective with your progress monitoring and accountability practices? Reflect on the following questions:

Goal Setting: Have I clearly defined and communicated learning goals and expectations to my students?

Frequency: How often do I assess student progress through formal or informal assessments?

Feedback: Do I provide timely and constructive feedback that helps students understand their strengths and areas for improvement?

Record Keeping: Am I consistently keeping track of student progress to inform my instruction?

Student Involvement: Do I involve students in tracking their own progress and setting personal learning goals?

Adaptability: Am I adjusting my teaching strategies based on the progress monitoring data to better meet the needs of all students?

Equity: Am I ensuring that all students are held accountable in a fair and supportive manner?

Impact Statement

Progress monitoring and accountability drive effective teaching by providing timely, actionable data that guides instructional decisions, ensuring all students are on track to meet their learning goals.

PROGRESS MONITORING & ACCOUNTABILITY
Lessons Included in Section 2

The following lessons provide a way to communicate to students the purpose of progress monitoring and accountability so they may be a part of the process. The lessons in Section 2 provide a springboard of ideas. Use them as they are or adjust them to fit the group of students in front of you.

PM.1 Goal Setting

PM.2 Self-Assessment Skills

PM.3 Understanding Feedback

PM.4 Planning Template

Section 2

This section of the book provides ready-to-go, easy-to-use lessons from each of the eight components covered in Section 1. Drumroll please . . . Here's what you have been waiting for! Before you jump straight to the lessons, read the next two pages to see how they work! These lessons follow a template that divides the information into four sections, and we include extra planning templates along with each set of lessons so you can add your own based on the needs of your students and curriculum.

Section 2: Lessons—How This Will Work

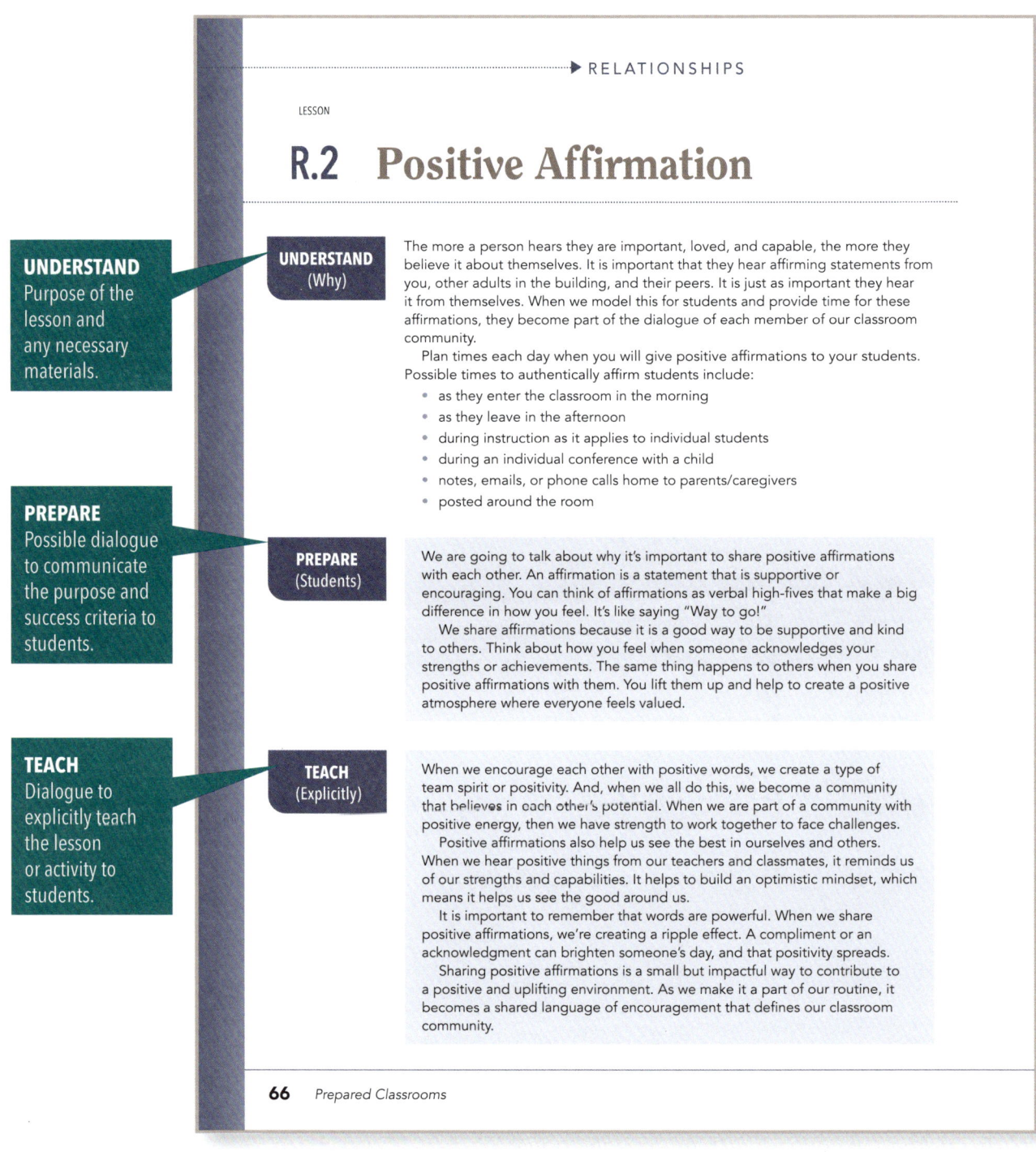

▶ RELATIONSHIPS

LESSON

R.2 Positive Affirmation

UNDERSTAND
Purpose of the lesson and any necessary materials.

UNDERSTAND (Why)

The more a person hears they are important, loved, and capable, the more they believe it about themselves. It is important that they hear affirming statements from you, other adults in the building, and their peers. It is just as important they hear it from themselves. When we model this for students and provide time for these affirmations, they become part of the dialogue of each member of our classroom community.

Plan times each day when you will give positive affirmations to your students. Possible times to authentically affirm students include:

- as they enter the classroom in the morning
- as they leave in the afternoon
- during instruction as it applies to individual students
- during an individual conference with a child
- notes, emails, or phone calls home to parents/caregivers
- posted around the room

PREPARE
Possible dialogue to communicate the purpose and success criteria to students.

PREPARE (Students)

We are going to talk about why it's important to share positive affirmations with each other. An affirmation is a statement that is supportive or encouraging. You can think of affirmations as verbal high-fives that make a big difference in how you feel. It's like saying "Way to go!"

We share affirmations because it is a good way to be supportive and kind to others. Think about how you feel when someone acknowledges your strengths or achievements. The same thing happens to others when you share positive affirmations with them. You lift them up and help to create a positive atmosphere where everyone feels valued.

TEACH
Dialogue to explicitly teach the lesson or activity to students.

TEACH (Explicitly)

When we encourage each other with positive words, we create a type of team spirit or positivity. And, when we all do this, we become a community that believes in each other's potential. When we are part of a community with positive energy, then we have strength to work together to face challenges.

Positive affirmations also help us see the best in ourselves and others. When we hear positive things from our teachers and classmates, it reminds us of our strengths and capabilities. It helps to build an optimistic mindset, which means it helps us see the good around us.

It is important to remember that words are powerful. When we share positive affirmations, we're creating a ripple effect. A compliment or an acknowledgment can brighten someone's day, and that positivity spreads.

Sharing positive affirmations is a small but impactful way to contribute to a positive and uplifting environment. As we make it a part of our routine, it becomes a shared language of encouragement that defines our classroom community.

66 *Prepared Classrooms*

Here's an example. "Mason, when you came over to the carpet this morning I noticed you were quiet and respectful to those around you. And, you were smiling. It made me smile when I saw you happy and ready to learn."

I am going to give you a minute to look at the person to your right and think of a positive affirmation you can share with them. Then, we will go around the group and share. (Go around the group so each child has a chance to share and receive a positive affirmation.)

Let's make it a point to share positive affirmations with each other. Whether it's acknowledging someone's hard work, their creativity, or appreciating who they are, these affirmations have the power to make our shared journey through school an even more positive and enjoyable experience for everyone.

SUPPORT (Pivots)

- It is important to keep any affirmative statement true, authentic, and intentional.
- You may choose to have a mirror in your classroom with affirmative statements around it that help to remind children all the great qualities about them. (See image below.)
- Peter Reynolds and Susan Verde have a whole series of books (the "I Am" series) you can use to launch this way of thinking. Wouldn't it be great if students said, "I am enough!" "I am worthy!" "I am loved!" And "I have got this!" on a daily basis!?

SUPPORT: Possible pivots or next steps to enhance learning.

AFFIRMATIONS

- You worked hard on that!
- You must be proud of yourself!
- That required some deep thinking!
- Very creative!
- You always do the best you can.
- you learned a lot today.
- You are dedicated.
- Look at how you persevered through that!
- That was very kind.
- Anything is possible.
- You make me smile.
- You are strong.
- You are capable
- You are confident.
- You are persistent and never give up!
- You are unique and valuable.
- You have a positive attitude.
- You are focused.
- You are resilient.
- You are an important part of our classroom community.

HELPFUL HINT See the print in the shaded boxes? This optional language is included to get you started. You can read it as is or adjust as needed.

SECTION 1 Relationships **67**

2.1 RELATIONSHIPS

RELATIONSHIPS

LESSON

R.1 Name Pronunciation

UNDERSTAND (Why?)

Names are a core part of identity. Family names may be handed down from one generation to the next and can have a special meaning or be a source of pride. Be intentional to take the time to learn each child's name as quickly as possible, and provide opportunities for them to learn each other's names, too.

Select a book for a read aloud that highlights the importance of an individual's name. Any of these books are a good place to start:

- *Alma and How She Got Her Name* by Juana Martinez-Neal
- *Always Anjali* by Sheetal Sheth
- *Calvin* by JR Ford and Vanessa Ford
- *Shin-Chi's Canoe* by Nicola I. Campbell
- *The Boy Who Tried to Shrink His Name* by Sandhya Parappukkaran
- *The Name Jar* by Yangsook Choi
- *Your Name is a Song* by Jamilah Thompkins-Bigelow

PREPARE (Students)

Our names are a very important part of who we are. When meeting someone, it's important to pay close attention to their name and the way they want their name said, which is called the pronunciation. Today we're going to learn about names and then you will have a chance to share your name with our class and how to say or pronounce your name. We'll practice saying each other's names so that we're able to learn them. We'll know we're successful when we can identify each classmate by their name, saying it correctly.

TEACH (Explicitly)

Share a read aloud with your students that highlights the importance of an individual's name. Have a conversation about the book, the feelings of the character, what's learned from the story, etc.

If you have an example of a time your name was mispronounced or unknown, share your story and how you felt.

Have students go around and share their name. As they say their name, take notes on the pronunciation that will help you to remember how to say it correctly. Have the student say their name and the class repeat it. Do this with each member of the class, providing brain breaks if necessary.

We just learned how each classmate says their name. We learned the correct pronunciation. In the days and weeks to come we'll continue to practice saying each other's names so we can be sure to say them correctly.

SUPPORT (Pivots)

- Refer to your notes to be sure you're pronouncing student names correctly.
- For three to five days, go around the room having each child say their name and the class repeat it.

#	Student Name	Pronunciation
1		
2		
3		
4		
5		
6		
7		
8		
9		
10		
11		
12		
13		
14		
15		
16		
17		
18		
19		
20		
21		
22		
23		
24		
25		
26		
27		
28		
29		
30		

RELATIONSHIPS

LESSON

R.2 Positive Affirmation

UNDERSTAND (Why?)

The more a person hears they are important, loved, and capable, the more they believe it about themselves. It's important that they hear affirming statements from you, other adults in the building, and their peers. It's just as important they hear it from themselves. When we model this for students and provide time for these affirmations, they become part of the dialogue of each member of our classroom community.

Plan times each day when you will give positive affirmations to your students. Possible times to authentically affirm students include:

- as they enter the classroom in the morning
- as they leave in the afternoon
- during instruction as it applies to individual students
- during an individual conference with a child
- notes, emails, or phone calls home to parents/caregivers
- posted around the room

PREPARE (Students)

We're going to talk about why it's important to share positive affirmations with each other. An affirmation is a statement that's supportive or encouraging. You can think of affirmations as verbal high fives that make a big difference in how you feel. It's like saying "Way to go!"

We share affirmations because it's a good way to be supportive and kind to others. Think about how you feel when someone acknowledges your strengths or achievements. The same thing happens to others when you share positive affirmations with them. You lift them up and help to create a positive atmosphere where everyone feels valued.

TEACH (Explicitly)

When we encourage each other with positive words, we create a type of team spirit or positivity. And, when we all do this, we become a community that believes in each other's potential. When we're part of a community with positive energy, then we have strength to work together to face challenges.

Positive affirmations also help us see the best in ourselves and others. When we hear positive things from our teachers and classmates, it reminds us of our strengths and capabilities. It helps to build an optimistic mindset, which means it helps us see the good around us.

It's important to remember that words are powerful. When we share positive affirmations, we're creating a ripple effect. A compliment or an acknowledgment can brighten someone's day, and that positivity spreads.

Sharing positive affirmations is a small but impactful way to contribute to a positive and uplifting environment. As we make it a part of our routine, it becomes a shared language of encouragement that defines our classroom community.

Here's an example. "Mason, when you came over to the carpet this morning I noticed you were quiet and respectful to those around you. And, you were smiling. It made me smile when I saw you happy and ready to learn."

I'm going to give you a minute to look at the person to your right and think of a positive affirmation you can share with them. Then, we'll go around the group and share. *(Go around the group so each child has a chance to share and receive a positive affirmation.)*

Let's make it a point to share positive affirmations with each other. Whether it's acknowledging someone's hard work, their creativity, or appreciating who they are, these affirmations have the power to make our shared journey through school an even more positive and enjoyable experience for everyone.

SUPPORT (Pivots)

- It's important to keep any affirmative statement true, authentic, and intentional.
- You may choose to have a mirror in your classroom with affirmative statements around it that help to remind children of all the great qualities about them. (See image below.)
- Peter Reynolds and Susan Verde have a whole series of books (the "I Am" series) you can use to launch this way of thinking. Wouldn't it be great if students said, "I am enough!" "I am worthy!" "I am loved!" and "I have got this!" on a daily basis!?

AFFIRMATIONS

- You worked hard on that!
- You must be proud of yourself!
- That required some deep thinking!
- Very creative!
- You always do the best you can.
- You learned a lot today.
- You are dedicated.
- Look at how you persevered through that!
- That was very kind.
- Anything is possible.
- You make me smile.
- You are strong.
- You are capable.
- You are confident.
- You are persistent and never give up!
- You are unique and valuable.
- You have a positive attitude.
- You are focused.
- You are resilient.
- You are an important part of our classroom community.

RELATIONSHIPS

LESSON

R.3 Teach Read-Aloud Behaviors

UNDERSTAND (Why?)

Classroom read-aloud sessions provide opportunities for students and teachers to engage in shared literary experiences, fostering a sense of connection and community. Through read alouds, educators can model effective communication, active listening, and empathy, contributing to stronger relationships. These interactive sessions create a positive and inclusive classroom culture centered around a love for reading and learning together.

PREPARE (Students)

Set a purpose for the read aloud by choosing a text for enjoyment, information, or a shared literary experience. Tell students:

> Read alouds help us build community and make sense of the world around us. To get the most from a read aloud, we must learn how to be active listeners. We do this because it shows respect for others and allows us to learn and enjoy what's being read.

TEACH (Explicitly)

Establish clear expectations for behavior during a read-aloud session.

> We listen to someone read aloud for many reasons. Sometimes it's for enjoyment. Other times it's for information and to learn something new. And sometimes it's so we can all be part of the same experience and discuss it. Whatever the reason, it's important to be active listeners when someone is reading so that we can get the most out of it and it's respectful.

Using an anchor chart, list the expected active listening behaviors during a read aloud.

> When listening to someone read aloud, it's important to make eye contact with the reader, sit quietly, keep your hands and body to yourself, focus your listening on what the reader is saying, and ignore distractions.

Select a student to demonstrate active listening by modeling appropriate behaviors while you read a short passage. When finished, reflect on student behaviors. Ask the class:

> Did ___ sit quietly? Did they make eye contact? Did they keep their hands and body to themselves? Did they focus on what was being read? Did they ignore distractions? If this is how you actively listen, is it respectful to the reader? (Yes.) Do you have a better chance to understanding what's being read? (Yes.)

Have students practice active listening behaviors as a whole class while you read another passage. Now we're going to practice as a class. I'm going to read another passage and I want you to practice being an active listener. Remember, that means you will sit quietly, make eye contact with the reader, keep your hands and body to yourself, focus on what the reader is saying, and you will work to ignore distractions. *Read a passage so the class can practice their listening skills.*

When finished, ask students to self-reflect on their behaviors as you review the I-chart.

Okay, now I want you to think about yourself during that read aloud. Show me thumbs up for yes and thumbs sideways if it's something you want to work on. Did you sit quietly? Did you make eye contact? Did you keep your hands and body to yourself? Did you focus on what was being read? Did you ignore distractions? If this is how you actively listen, is it respectful to the reader? (Yes.) Do you have a better chance to understanding what's being read? (Yes.)

Way to go! You will hear read alouds many times during the school year. And sometimes many times in one day. When someone is reading aloud to you, it's important to make sure to follow these behaviors so you can understand what's being read.

SUPPORT (Pivots)

- Continue to review the anchor chart and practice behaviors. Recognize positive behavior and acknowledge when students demonstrate active listening, contribute thoughtfully, or follow the established procedures.
- If disruptive behavior occurs, remind students of expectations and the importance of active listening during read alouds. Have a private conversation including engagement goal setting if needed.
- Overall, celebrate successful read-aloud sessions by recognizing the collective efforts of the class in maintaining positive behavior and emphasize the enjoyment and learning that come from shared reading experiences.

{Increase Understanding} **Read Aloud** *{Respectful / Fun}*
Active Listening
- Sit quietly
- Make eye contact
- Think about what is being read
- Keep hands and body to yourself
- Ignore distractions

RELATIONSHIPS

LESSON

R.4 Turn, Listen, and Talk

UNDERSTAND (Why?)

Incorporating the Turn, Listen, and Talk strategy into the school day helps to establish a conducive and engaging learning environment, fostering effective communication and active participation among students. This increased communication and participation enhances relationships by creating opportunities for building trust, fostering collaboration, enhancing understanding, and promoting inclusivity, ultimately creating a supportive and engaging learning community.

PREPARE (Students)

We're going to learn a strategy that will make our class discussions even better. It's called "turn, listen, and talk." Imagine it like a superpower for communication! We're going to learn this strategy because it helps our brains learn and remember what's being taught. When we actively listen, we're thinking, processing, and engaging with the information. When we're active listeners, we're respectful to those who are talking.

TEACH (Explicitly)

Establish classroom norms and expectations for turn, listen, and talk. Clearly communicate when and how you expect students to use this strategy by writing behaviors down on an anchor chart.

When someone is speaking, we realize it's their "turn" and we respect that, right? We work to give them our full attention. We turn to face them and make eye contact. That's the first part of this strategy—"turn." *(Write on anchor chart.)*

Then comes the next part—"listen." This is when our ears have an important job. We listen actively, not just hearing the words, but paying attention to what's being said and understanding the ideas and feelings behind them. To do this, we face the person who is talking, make eye contact, and ignore any distractions so they have our full attention. This is respectful to the speaker and helps you understand what they are saying. *(Write on anchor chart.)*

Now, here's where we become communication champions. After we have taken our turn to listen, we switch roles. It's now our turn to "talk" and while the other listens. But not just any talk—it's thoughtful, respectful sharing. We build on what others have said, ask questions, and express our own ideas. This way, everyone's voice gets heard, and our discussions become a powerhouse of ideas and we'll learn so much. *(Write on anchor chart.)*

Now I'm going to ask someone to come up here and model the strategy "Turn, Listen, and Talk" with me.

Call on a student to model with you. Tell them they are going to be the speaker and are going to tell you about what they did last night. When they are talking, model active listening. Stand in front of the class, make eye contact, face the speaker, and engage in the act of listening. When they are finished speaking, respond thoughtfully. This visual demonstration helps students understand the behavior. When finished, review the behaviors and reflect on the outcome.

> Let's reflect on what you noticed when we were modeling the turn, listen, and talk strategy. Did I turn to face the speaker and make eye contact? Did I actively listen? Did I ignore distractions? When the speaker was finished, did I respond thoughtfully? (Yes.) If we use the strategy turn, listen, and talk like this will we be successful at active listening and communication? (Yes!)
>
> We call this strategy, "Turn, Listen, and Talk." It will help us to create a classroom where everyone feels heard and valued. Who is ready to try this out in our next discussion?

Then, pair students up and give them a specific prompt or discussion topic. Have them practice taking turns being the speaker and the listener. Encourage them to practice turning toward each other, actively listening, and responding respectfully.

SUPPORT (Pivots)

- After practice sessions, engage the class in reflective discussions. Ask students to share their experiences with the strategy and discuss how it helped their understanding of others and their understanding of the content. Post the anchor chart in the room to serve as a visual reminder to reinforce the concept.
- Review and practice so that students build behaviors with consistent implementation. Encourage students to self-monitor their use of the strategy.
- Review the anchor chart as needed.

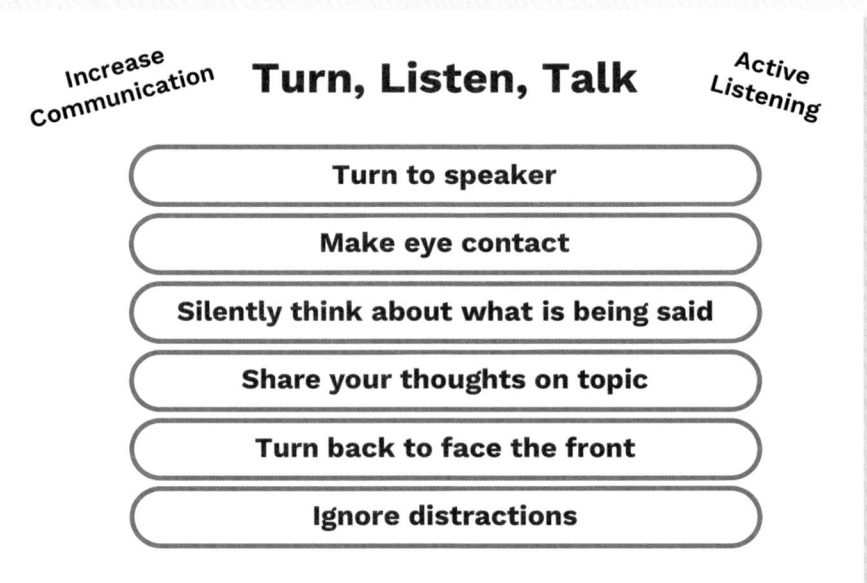

126 Prepared Classroom

RELATIONSHIPS

LESSON

R.5 Me Too!

UNDERSTAND (Why?)

This activity helps students get to know each other better while also providing an element of movement and engagement. It works great as an icebreaker or a brain break during a lesson and fosters a sense of connection and commonality that helps encourage stronger relationships among your learning community.

PREPARE (Students)

Have a space large enough for students to stand in a circle or sit in a group.

> We're going to play a fun and interactive game called "Me Too"! We're going to play this because it's a great way for us to learn more about each other and find out what things we have in common, and we may use it at times for a brain break.

TEACH (Explicitly)

> Here's how it works:
> One person at a time will stand up and share something interesting or cool about themselves. For example, "I love playing the guitar." If that's true for you too, you stand up and say, "Me too!"
>
> We're going to keep it light, positive, and inclusive, so feel free to share something you're proud of or excited about. We want to learn about each other and be open and accepting. Are we ready? Who would like to go first and share something about themselves?

One student at a time steps forward or stands up and shares a personal fact about themselves. For example, "I play the piano." Other students who share the same fact respond by standing up, saying, "Me too!" Everyone returns to the starting position, and the next student takes their turn to share a fact. Repeat the process, allowing each student to share something about themselves, and others respond with "Me too!" if it applies to them.

> We just had a chance to learn more about the friends in our class. What's one thing new you learned about someone? We'll do this again another time. I can't wait to keep learning more about you!

SUPPORT (Pivots)

- Emphasize the importance of positive and supportive reactions when someone shares a fact. Encourage students to celebrate similarities and embrace differences. Pay close attention to the responses to ensure that all students feel included. If a particular statement excludes some students, consider modifying or balancing it with statements that cater to a broader range of experiences.
- After the activity, take a moment to reflect on the experience with the students. Discuss what they learned about each other and how the activity contributed to building a sense of community within the group.

Possible Starting Statements for "Me Too!"

- I play the piano
- I have a pet dog.
- I speak more than one language.
- I have a sibling.
- I love playing video games.
- I have broken a bone.
- I enjoy listening to music.
- I have seen the movie Batman.
- I like to eat pizza.
- I like seafood.
- I enjoy playing basketball.
- On the weekends I like to wake up early.
- I like rainy days.
- I like to read.
- I have traveled out of the state.
- I have traveled out of the country.
- I have a pet cat.
- I like to eat or want to try sushi.
- I like broccoli.
- I enjoy watching cartoons.
- I have flown on an airplane before.

RELATIONSHIPS

LESSON

R.6 Morning Message

UNDERSTAND (Why?)

A morning message is typically a greeting written by the teacher and displayed or projected for all to see. Morning messages are a powerful and efficient way to integrate various concepts and skills while establishing a positive and supportive learning environment. The brief daily routine contributes to a sense of purpose for the day, consistency, and coming together as a community, making it a valuable part of building classroom relationships.

PREPARE (Students)

Good morning, everyone! I hope you're ready for a fantastic day ahead. It's time for our morning message, where we get to share important updates, interesting facts, and some words of encouragement. This helps to prepare us for our day. So, let's get started. Are you ready? Great!

TEACH (Explicitly)

You may choose to write the message in front of the students and think aloud while writing, or you may wish to already have the message written and read it with the class. The example below is if it was written ahead of time.

Let's read our message together. *(Point to the words as you read or call on a student to come and lead the reading.)*

Dear Class,

Today is Tuesday, November 19. After lunch we have music. In science we'll continue learning about the water cycle, and in social studies we'll talk about the difference between needs and wants. It will be a wonderful day!

Love, (your name)

Great! Does anyone have any questions about our day? *(Allow time for questions and follow-up.)* Let's make it a great one!

SUPPORT (Pivots)

- Each day consider the purpose of your message. Is it to provide information, inspire, set goals, or build community?
- Take a moment to reflect on the effectiveness of your morning messages. Are students engaged? Do they respond positively? Use feedback to refine and improve your approach.
- Make the message relevant to your students' lives or current happenings in the school. This can help them connect to the message on a personal level.
- Keep the message concise and consider incorporating students in ways such as shout-outs, recognizing achievements, or sharing something interesting a student did.

Possible Morning Message Elements

A morning message provides a versatile platform for teaching various concepts and skills. Here are ways you can incorporate different elements into your morning messages:

1. **Vocabulary:**
   - Introduce and reinforce new vocabulary words relevant to the day's lessons or thematic units.

2. **Sentence Structure:**
   - Model different sentence structures to help students understand the components of a well-structured sentence.
   - Practice varying sentence lengths and types for writing fluency.

3. **Content:**
   - Reinforce content-related concepts by integrating them into the morning message.
   - Summarize previous lessons or introduce new topics, creating anticipation for the day's learning.

4. **Schedule Considerations:**
   - Review the daily schedule to help students anticipate activities and transitions throughout the day.
   - Discuss any special events, projects, or changes in routine to provide a sense of structure and reduce anxiety.

5. **Math Concepts:**
   - Integrate math concepts by incorporating relevant problems or scenarios.
   - Pose math-related riddles or challenges that encourage problem solving.

6. **Current Events:**
   - Connect the morning message to current events, fostering an awareness of the world outside the classroom.
   - Discuss age-appropriate news or events and encourage students to share their thoughts.

7. **Positive Affirmations:**
   - Include positive affirmations or motivational messages to promote a growth mindset and boost students' confidence.

8. **Interactive Elements:**
   - Add interactive elements such as questions, prompts, or challenges to encourage student engagement.
   - Create opportunities for students to share their thoughts, experiences, or responses with the class.

9. **Seasonal Themes:**
   - Tie morning messages to seasonal themes, holidays, or special events to make learning more enjoyable and relevant.

RELATIONSHIPS

LESSON

R.7 True, True, False

UNDERSTAND (Why?)

This is a popular game or brain break where students take turns making three statements about themselves—two of which are true, and one is false. The other students then try to guess which statement is false.

PREPARE (Students)

Have students come to the gathering area where they can sit in a circle or group. We're going to play a game called "True, True, False." It's a game that will challenge our thinking a bit and help us to learn some interesting facts about each other. Remember, something that's true means it really happened, and something that's false means it isn't true and didn't really happen. For example, if I said I ate breakfast this morning, it's true because I really did eat breakfast. If I say I ate pizza for breakfast, that's false because I didn't eat pizza, I ate cereal. Show me thumbs up if you're ready.

TEACH (Explicitly)

I'll go first. Here's how it works: I'm going to make three statements about myself. Two of them will be true, and one will be false. Your job is to figure out which statement is the false one.

After I share my statements, you will decide which statement you think is false.

But here's the twist—once we have revealed the false statement, it's your turn! You will have a chance to share three statements about yourself, two that are true and one that's false. Then, we'll try to guess the false one.

We might not get to everyone right now, but we'll come back to this the next few days until everyone has had a chance to share.

It's a fantastic way to get to know each other better and have some fun along the way. So, are you ready for a round of "True, True, False"? Let's dive in and see how well we know each other!

Here are my statements. *(Provide two true statements and one false—not necessarily in that order. Then have students show which they think is false by a show of hands. Let them know the correct answer.)*

Okay! Now it's your turn. Who would like to go first? *(Call on a student to share and continue with a few others.)*

SUPPORT (Pivots)

- If there were particularly surprising or unexpected truths revealed during the game, use them as conversation starters. Ask follow-up questions or encourage others to share similar experiences.
- You may wish to take a moment to reflect on any commonalities or shared interests that emerged during the game. This can be a great way to strengthen connections within the group.

▶ RELATIONSHIPS

LESSON

R.8 Would You Rather?

UNDERSTAND (Why?)

This is a conversational game that provides a fun way for students to express their preferences while also promoting communication social interaction, and relationship building.

PREPARE (Students)

Have students come to the gathering area where they can sit in a circle or group—whatever allows for easy communication.

> Today we're going to play a game that will help us learn more about each other. You may have heard of it before or maybe you have even played it. It's called "Would You Rather."
>
> Our goal is to have fun and learn more about the friends in our room.

TEACH (Explicitly)

> Here's how we play: I'll ask you a series of questions, and each question will have two options. Your job is to choose the option that you would rather go for. Some of them will be a tough decision and others will be easy, but that's part of the fun!
>
> Let's start with an example. Would you rather have the ability to fly or be invisible? Okay, now I'm going to give you a moment to think about it and then I'll give you directions. *(Pause.)* If you would rather have the ability to fly, stand up. If you would rather have the ability to be invisible, sit down. Ahhh… look around at your friends and see what they think.
>
> Okay, here's another. For dinner would you rather eat spaghetti or tacos? Think about it. If you would rather eat spaghetti, stand up. If you would rather eat tacos sit down.

Continue with your own questions or any on the suggested list of questions that follow this lesson.

When finished:

> Wasn't that fun! I learned some interesting things about you and hope you did too! We'll do this again another time and continue to learn about each other. Thanks for playing!

SUPPORT (Pivots)

- Adjust questions based on the age of the students and the context of the conversation. You also may wish to encourage students to share reasons behind their choices. Optionally, you can have students reflect and share something interesting they learned about their classmates during the activity.
- You might choose to have students stand and sit or move to two different sides of the room or any variety of movement.
- Prepare a list of questions to ask. If using this solely as a relationship builder, you may wish to include a mix of lighthearted, funny, and thought-provoking questions. If you're covering a certain theme or topic in class, you may wish to incorporate related questions. And, you might consider having students come up with their own questions to add an extra layer of personalization to the activity.

Possible Questions: Would You Rather

Would you rather ...

have pizza for breakfast or cereal for dinner?

travel to the past or the future?

have the ability to fly or be invisible?

spend a day at the beach or in the mountains?

have a pet dinosaur or a pet dragon?

always have to whisper or always have to shout?

read a book or solve a math problem?

be a famous actor or a famous musician?

live in a treehouse or a houseboat?

have the power to teleport or time travel?

live without the Internet or without air-conditioning and heating?

be able to control fire or water?

go to a concert or a movie?

play a game or watch television?

be able to change the past or see into the future?

have a rewind button for your life or a pause button?

have the ability to freeze time or fast-forward it?

live in a world where it's always daytime or always nighttime?

play soccer or basketball?

sing or dance?

go on a walk or go for a swim?

RELATIONSHIPS

LESSON

R.9 Exit Slips

UNDERSTAND (Why?)

The end-of-day exit slip not only provides a valuable opportunity for formative assessment but also fosters a positive and supportive classroom environment. It allows you to connect with your students on a personal level and helps them feel heard and valued. Additionally, it encourages reflection and self-awareness.

PREPARE (Students)

Today we'll be doing our end-of-day exit slip. This helps us to think about our day and share our thoughts.

TEACH (Explicitly)

I'll ask a question and you will take a moment to write your thoughts on the paper I give you. Remember, there are no right or wrong answers—this is a chance to express yourself. Today's question is, "What was something new you learned today?" Please take a few minutes to think about your response. Think about what we did today *(maybe provide a brief recap)* and write down at least one thing new that you learned. Go ahead.

When you're finished, please hand it to me and *(give them their next directive)* get your bookbag and return to your seat.

SUPPORT (Pivots)

- Determine the purpose of your exit slip. Is it to gauge understanding, build relationships, or reflect on the day?
- Choose questions that align with your purpose. Consider a mix of academic, personal, and social questions to get a holistic view of the students' experiences. Make sure questions are age appropriate and relevant to your classroom context.
- Determine whether students will write their reflection or share verbally. If they are writing, what will write on and where they will place their slip when they are finished?
- Take time to review student responses. Provide feedback if they shared something personal or if there are opportunities for positive reinforcement.
- Regularly reflect on the effectiveness of the end-of-day exit slips and be open to adapting questions or the process based on your observations.

Possible Exit Slip Questions

1. **Academic Reflection:**
   - What was something new you learned today?
   - What concept or skill did you find challenging?
   - Is there anything you still have questions about?
2. **Personal Reflection:**
   - What's something positive that happened to you today?
   - What made you smile or laugh today?
   - Did you face any challenges today? How did you overcome them?
3. **Social Interaction:**
   - Share one kind thing someone did for you today.
   - Describe a moment when you helped someone else today.
   - Who did you collaborate with today, and what did you accomplish together?
4. **Future Outlook:**
   - What are you looking forward to tomorrow?
   - Is there anything you would like to learn more about in our upcoming lessons?
   - How can you make tomorrow a great day?
5. **Character and Values:**
   - Share one way you demonstrated kindness or empathy today.
   - Reflect on a situation where you showed resilience or perseverance.
   - How did you contribute to creating a positive classroom environment today?
6. **Reading and Hobbies:**
   - What book are you currently reading, and what do you like about it?
   - If you could recommend a book, what would it be and why?
   - What's something interesting you discovered or learned outside of class today?
7. **Home and Family:**
   - How do you plan to help out at home tonight?
   - Share one thing you appreciate about your family.
   - Is there something special you would like to share about your day with your family?
8. **Reflection on Classroom Environment:**
   - What's something you appreciate about our classroom?
   - Is there anything you think we can do to make our classroom even better?
   - How can we make everyone feel included and valued in our class?

GET OUT OF CLASS PASS

WHAT IS ONE THING YOU LEARNED TODAY?

_____

_____

_____

_____

COULD YOU TEACH THIS TO ANOTHER STUDENT?   YES   NO

EXIT TICKET

A question I have about today's learning is

A statement I have about today's learning is

Lightbulb Moments!
Two things I learned today are:

1. _____

_____

2. _____

_____

▶ RELATIONSHIPS

LESSON

R.10 I PICK Book Talk

UNDERSTAND (Why?)

I PICK Book Talks provide a platform for students to share what they are reading, along with their thoughts, interests, and recommendations with their peers, creating meaningful discussions and connections around literature. These conversations foster a sense of camaraderie, mutual respect, and shared enthusiasm for reading, enhancing relationships within the classroom.

Before using this strategy: Teach students how to select a good-fit book using the acronym I PICK. (See Lesson IL 1.4, page 198.)

PREPARE (Students)

Let's talk about I PICK. Who remembers what the I stands for? (I pick up a book). What about the P? (Purpose) I? (Interest) C? (Comprehend) K? (Know most of the words). Right! Well, it can be fun to share what we're reading and see what our friends are reading. Throughout the year when we have a few extra minutes I'm going to ask one or two of you to select a book from your book box and share with us how it's a good-fit book using I PICK. This gives us a chance to share what we're reading and also, we get to see what our friends are reading and maybe get some ideas for future books we might be interested in.

TEACH (Explicitly)

We have a few extra minutes right now so I would like to ask _____ to go choose one book from their book box to share with us. *(That student goes to get their book and holds it up for the class to see.)*

Perfect! Would you please tell us the title of the book?

We see you have Picked a book, let's go look at the I in I PICK. Does this book interest you and why? *(let student share.)*

Okay, let's look at the C. Comprehend. Do you understand what you're reading? Can you tell us a little bit about what the book is about? *(student response.)*

Now the K. Know the words. Do you know most of the words? Can you read a few sentences for us? *(student response.)*

Great! Thank you for sharing!

Then, move to another student if there's time.

SUPPORT (Pivots)

- Students may wish to make note of book titles they are interested in reading later.

▶ RELATIONSHIPS

LESSON

R.11 I Wish My Teacher Knew

UNDERSTAND (Why?)

This is a meaningful and insightful activity that aims to deepen the understanding between teachers and students by creating an open space for them to share their thoughts, experiences, and personal or academic concerns. Encouraging students to share personal thoughts and feelings helps build trust between you and your students. If hidden challenges are revealed, you can support students by tailoring your teaching to better meet their needs and preferences.

PREPARE (Students)

We're going to do an activity called "I Wish My Teacher Knew." We're doing this because it will help me to better understand you. I want you to know that your answers will only be read by me. You can share as much or as little as you want. I know the days can be busy and I want to make sure you have time to tell me the things you want me to know. This activity will help with that. Only share what you're comfortable sharing.

TEACH (Explicitly)

As I mentioned, this activity is called "I Wish My Teacher Knew." It's an opportunity for each of you to share something with me that you might not have had a chance to share before. It could be something you're proud of, something you're struggling with, or just something about you that you think is important for me to know. For example, maybe you want me to know you miss a friend that moved away last year or that you're excited about a new friend you have met or maybe you have something to share that's going on at home, or something that's happening with a team you play on, and it could be what you're excited to learn about, or even that you really want to do more math or reading.

Take a moment to think about something you would like me to know, and let's get started. *(Have students write on a designated slip, in a notebook, or wherever is best for you.)* When you're finished you can place what you're sharing in the basket on the counter (. . . or wherever you would like their response to go).

SUPPORT (Pivots)

- Thank your students for sharing their thoughts and being open with you.
- After collecting the notes, take the time to read and reflect on the responses. Consider how you can incorporate this information into your teaching practices or classroom environment. If there are common themes, share them (anonymously) with the class to reinforce a sense of community.
- If any response requires further discussion you may choose to provide a written response or meet for a conference with a child.

RELATIONSHIPS

LESSON

R.12 Planning Template

UNDERSTAND
(Why?)

PREPARE
(Students)

TEACH
(Explicitly)

SUPPORT
(Pivots)

2.2 ENVIRONMENT

ENVIRONMENT

LESSON

E.1 Respectful Communication

UNDERSTAND (Why?)

Respectful communication promotes empathy, understanding, and constructive dialogue among students, leading to stronger relationships and a sense of community. In this lesson we share language that's posted in the room for students to refer to throughout the year. It equips students with critical social and emotional skills that are essential for navigating diverse and collaborative environments.

PREPARE (Students)

Today, we're going to learn about something very important: respectful communication. Respectful communication is all about treating others with kindness, listening carefully to what they have to say, and considering their feelings. It helps us build positive relationships and create a supportive classroom environment.

TEACH (Explicitly)

I'm going to share what respectful communication looks and sounds like. Imagine you're having a conversation with a friend. How do you want them to speak to you? (Possible student responses: "I want them to listen to me," "I want them to use nice words," "I want them not to interrupt.") Exactly! Respectful communication means listening when others speak, using kind words, and not interrupting. It's about making people feel valued and respected. We do this many times throughout the day, and we can do it during class discussions as well. There are some go-to phrases that we can use to help us be respectful communicators. For example, if you agree with something someone says and have something to add to it, you might say, "I agree with _____, and I would like to add _____." Or, if you do not agree with what someone says, you might say, "I respectfully disagree because _____." *(Write example statements as you share.)*

If you need more information to help you understand what's being said, you might say, "Please give me an example." or "Please explain what you mean by _____."

Let's practice respectful conversations! I'm going to ask an opinion question, and you will share your answer with your partner. They will respond with a respectful comment such as "I agree with you and I would like to add _____," or they might respond with "I respectfully disagree because _____." Are you ready? Turn to your partner and tell them which TV show you think is the funniest. Remember to listen, use kind words, and take turns speaking. *(Students engage in a conversation in which they practice respectful communication.)*

Great! Think to yourself what made your conversation respectful. Was it the kind words? Was it that your partner listened to what you had to say? Was it that you each had a chance to share? *(Pause for students to self-reflect.)* How did it feel to have a respectful conversation? Show me a thumbs-up if it felt good. *(Wait for student response.)* When we communicate respectfully, we build a positive classroom environment. We'll continue to practice respectful communication every day and learn more statements to help you communicate respectfully.

SUPPORT (Pivots)

- Designate a space on the wall or bulletin board to write respectful communication stems for children to use as springboards for their conversations. Templates are provided on the following pages.

SECTION 2 Environment

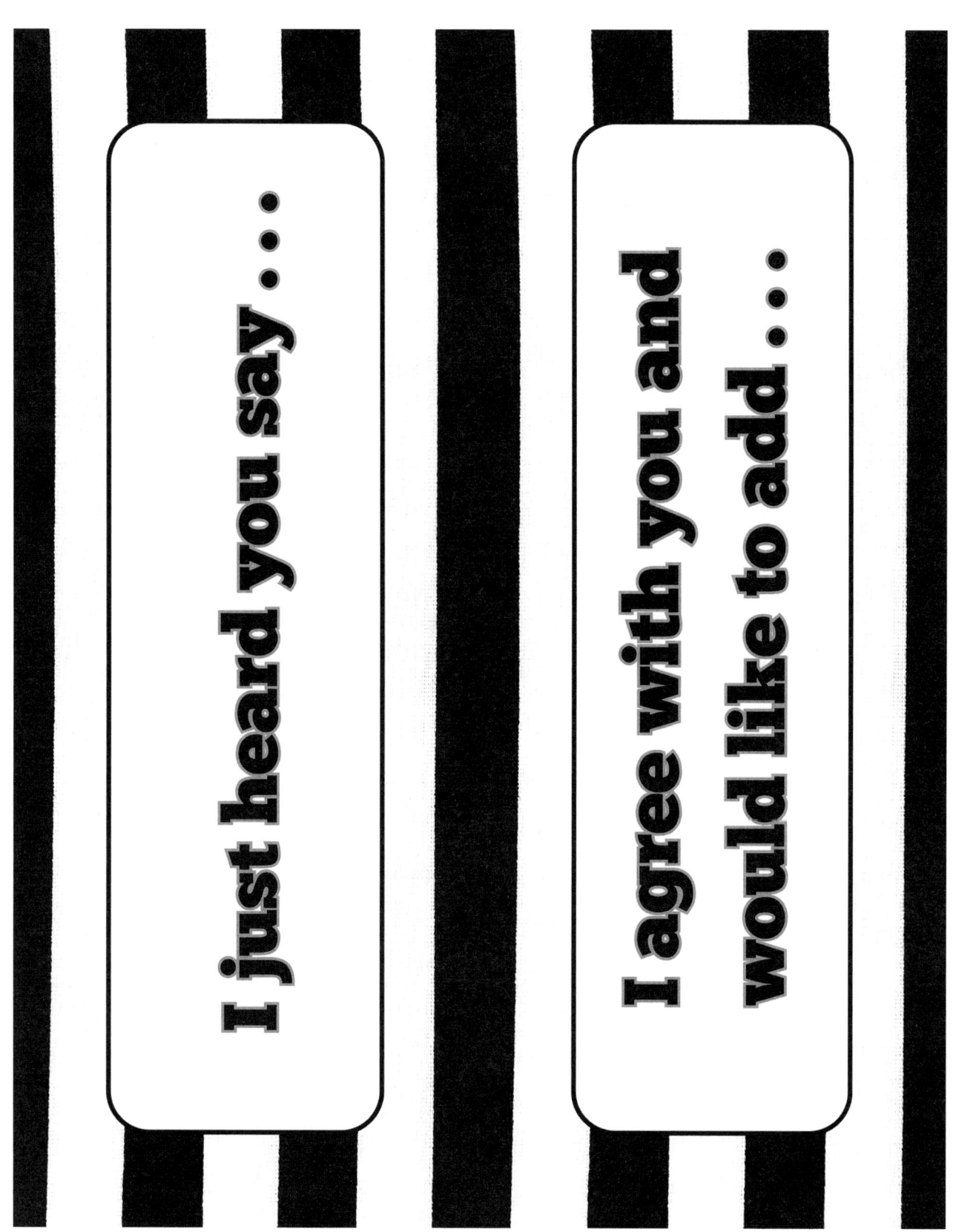

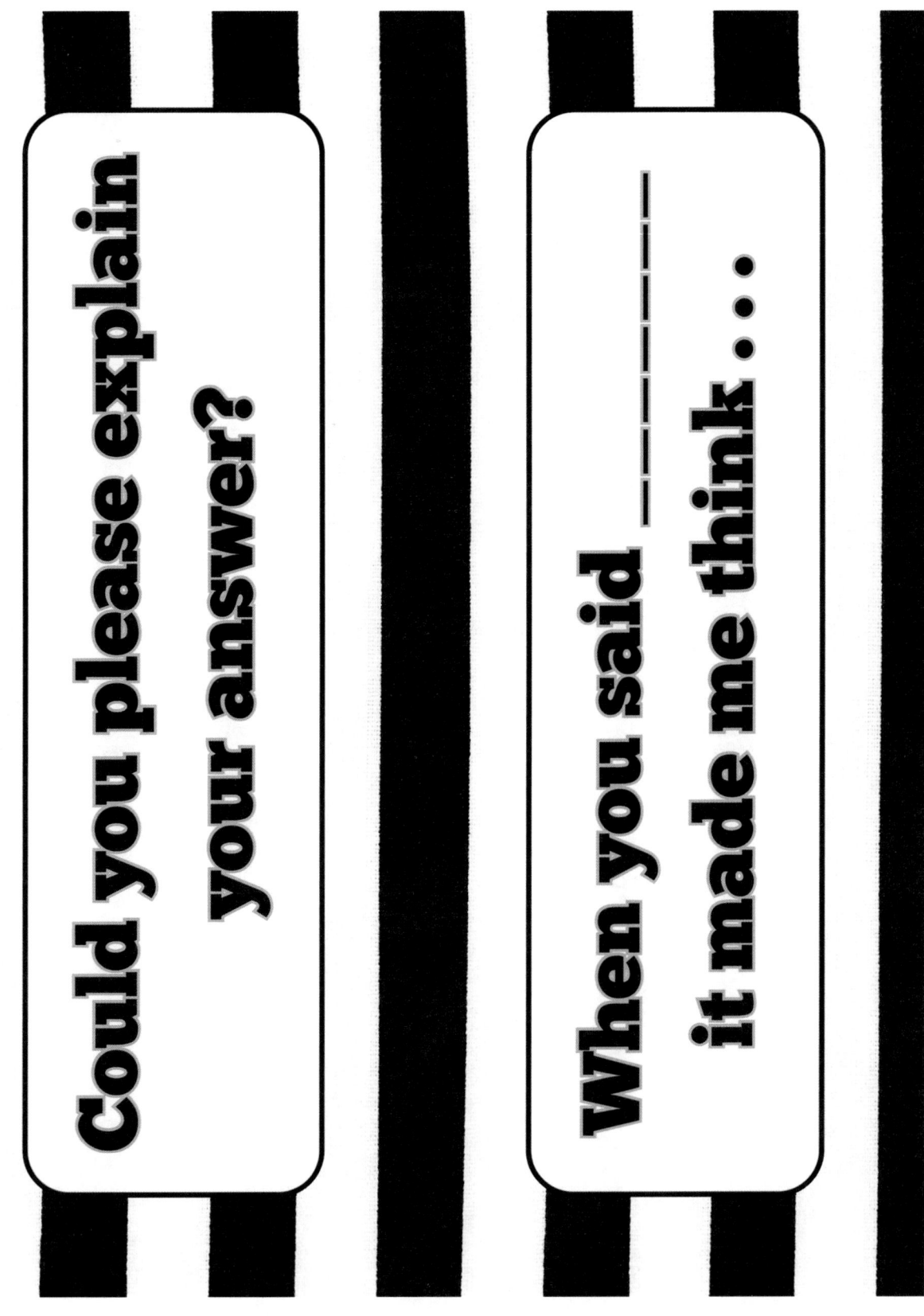

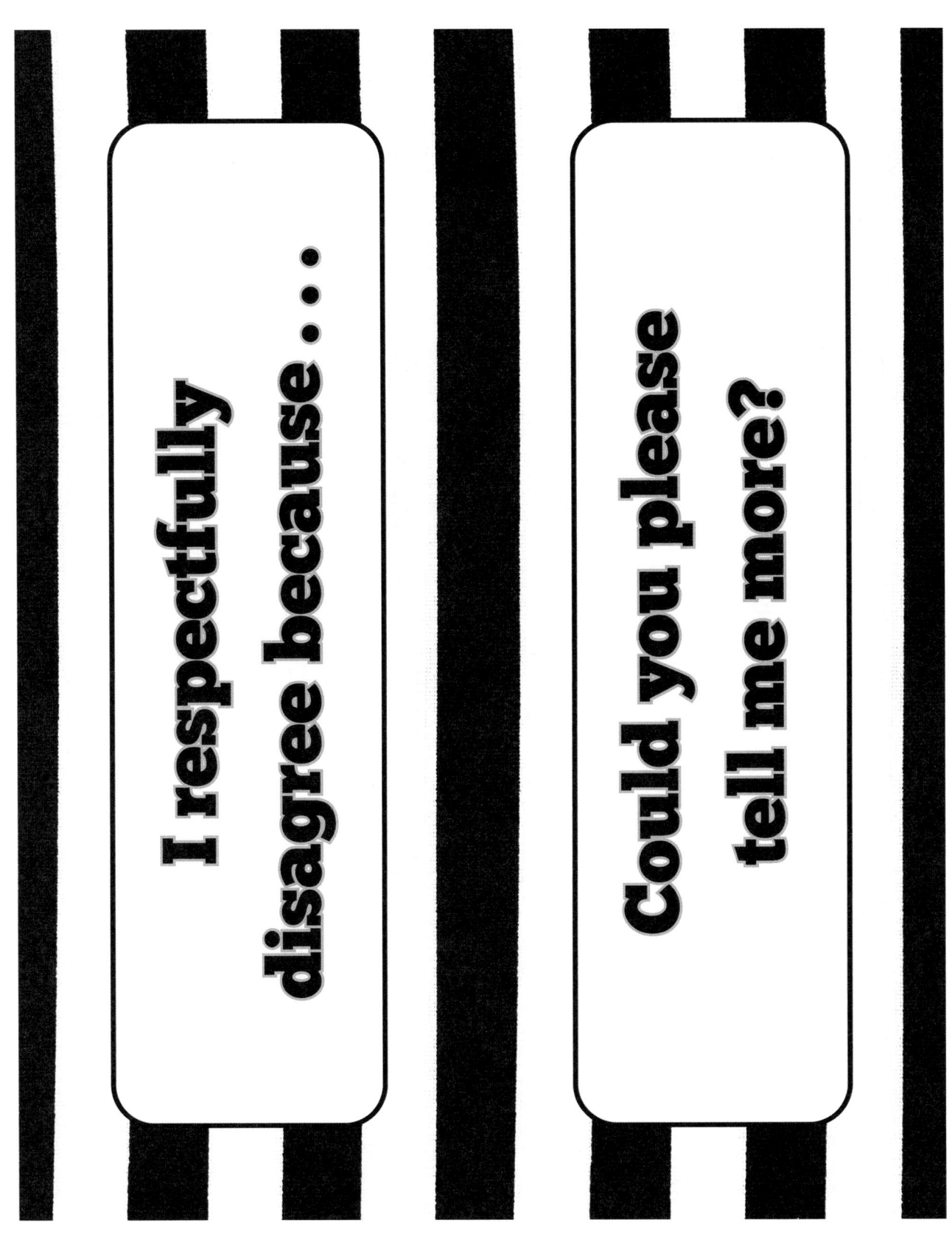

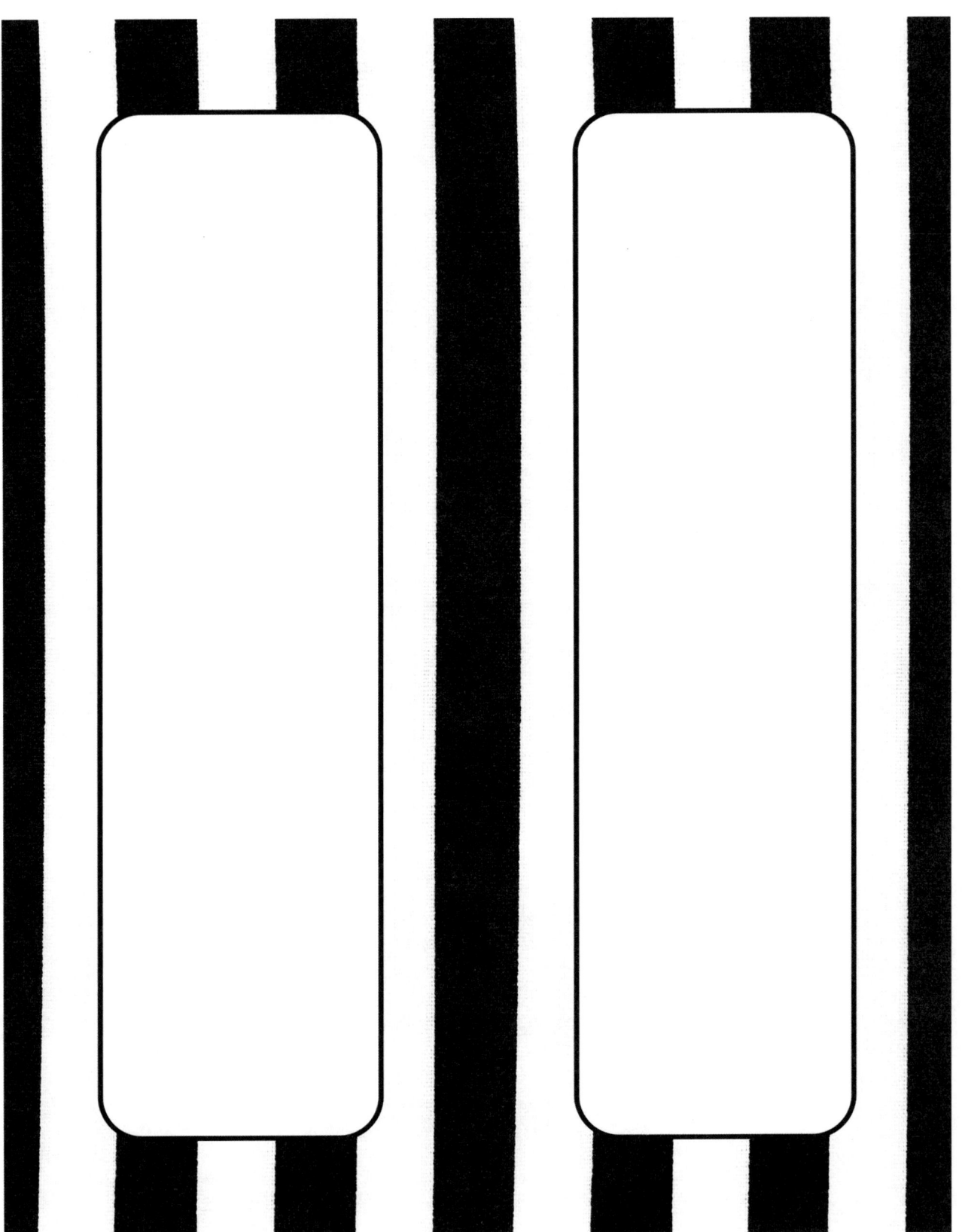

▶ ENVIRONMENT

LESSON

E.2 Stress Management

UNDERSTAND (Why?)

Teaching stress management techniques empowers students to regulate their emotions effectively, fostering a positive emotional environment in the classroom where students feel supported, resilient, and able to focus on learning. These strategies help students cope with academic pressures, social challenges, and personal stressors, improving their overall mental health and ability to succeed in school. By learning healthy coping mechanisms early on, students develop lifelong skills for managing stress and navigating life's challenges effectively.

PREPARE (Students)

Today, we're going to learn some important skills for managing stress and staying calm when things get tough. Stress is a feeling we sometimes have when we're worried or overwhelmed. We can learn strategies to help us feel better when we feel this way. When we feel calm, it's easier to learn new things. Let's explore some fun and helpful ways to take care of our minds and bodies!

TEACH (Explicitly)

The first thing we're going to do is practice taking deep breaths. Sometimes when you're faced with challenges or are worried about something it can help to take deep breaths. We're going to practice doing this together. First, sit comfortably and if you want, you can close your eyes. Now, take a slow, deep breath in through your nose, counting to three silently in your head. Hold the breath for a moment, and then slowly exhale through your mouth, counting to three again. Let's do that a few more times, inhaling deeply (one, two, three) and exhaling slowly (one, two, three). Notice how your body feels more relaxed with each breath. *(Practice breathing with students.)*

    The next strategy we'll practice is to refocus by using our senses. Our five senses are touch, taste, see, hear, and smell. When we feel stressed, our minds can become overwhelmed, and it becomes harder to think clearly. By refocusing our attention on our senses, we can help calm our minds and bring ourselves back to a more relaxed state. This can help us feel better and more in control when faced with challenging situations.

    To use your senses as a way to calm yourself, first you're going to find a comfortable place to sit. Then, take a deep breath in and out. Focus on what you can see around you. Notice the colors, shapes, and textures of objects in the room. *(Pause for students to notice.)* Take a moment to really observe. Now, shift your attention to what you can hear. Listen closely to the sounds around you, both near and far. Notice any sounds that are soothing or calming. *(Pause for students to listen.)* Next, pay attention to what you can feel. Wiggle your toes and fingers and notice the sensation of your clothes against your skin. *(Pause for students to notice what they feel.)* Finally, take a deep breath in, focusing on the smell of the air around you. Notice any scents that you hadn't noticed before. *(Pause for students to use their sense of smell.)* As you practice calming strategies using your senses, remember that this is a strategy you can use any time you feel stressed or worried and you want to calm your mind and body.

The final strategy I want to teach you today is how to use your words when you find yourself feeling upset or worried. Sometimes, when a person feels upset or worried, they have so many emotions it's hard to keep them under control. This happens to a lot of people when they are stressed. One helpful thing we can do when we feel this way is to use our words to express how we're feeling. For example, you can say something like, "I'm feeling upset because ..." or "I'm feeling worried about ..." It's important to use "I" statements to talk about your own feelings. And, if you need help or support, you can also say, "Can I talk to you about something?" or "I need some help with this." Remember, it's okay to ask for help when you need it, and using your words can help others understand how they can support you.

Let's practice using our words to express our feelings. Take a moment to think about a time when you felt upset or worried and think about how you could have used your words to communicate how you were feeling. Turn and talk with a partner to share how you could use your words to communicate your feelings. *Pause for students to share.*

We just learned three ways to help us manage stress when we start to feel upset or worried. We can use deep breathing, focus on our senses, or use our words to express how we feel.

SUPPORT (Pivots)

- Respect cultural norms around expressing emotions. In some cultures, direct verbal expression of stress or distress may be less common, while nonverbal cues or subtle communication styles are more prevalent. Encourage students to express themselves in ways that feel comfortable and authentic to them, whether through words, art, movement, or other means.
- Stress management is a skill that improves with practice. Encourage students to integrate stress management techniques into their daily routines and provide opportunities for regular practice and reinforcement.

▶ ENVIRONMENT

LESSON

E.3   S.P.A.C.E.

UNDERSTAND (Why?)

It's important to teach students to find a good-fit space to work because it enhances their ability to concentrate and engage with tasks effectively. S.P.A.C.E. is an acronym that stands for:

- Sound: Is it quiet enough?
- People: Can I ignore the people around me?
- Area: Am I physically distanced?
- Comfort: Am I comfortable?
- Eyes: Can I see the text?

By understanding their optimal work environment, students can improve their productivity and overall learning outcomes. Additionally, this skill fosters independence and self-regulation, preparing students for success in future endeavors.

PREPARE (Students)

We're going to learn about finding a good-fit space to work. It's important to think about where we work best during our learning time. Think about times when you have felt focused and able to do your best work. What was your environment like? Was it quiet? Did you have everything you needed within reach? Were you comfortable? Finding a good-fit space means finding a place that helps us concentrate, feel comfortable, and be productive. It's like finding the perfect spot to read a book or play a game. Today, we'll learn how to find a workspace that suits us best.

TEACH (Explicitly)

We're going to use the word, S.P.A.C.E., an acronym, to help us learn how to choose a good-fit space to work. *(Write SPACE vertically down the board or chart paper.)* Listen as I tell you each letter, what they mean, and how to use that word to learn about spaces to work.

   The S stands for Sound. *(Write Sound next to the S.)* Look around the room and think about the noise level and where might be the best place to work. For example, is there a fan on or a radio, or are there people working together talking? Will this affect my productivity? I want to find a space where the sound level allows me to concentrate and work without disruption.

   The P stands for People. *(Write People next to the P.)* Where are people sitting in the room and will you be distracted if you sit too closely to them? Take notice and choose a place that will allow you to be successful in your work.

   The A stands for Area. *(Write Area next to the A.)* Think about the area you have to work. Do you need to be physically distanced from others? Do you have enough room to be comfortable and work effectively?

   The C stands for Comfort. *(Write Comfort next to the C.)* Being comfortable promotes focus, reduces distractions, and enhances productivity, ultimately leading to better learning outcomes. We want to make sure where we choose to work is a comfortable space for us so that we can work the whole time, focused on our learning.

The E stands for Eyes. *(Write Eyes next to the E.)* We look at the workspace in front of us to make sure the lighting is appropriate, and we can see okay. It's important that we avoid straining our eyes so we need to make sure we can clearly see the text we're reading or the work we're doing.

Let's try using the S.P.A.C.E. acronym first by imagining it. Close your eyes and imagine your ideal workspace for reading a book. What do you see? Is it quiet and cozy? What do you notice that makes it perfect for you? Now, think about the acronym S.P.A.C.E. What's the sound level of the ideal workspace you imagine? *(Pause.)* Where are people sitting? *(Pause.)* How much area do you have around you? *(Pause.)* What makes it comfortable? *(Pause.)* Does the lighting help your eyes see clearly? *(Pause.)* This will help you think about the best workspace for you.

Look around our classroom. You will see many different spaces to work. In the next few days I'm going to place you in different spaces around the room to work and during that time you can think about sound, people, area, comfort, and eyes. This will help you to find your own good-fit workspace when it's your turn to choose.

SUPPORT
(Pivots)

- Allow for flexibility in workspace arrangements, such as movable furniture or alternative seating options like standing desks or beanbag chairs. This accommodates students who may prefer different postures for optimal focus and comfort.
- Teach students organizational skills and provide easy access to necessary resources and materials within their workspace. This includes having storage solutions for supplies and keeping the workspace clutter free to minimize distractions.

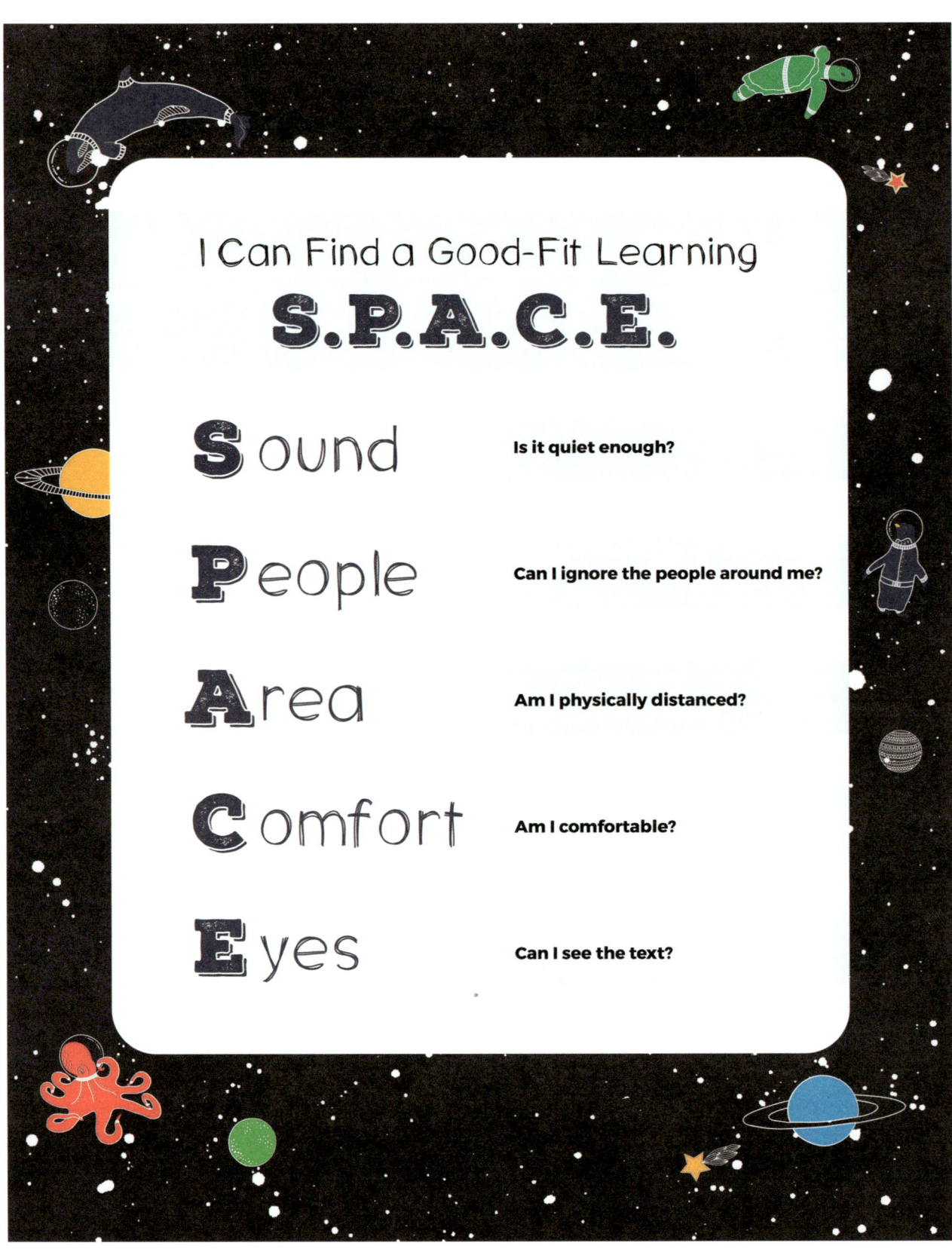

ENVIRONMENT

LESSON

E.4 Flexible Seating

UNDERSTAND (Why?)

Flexible seating refers to classrooms that have a variety of seating choices that support students' preferences and needs. Instead of only having regular desks and chairs, flexible seating gives options to pick from. It promotes active learning and facilitates collaboration and group work by providing adaptable seating arrangements that can be easily rearranged. Additionally, flexible seating enhances students' comfort, well-being, and sense of ownership over their learning environment, contributing to a more engaging and inclusive classroom atmosphere.

PREPARE (Students)

Today we're going to talk about the different seating options in our classroom. It's called flexible seating. Flexible seating means having a variety of seating options that you can choose from based on what helps you learn best. We're all different and because of this we have different preferences for how we like to sit and work. So today I'm going to share some of the options we have available in our room.

TEACH (Explicitly)

I'm going to introduce three of the flexible seating options we have in our classroom. First, we have carpet squares. These are perfect for students who like a cozy and soft surface to sit on. They are great for group activities, reading corners, or even just finding a comfortable spot to work independently. If you choose to use a carpet square you will simply walk to pick one up, place it where you choose to sit, then sit down and work. When time is up, you will put it back where you got it.

Next, we have the couch and the chairs. The couch or the chairs are great when you prefer a relaxed and soft seat. If you're able to ignore distractions and work without a table, this might be a good choice for you.

The third option I want to share with you today are our scoop chairs. Scoop chairs have a unique curved shape that cradles your body, some people find this very comfortable for extended periods of sitting.

As we continue to explore flexible seating options, remember that each option is here to support your learning. Whether you prefer carpet squares, the couch, the chairs or scoop chairs, the goal is to create a classroom environment where you're comfortable and have a workspace that helps you be successful. So, think about which seating option would help you learn and work your best. As we get used to these options, I'll share a few more.

SUPPORT (Pivots)

- Set clear expectations and guidelines for using flexible seating to ensure a smooth and productive learning environment. Communicate to students how they can choose their seating, when it's appropriate to move seats, and how to respect others' choices and space.
- Encourage students to reflect on their experiences with flexible seating and provide opportunities for feedback. Ask students to reflect using this question: Was this a place where you and others were successful?

▶ ENVIRONMENT

LESSON

E.5 Gathering Area

UNDERSTAND (Why?)

Meeting in a gathering area promotes engagement, collaboration, and active participation. It provides a comfortable and conducive environment for discussions, group activities, and interactive learning experiences. Most classrooms gather on the floor with the teacher sitting in front and the students facing the teacher. There may be times students need to stay at their desks or learning spots instead of gathering.

PREPARE (Students)

Good morning, everyone! Today, we're going to learn about gathering in our classroom's gathering area. The gathering area is a comfortable space where it's easier to hear each other and to stay focused. Here we can have discussions, do group activities, and enjoy learning together. Typically, our gathering area is on the floor with me sitting in front and all of you facing me. However, there may be times when you need to stay at your desks or learning spots instead of gathering, and that's okay too. Today, we'll practice how to gather in the gathering area smoothly and respectfully, so we can make the most out of our time together.

TEACH (Explicitly)

When you're at the gathering area, you will show certain behaviors as students, and I'll show certain behaviors as the teacher so that all of us can learn by listening, sharing, and having fun. When we're at the gathering spot, I might ask you to do different activities. This could be listening to a story, working with a partner, participating in a discussion, or sharing with the group.

When working at the gathering area, you will:

- work and participate the whole time *(write on chart under students)*,
- stay in one spot *(write on chart under students)*,
- look at the person speaking *(write on chart under students)*, and
- sit up quietly *(write on chart under students)*.

While you students are showing these behaviors, I'll be:

- working with students *(write on chart under Teacher)*

Select a student to come to the front of the gathering area and model the correct behaviors. Direct the class's attention toward the student who is modeling and point out each of the behaviors listed on the I-chart. Ask the class: Is _____ [student name] working and participating the whole time? Is _____ staying in one spot? Is _____ looking at the speaker? Is _____ sitting quietly? Then say, if _____ continues to do these things, will they learn by listening and sharing?

156 *Prepared Classroom*

Then have a student model the incorrect behaviors. Stop and review each of the behaviors and ask the question: If this is what we do at our gathering spot will _____ learn by listening and sharing? (No.) Now show us the correct way.

The same student then models the correct behaviors. Again, point out each of the behaviors listed on the chart and ask the class: If this is what we do at our gathering area will _____ learn by listening and sharing? (Yes!)

Now, we're all going to practice. I'm going to read a story and you're each going to practice using the correct behaviors we just learned.

Read a short read aloud, paying attention to the gathering spot behaviors of the students. When you see students have less stamina, stop the read aloud.

Let's check in to see how each of us did with the behaviors on our chart. This check-in is only for you and will help you decide which behaviors you're doing well and which will be your goal for the next time we meet in the gathering spot. Please put your hand in front of your chest. I'm going to point to each of these behaviors, and you're going to indicate how proficient you were in practicing that behavior. You will hold up one finger if you found it hard to be independent with that behavior, but you're going to work on it; two fingers if you feel you did okay at being independent with that behavior, but you think you can do better; or three fingers if you were very independent with that behavior.

Have students rate themselves for working and participating the whole time, staying in one spot, looking at the person speaking, and sitting up quietly.

Based on how you checked in, what's your goal for the next time we prepare for a read aloud? What would you like to work on? *Call on one or two volunteers to share their goal.* Please tell your elbow partner what your goal is for the next time we're in our gathering area.

SUPPORT
(Pivots)

- Teach students about the importance of respecting personal space when sitting in the gathering area. Encourage them to sit comfortably while also being mindful of not encroaching on others' space, which helps maintain a positive and comfortable atmosphere.
- Emphasize the importance of active listening and participation while sitting in the gathering area. Encourage students to listen attentively to the speaker, raise their hands to contribute to discussions, and engage in group activities or discussions to make the most out of the learning experience.

Learn by listening and sharing

Gathering Area

Fun

Independent

Students	Teacher
Work and participate the whole time **Stay in one spot** **Look at the person speaking** **Sit up quietly**	**Work with students**

ENVIRONMENT

LESSON

E.6 Word Collector

UNDERSTAND (Why?)

A Word Collector creates an interactive display of vocabulary words, phrases, and concepts. It creates a rich vocabulary environment where students can actively engage with language and expand their word knowledge to improve reading comprehension, enhance writing skills, and boost speaking abilities. A class Word Collector adds color, interest, and engagement to the classroom environment, making learning more visually stimulating and memorable for students.

PREPARE (Students)

Today we're going to start our journey as word collectors. Our class Word Collector is a special place where we'll gather interesting and exciting words to explore together throughout the year. As we gather fascinating words we'll expand our vocabulary, improve our communication skills, and make our writing more colorful and expressive.

TEACH (Explicitly)

I'm going to read a sentence to you and I want you to identify an interesting word in the sentence. Okay, are you ready? **The magnificent castle stood proudly atop the hill.** *(You may wish to write this sentence on chart paper or the board in front of you.)* Take a moment to think about the words in this sentence and see what words are interesting that you would like to add to our Word Collector. Raise your hand when you're ready to share.

Students may share the word "magnificent" or the word "proudly." Have a discussion about the word they share and add it to the class Word Collector. The discussion might sound like this:

Student: "I found the word 'magnificent' interesting!"
Teacher: "What makes the word 'magnificent' stand out to you?"
Student: "It makes me think of something really grand and impressive."
Teacher: "'Magnificent' is a powerful word that describes something extraordinary and awe-inspiring. Let's add it to our Word Collector and remember to use it in our writing to make our descriptions more vivid and engaging."

As we go through the year, we'll discover new words from our readings, discussions, and experiences to make our Word Collector even more exciting and diverse. We'll continue to grow our Word Collector so that we have new words we can use in our speaking and writing.

SUPPORT (Pivots)

- Use engaging activities, such as brainstorming interesting words from sentences or sharing personal experiences related to words, to encourage active participation and enthusiasm among students for the Word Collector.
- Refer to the Word Collector often throughout the year so students get used to using their new words and adding more to the chart.
- Consider creating personal word collectors for each student.

SECTION 2 — Environment

WORD COLLECTOR

Aa	Bb	Cc	Dd	Ee
Ff	Gg	Hh	Ii	Jj
Kk	Ll	Mm	Nn	Oo
Pp	Qq	Rr	Ss	Tt
Uu	Vv	Ww	Xx/Yy	Zz

ENVIRONMENT ◂

LESSON

E.7 Classroom Tour

UNDERSTAND (Why?)

The classroom tour is all about making students comfortable, confident, and excited about the learning space. It helps students know where everything is and become more independent learners. After all, the classroom is the students' space and the tour introduces important resources, tools, and even procedures that set the tone for the coming year.

PREPARE (Students)

We're going to take some time for a classroom tour to familiarize ourselves with the space we'll work and learn in each day. It's important because knowing where everything is and how things work will help us feel comfortable and ready to learn.

TEACH (Explicitly)

Each tour will be different, depending on the areas of your individual room and the resources available to students. It's important to tour all areas of the room even though you may think students already know the space. You're reinforcing expectations and want all students to hear and experience them. Some areas you will want to consider sharing include reading corner, library, math or science area, writing material area, technology, interactive whiteboard, group work areas, supply area, coat hooks or lockers, attendance/lunch count, etc. The following is an example of what a room tour might sound like.

> As we walk around, you will get to know our learning environment better. Starting here at the front, we have our whiteboard where we'll write important announcements and display our daily schedule.
>
> Over here is our cozy reading nook, filled with a variety of books for you to enjoy during independent reading time. You will see our books are organized by subject/genre/author.
>
> Moving on to the center of the room, you will find our desks and tables arranged in groups for collaborative activities. Each group has a supply caddy with pencils, markers, and other materials you might need.
>
> Now, let's head to the back of the room. Here, you will see shelves with book boxes. This is where you will store your book box each day. Your book box will have the books you have chosen to read, along with your writing journal, pencil, and a few other resources I'll give you as we work together.
>
> Are there any questions? I'll share more as the year goes on! This is our space and we want it to feel like a special place for everyone.

SUPPORT (Pivots)

- Ensure that you clearly communicate the purpose of each area in the classroom and how it contributes to the learning environment. Use simple language and provide examples or demonstrations to help students understand the functionality of each space.
- Encourage students to actively participate during the tour by asking questions, modeling desired behaviors, and sharing their thoughts. This helps to make the tour interactive, engaging, and memorable for students.

› ENVIRONMENT

LESSON

E.8 Introduce What's on the Walls

UNDERSTAND (Why?)

The walls of the classroom reflect our shared experiences. introducing students to what's on the walls of your classroom is important because it provides visual cues and reminders of key concepts, rules, and learning objectives. It helps create a print-rich environment and reinforces content knowledge. Additionally, showcasing student work and achievements on the walls fosters a sense of pride, motivation, and ownership in their learning environment.

PREPARE (Students)

Class, I'm excited to share with you what's on the walls of our classroom. The visuals around us help us remember important information, stay organized, and create a welcoming environment where we can all learn and grow together. As the year goes on and we add more, I'll share about that, too.

TEACH (Explicitly)

The wall space in every classroom will be different. What's important is to avoid posting anything on the wall that doesn't connect to a learning experience. Any preprinted posters or bulletin boards that are posted without attached learning won't serve an educational purpose. Areas of wall space you may want to include in your tour of the walls include the Word Collector, CAFE Menu (Boushey & Behne, 2020), anchor charts, displayed student work, communication stems, calendar, morning message, etc. A room tour might sound like this:

> Our walls look a little bare now, and that will change as we learn throughout the year. One thing you will notice on the wall are the letters C, A, F, and E. This spells CAFE. A CAFE is a place where people go to eat. So why would we have the word CAFE on our classroom wall? Well, it's because when you go eat you have a menu to order from, and here in our classroom we do a lot of reading, and sometimes when we read we need strategies to help us; our CAFE is a menu for reading. I'll explain more about this later, but for now know that our CAFE Menu will have strategies for helping us with our reading.
>
>   You will also see our Word Collector, where we'll write down words we find interesting and that we want to start using in our speaking and writing. And you will see an area to help us with our respectful communication. Here there will be phrases we can use to help us communicate with our peers in a kind and respectful way.
>
>   Finally, we have an area that highlights your work. Here you will see work you have completed that you chose to share with us all. As the year goes on, we'll add to what's on the walls. It's important to know that if it goes on the wall, that means it's important and therefore we'll refer to it and use it often. So, yes, you may think the walls look bare now, but they won't for long! I'm excited to create our wall space with you this year.

SUPPORT
(Pivots)

- Ensure that the items displayed on the walls serve a clear educational purpose and are relevant to the students' learning. This could include anchor charts, visual aids, student work, and inspirational quotes that support classroom objectives and curriculum.
- Encourage students to interact with the wall space by referencing it during lessons, discussions, and activities. Create opportunities for students to contribute to the wall displays, such as adding their own work, ideas, or reflections, to promote a sense of ownership and engagement with their learning environment.

> ENVIRONMENT

LESSON

E.9 Intro to CAFE Menu

UNDERSTAND (Why?)

Posting learning on the walls of the classroom is important because it serves as a visual reinforcement of concepts and information, helping students retain and recall knowledge more effectively. Using a menu creates an interactive and engaging learning environment that encourages students to actively participate, reference visual aids during lessons, and make connections between different topics or ideas.

PREPARE (Students)

As we have already learned, what's on the walls of our classroom is intentional because it can help us remember important information and stay organized. Today I'm going to share about a part of our classroom that will help us to remember and use different strategies that will help us become better readers.

TEACH (Explicitly)

Earlier I showed you the CAFE Menu in our room and shared why it's called CAFE. We know that when we go out to eat at a CAFE, we have a menu to order from, and here in our classroom we do a lot of reading, and sometimes when we read, we need strategies to help us; our CAFE is a menu for reading. Here's how it works: The C stands for Comprehension. Comprehension means I understand what I read. Sometimes when you're reading you might find that you don't understand what you have read. Here, under the C of our CAFE Menu we'll add comprehension strategies throughout the year that can help you deepen your understanding of what you read.

The next letter on our CAFE menu is the A. The A stands for Accuracy. In reading, accuracy means that we can read the words. Sometimes when we're reading, we come to a word or words we don't know. When this happens, we can use our phonics skills to help us to read the word accurately.

The third letter on our CAFE Menu is the F, which stands for Fluency. Fluency is the ability to read accurately, with expression, and understand what you read. Sometimes we might notice our reading isn't smooth or even sounds a little choppy. The strategies under the F of the CAFE Menu will help us to be fluent readers so our reading sounds smooth.

And finally, the E stands for vocabulary. (Pause.) Wait? Does that make sense? How would the E stand for Vocabulary? (Laugh.) It doesn't. It stands for Expand Vocabulary. We don't just want to have a regular vocabulary, but we want to continually grow, or expand, our vocabulary. The strategies under the E of the CAFE menu will help us to focus on interesting words, learn more about them, and use them in our speaking and writing.

So that's our CAFE Menu. It's a menu of strategies that we'll add to throughout the year that will help us with comprehension *(point to the C.)*, accuracy *(point to the A.)*, fluency *(point to the F.)*, and expanding vocabulary *(point to the E.)*. I can't wait to add our first strategy to the menu so we can start to use it!

SUPPORT (Pivots)

- Be sure the menu is accessible to students. You will add to it throughout the year and your students will refer to it frequently.
- In order to anchor learning to the menu, post strategies as they are introduced.

ENVIRONMENT

LESSON

E.10 Planning Template

UNDERSTAND
(Why?)

PREPARE
(Students)

TEACH
(Explicitly)

SUPPORT
(Pivots)

2.3 DAILY ROUTINES

DAILY ROUTINES

LESSON

DR.1 Quiet Signal

UNDERSTAND (Why?)

A quiet signal is a soft sound that's easy on the ears, made to alert students that their attention is required. This signal is meant to gather the attention of students and save the teacher's voice for instruction. Introducing the procedure for what to do when students hear the quiet signal promotes a smooth transition to quiet and focused learning environments, minimizing disruptions and maximizing instructional time.

PREPARE (Students)

We have many signals in our world. Traffic signs give us the signal to stop or go, telephone rings signal that someone is calling, and when someone holds their finger to their lips and says "Shh," that's a signal to be quiet. At times I'll need your attention, such as when I have an announcement, or a routine to follow for a new activity. It's important to learn what to do when you hear the quiet signal because it helps create a focused atmosphere for learning, allowing everyone to concentrate and participate effectively. Responding appropriately to the quiet signal also helps us show respect for others.

TEACH (Explicitly)

This is our signal *(Show chime.)*. I'm the only one to sound the signal. The first thing you will do when you hear this sound is stop *(Hand gesture.)* the activity you're doing and look up *[point to eyes]* and listen *(Gesture to ear.)*. It's important that when you stop and listen, you either wait for directions or follow the routine and move. Sometimes I'll give you directions for what you will need to do next. Other times you will simply clean up and return to the gathering area.

So, when you hear the signal, you're going to stop. *(Write <u>stop</u> on the anchor chart.)* Then you're going to look up *(Write <u>look up</u> on chart.)*, and then you will listen to see if there are specific directions or if you should just go to the gathering area. *(Write <u>listen</u> on the anchor chart.)* Then you're going to follow directions. *(Write <u>follow directions</u> on the chart.)*

Now I'm going to have two friends model this for us. *(Call on two students to show what it should look like and sound like when they hear the quiet signal. Have them start to talk to each other and then sound the signal so they can follow the behaviors listed on the chart. When they finish, review the behaviors on the chart.)*

When they heard the signal did they stop right away? (Yes.) Did they look up and listen for directions? (Yes.) Did they follow the directions given? (Yes.) If they follow these steps when they hear the quiet signal will we minimize disruptions and maximize our learning time? (Yes.) Is it respectful to those around us? (Yes.)

Okay, now I want us to see what it doesn't look like. *(Call on two students to show what it wouldn't look like. Tell them when they hear the signal they won't stop or listen. Have them start to talk to each other and then sound the signal. Wait a few seconds as they continue to talk and not follow directions.)*

Did you see a difference? When they heard the signal, did they stop right away? (No.) Did they look up and listen for directions? (No.) Did they follow directions given? (No.) If they do this when the quiet signal sounds, will they minimize disruptions and maximize their learning? (No!) Is it respectful to those around them? (No!) Oh, my! Now, I want them to show us what it does look like. *(Ask the same students to model again, only this time following the behaviors from the chart. Have them start talking and sound the signal.)*

This time when they heard the signal did they stop right away? (Yes.) Did they look up and listen for directions? (Yes.) Did they listen for and follow the directions given? (Yes.) If they follow these steps when they hear the quiet signal will we minimize disruptions and maximize our learning time? (Yes.) Is it respectful to those around us? (Yes.) Thank you!

Now we're all going to practice. I want you to turn to the person next to you and start talking. When you hear the signal, you're going to stop, look up, and listen for directions.

(Have students start to talk and when ready, sound the signal. After they follow the behaviors on the chart, stop and review.)

Okay, now let's reflect. When you heard the signal did you stop right away? (Yes.) Did you look up and listen for directions? (Yes.) Did you follow the directions given? (Yes.) Great! If we all follow these steps when we hear the quiet signal will we minimize disruptions and maximize our learning time? (Yes.) Is it respectful to those around us? (Yes.) Great!

SUPPORT (Pivots)

- It's important to provide ample practice opportunities for students to learn and internalize the expected response to the quiet signal.
- Recognize that students may respond differently to the quiet signal based on factors such as age, learning style, and individual needs. Consider using differentiated approaches to teaching and reinforcing the expected response, such as providing visual supports for younger students or offering alternative strategies for students who may struggle with self-regulation.

Quiet Signal

Signal for attention
Learn what to do next
Respectful
Independent

Students	Teacher
Stop	Sound the signal
Look at teacher	Give directions
Listen	
Follow directions	

DAILY ROUTINES

LESSON

DR.2 Brain Breaks

UNDERSTAND (Why?)

Brain breaks provide students with opportunities to recharge and refocus, leading to increased engagement and attentiveness in learning activities. These breaks help reduce stress and fatigue, allowing students to manage their emotions effectively and maintain a positive attitude toward learning. Additionally, brain breaks encourage social interaction, teamwork, and positive peer relationships, contributing to a supportive and inclusive classroom environment.

PREPARE (Students)

At times our brains and bodies need a minute or two to energize and refocus. At those times, we'll take a brain break. Not all brain breaks will look and sound the same, but we need to learn how to do them quickly, quietly, and safely. Today we're going to learn what it looks like and sounds like when we take a brain break.

TEACH (Explicitly)

We'll need brain breaks multiple times throughout the day. When it's time to take a brain break, I'll make the quiet signal to let you know. You will stop your activity *(Write* stop activity *on chart.)*, look at me *(Write* look at teacher *on chart.)*, and listen *(Write* listen for directions *on chart.)*. Then, you will quickly and safely participate in the brain break *(Write* quickly and safely participate *on chart.)*. After the brain break, you will settle your body quickly so we can continue your work and learning *(Write* settle body *and* continue your work *on chart.)*.

   Select a student to model a particular brain break. The student will listen for the quiet signal, stop their activity, listen for directions, and follow them. When they finish modeling, ask, Did _____ listen for the quiet signal (Yes.); stop the activity they were working on (Yes.); look at me (Yes.); listen for directions (Yes.); and participate quickly, quietly, and safely? (Yes.) _____ has given their brain and body a quick, energizing break and is ready to get back to work. If they follow these steps when doing a brain break will they be reenergized, refocused, and have fun? (Yes.)

   Select a student to model the incorrect brain break behaviors and then the correct behaviors. End each practice time reviewing the behaviors and asking the question, Did _____ listen for the quiet signal, stop the activity they were working on, look at me, listen for directions, and follow them quickly, quietly, and safely? (No.) If this is how we engage in brain breaks, will we be energized and ready to get back to work? (No.) *(Ask the same students to model again, only this time following the behaviors from the chart.)* Much better! This time, did _____ listen for the quiet signal (Yes.), did they stop the activity they were working on (Yes.), did they look at me (Yes.), did they listen for directions (Yes.), and did they participate quickly, quietly, and safely? (Yes.) _____ has given their brain and body a quick, energizing break and is ready to get back to work. If they follow these steps when doing a brain break will they be reenergized, refocused, and have fun? (Yes.)

Now we all get to show what it will look like and sound like when we take a brain break.

Students move to different spaces throughout the room. When you make the quiet signal, students will stop, look, listen, and quickly, quietly, and safely follow directions for the brain break. After the group practice follow up with a check-in:

Let's check in to see how each of us did when we took a brain break. This check-in is only for you and will help you decide which behaviors you're doing well, and which will be your goal for the next time we take a brain break. Please put your hand in front of your chest and indicate how proficient you were in practicing that behavior. You will hold up one finger if you found it hard to be independent with that behavior, but you're going to work on it; two fingers if you feel you did okay at being independent with that behavior, but you think you can do better; or three fingers if you were very independent with that behavior.

Begin by pointing to each behavior on the chart and ask students to check in.

Based on how you checked in, what's your goal for the next time we take a brain break? What would you like to work on? *Call on one or two volunteers to share their goal.*

SUPPORT
(Pivots)

- Provide clear and concise instructions for each brain break activity, including how to start, what movements or actions to perform, and when to end. Use visual cues or demonstrations to help students understand the steps involved.
- Offer a variety of brain break activities that cater to different interests and preferences, such as physical movements, mindfulness exercises, or quick games. Keep the activities engaging and interactive to maintain student interest and participation throughout the day. Some possible suggestions follow this lesson.

Energize *Refocus* **Brain Breaks** *Fun*
Independent

Students	Teacher
Listen for signal	**Give signal**
Stop activity	**Give directions**
Look at teacher	**Take a break with students**
Listen for directions	
Quickly and safely participate	
Settle body	
Continue your work	

172 Prepared Classroom

Brain Breaks

Brain breaks provide a physical, emotional, or cognitive shift for learners. This allows them to reset and refocus so they can continue with focused instruction. Here are some brain break ideas:

1. **Music**—Play or sing a short song.

2. **Dance**—A thirty-second dance break where students stand and get their wiggles out.

3. **Stretching or short exercise**—Reach for the ceiling, touch your toes, twist side to side, jumping jacks, march in place, high knees, toe raises, squats, jump, etc.

4. **Breathing exercises**—Deep breath, hold for five seconds, release.

5. **Gratitude**—Students share one thing for which they are thankful.

6. **Wave**—Start the wave and have it ripple through the class. (This will need to be taught ahead of time, so they know what to expect when you start it.)

7. **Sign language**—Teach students the alphabet in sign language and have them stand and sign the ABCs as a cognitive and kinesthetic shift.

8. **Doodle**—Play music for one to two minutes while students doodle on a sheet of paper.

9. **Jokes**—Students share jokes of their own or you may choose to read from a joke book.

10. **Mirror**—Students mirror the body actions or facial expressions of the leader.

11. **Emotion**—Show students an emotion and fifteen seconds of think time. Then, students finish the sentence that goes with an emotion. Example: I'm (happy, nervous, sad, excited, etc.) when ….

12. **Class promise or mantra**—Decide on a class mantra together and add in some coordinating actions. Say (and perform) the mantra as a brain break during the day.

▶ DAILY ROUTINES

LESSON

DR.3 Morning Routines

UNDERSTAND (Why?)

When students learn how to start their morning with a morning routine, they have a smooth, predictable start to the day.

PREPARE (Students)

We're going to learn how to enter our room when you come to school each morning. We learn this so we know how to have a successful start to each day. Each morning, we arrive at school by car, by bus, or by walking, and we arrive at many different times. When you know how to enter the room, you're learning how to have a smooth, purposeful start to your day. You will know you're successful when you can independently enter the room and get started right away.

TEACH (Explicitly)

I'm going to teach you our morning routine. Here's the routine: *(Write each behavior on the I-chart as they are announced and discussed.)*

- **Walk quietly into the room.**
- **Greet others with a quiet voice.**
- **Hang up your coat.**
- **Hang up your backpack.**
- **Sign in for attendance.**
- **Report on lunch.**
  - **Ordering**
  - **Brought**
- **Get your book or book box.**
- **Choose a location.**
- **Sit down.**
- **Read quietly.**

Select a student to model entering the room and following the morning routine. The student will model the behaviors from the chart. When they finish modeling, ask, Did _____ walk quietly into the room (Yes.), greet others with a quiet voice (Yes.), hang up their coat and backpack (Yes.), sign in for attendance (Yes.), report on lunch (yes), get their book box (Yes.), choose a location (Yes.), sit down (Yes.), and read quietly? (Yes.) If _____ follows this morning routine as they enter the room each day, will they have a smooth, purposeful start to the day? (Yes.)

Select a student to model the incorrect morning routine behaviors and then the correct behaviors. End each practice time reviewing the behaviors and asking the question, If _____ follows this morning routine as they enter the room each day, will they have a smooth, purposeful start to the day? (With incorrect model they will respond no, with correct model they will respond yes.)

Now we all get to show what it will look like and sound like when we enter the room and follow our morning routine.

Students quietly grab their things, walk into the hallway, and practice entering the room. As they do, they will follow the directions on the chart. After the group practice follow up with a check-in:

> Let's check in to see how each of us did when following our morning routine. This check-in is only for you and will help you decide which behaviors you're doing well, and which will be your goal for the next time you follow our morning routine. Please put your hand in front of your chest and indicate how proficient you were in practicing that behavior. You will hold up one finger if you found it hard to be independent with that behavior, but you're going to work on it; two fingers if you feel you did okay at being independent with that behavior, but you think you can do better; or three fingers if you were very independent with that behavior.
>
> Point to each behavior on the chart and ask students to check in. Did you walk quietly into the room? *(Pause.)* Did you greet others with a quiet voice? *(Pause.)* Did you hang up your coat and backpack? *(Pause.)* Did you sign in for attendance? *(Pause.)* Did you report for lunch? *(Pause.)* Did you get your book box? *(Pause.)* Did you choose a location? *(Pause.)* Did you sit down? *(Pause.)* Did you read quietly? *(Pause.)* Based on how you checked in, what's your goal for the next time you follow the morning routine? What would you like to work on? *Call on one or two volunteers to share their goal.*

SUPPORT (Pivots)

- Establish a consistent and structured morning routine with clear expectations and steps that students can easily follow. Use visual aids, such as a visual schedule or checklist, to help students understand and remember the sequence of tasks.
- Encourage students to participate and complete the morning routine independently and on time. Celebrate their efforts and progress to reinforce desired behaviors and promote a positive start to the day.
- Revisit the morning routine anchor chart and behaviors throughout the year as needed.

Morning Routine

Smooth, purposeful start to the day — *Respectful* — **Independent**

Students	Teacher
Walk quietly into the room	Greet students
Greet others with a quiet voice	Work with students
Hang up your coat	
Hang up your backpack	
Sign in for attendance	

Report on lunch
  - Ordering
  - Brought	

Get your book or book box	
Choose a location	
Sit down	
Read quietly	

▶ DAILY ROUTINES

LESSON

DR.4 Line Up

UNDERSTAND (Why?)

We teach the daily routine of lining up because it helps promote order, safety, and efficiency during transitions between activities or locations. Additionally, teaching students how to line up encourages independence, responsibility, and respect for classroom procedures, contributing to a positive and organized learning environment.

PREPARE (Students)

We're going to learn how to line up. We're learning how to line up so we can go to other places in the school and be on time. We have many different places to travel to as a class, such as the library, recess, the lunchroom, and the music room. To get to these places, we need to line up. We want to make sure we know how to do this so we can do it quickly and safely, which will save time and help us get to our next destination on time.

TEACH (Explicitly)

When asked to line up, you will follow these steps: *(Write them on an anchor chart as you introduce them.)*

- Walk slowly and purposefully to the line.
- Use a quiet voice.
- Stand behind the person in front of you.
- Give that person space (an arm's length).
- Face forward.
- Wait for directions.

Select a few students to model lining up. When they finish modeling, read each of the behaviors on the anchor chart and ask the class if they did each behavior. Did they walk slowly and purposefully to the line? (Yes.) Did they walk quietly? (Yes.) Did each person stand behind the person in front of them? (Yes.) Did they give that person space? (Yes.) Did they face forward? (Yes.) Did they wait for directions? (Yes.) *Then, ask,* If this is how we line up, will we be able to travel to other places in the school and be on time? (Yes.)

Then, select a few students to model lining up incorrectly. When they finish modeling, read each of the behaviors on the anchor chart and ask the class if they did each behavior. For example, Did they walk slowly and purposefully to the line? (No.) Did they walk quietly? (No.) Did each person stand behind the person in front of them? (No.) Did they give that person space? (No.) Did they face forward? (No.) Did they wait for directions? (No.) *Then, ask,* If this is how we line up, will we be able to travel to other places in the school and be on time? (No.)

Okay, so we know these behaviors won't help us to save time, be independent, and transition effectively. Can you please show us the correct way to line up? *(Ask the same children to then model the correct way. When they are finished, revisit each of the behaviors again.)* Did they walk slowly and purposefully to the line? (Yes.) Did they walk quietly? (Yes.) Did each person stand behind the person in front of them? (Yes.) Did they give that person space? (Yes.) Did they face forward? (Yes.) Did they wait for directions? (Yes.)

Prepared Classroom

Then, ask, If this is how we line up, will we be able to travel to other places in the school and be on time? (Yes.)

Now we'll get to show what it will look like and sound like when we line up. When you hear the quiet signal, please follow this routine for lining up.

Sound the quiet signal and provide an opportunity for the class to practice lining up. When they finish, review as a class:

Let's check in to see how each of us did lining up. This check-in is only for you and will help you decide which behaviors you're doing well, and which will be your goal for the next time you line up. Please put your hand in front of your chest and indicate how proficient you were in practicing that behavior. You will hold up one finger if you found it hard to be independent with that behavior, but you're going to work on it; two fingers if you feel you did okay at being independent with that behavior, but you think you can do better; or three fingers if you were very independent with that behavior.

Point to each behavior on the chart and ask students to check in. Did you walk slowly and purposefully to the line? *(Pause.)* Did you walk quietly? *(Pause.)* Did you stand behind the person in front of you? *(Pause.)* Did you give the person in front of you space? *(Pause.)* Did you face forward? *(Pause.)* Did you wait for directions? *(Pause.)* Then ask, If this is how we line up, will we be able to travel to other places in the school and be on time? (Yes.)

Based on how you checked in, what's your goal for the next time you line up? What would you like to work on? *Call on one or two volunteers to share their goal.*

SUPPORT (Pivots)

- Clearly communicate the expectations for lining up, including where to line up, how to form the line (e.g., single file or in pairs), and the expected behavior during the lining-up process (e.g., staying quiet and orderly). Provide visual cues or reminders to reinforce these expectations.
- Offer multiple opportunities for students to practice lining up during non-transition times, such as during classroom activities or simulations. Recognize students who line up correctly and demonstrate the expected behaviors. Provide feedback and additional practice as needed to ensure students understand and can follow the lining-up routine consistently.

Line Up
Independent

Get ready to travel to another place in school

Be on time

Students	Teacher
Walk slowly and purposefully to line	Wait for students
Quiet voice	Give directions
Stand behind person in front of you	
Give space	
Face forward	
Wait for directions	

▶ DAILY ROUTINES

LESSON

DR.5 Walk in the Hall

UNDERSTAND (Why?)

It's important to teach kids the routine of walking in the hall to promote safety, respect, and orderliness in shared spaces. By learning how to walk quietly and in an organized manner, students contribute to a positive and focused learning environment for themselves and others.

PREPARE (Students)

We have many different places to travel to as a class, such as the library, recess, the lunchroom, and the music room. To get to these places, we need to walk in the hall. We want to make sure we know how to do this so we can do it quickly and safely. It will save time and help us get to our next destination on time while being respectful of others. Whether you're with our class or by yourself, most of the behaviors for walking in the hall are the same. Today, we're going to learn how to walk in the hall. We're learning how to walk in the hall so we can go to other places in the school, be on time, and be respectful to those around us.

TEACH (Explicitly)

Today I'm going to teach you how to walk in the hall. Many of these behaviors are the same as lining up. *(Teacher writes behaviors on I-chart while announcing them to the class.)*

When you walk in the hall, you will follow these steps:

- Walk slowly and purposefully.
- Walk quietly.
- Walk behind the person in front of you.
- Give that person space.
- Face forward.
- Stay on the right side of the hall.

Select a few students to model what it looks like walking in the hall. When they finish modeling, read each of the behaviors on the anchor chart and ask the class if they did each behavior. Did they walk slowly and purposefully? (Yes.) Did they walk quietly? (Yes.) Did each person walk behind the person in front of them? (Yes.) Did they give that person space? (Yes.) Did they face forward? (Yes.) Did they stay on the right side of the hall? (Yes.) Then, ask, If this is how walk in the hall, will we be able to travel to other places in the school, be on time, and be respectful? (Yes.)

Then, select a few students to model walking in the hall incorrectly. When they finish modeling, read each of the behaviors on the anchor chart and ask the class if they did each behavior. For example, Did they walk slowly and purposefully? (No.) Did they walk quietly? (No.) Did each person walk behind the person in front of them? (No.) Did they give that person space? (No.) Did they face forward? (No.) Did they stay on the right side of the hall? (No Then, ask, If this is how we walk in the hall, will we be able to travel to other places in the school, be on time, and respectful? (No.)

Prepared Classroom

Okay, so we know these behaviors won't help us to get to other spaces in the school on time and in a respectful way. Can you please show us the correct way to line up? *(Ask the same children to then model the correct way. When they are finished, revisit each of the behaviors again.* Did they walk slowly and purposefully? (Yes.) Did they walk quietly? (Yes.) Did each person walk behind the person in front of them? (Yes.) Did they give that person space? (Yes.) Did they face forward? (Yes.) Did they walk on the right side of the hall? (Yes.) *Then, ask,* If this is how we walk in the hall, will we be able to travel to other places in the school and be on time and respectful? (Yes.)

Now we all get to show what it will look like and sound like when we all walk in the hall. When you hear the quiet signal, please follow the routine for lining up. When you're ready, we'll start walking in the hall.

Sound the quiet signal and provide an opportunity for the class to line up and practice walking in the hall. When they finish, review as a class:

Let's check in to see how each of us did walking in the hall. This check-in is only for you and will help you decide which behaviors you're doing well, and which will be your goal for the next time you line up. Please put your hand in front of your chest and indicate how proficient you were in practicing that behavior. You will hold up one finger if you found it hard to be independent with that behavior, but you're going to work on it; two fingers if you feel you did okay at being independent with that behavior, but you think you can do better; or three fingers if you were very independent with that behavior.

Point to each behavior on the chart and ask students to check in. Did you walk slowly and purposefully? *(Pause.)* Did you walk quietly? *(Pause.)* Did you walk behind the person in front of you? *(Pause.)* Did you give the person in front of you space? *(Pause.)* Did you face forward? *(Pause.)* Did you walk on the right side of the hall? *(Pause.) Then ask,* If this is how we walk in the hall, will we be able to travel to other places in the school and be on time and respectful? (Yes.)

Based on how you checked in, what's your goal for the next time you walk in the hall? What would you like to work on? *Call on one or two volunteers to share their goal.*

SUPPORT
(Pivots)

- Teach children the importance of walking quietly, staying on the right side of the hall, and being aware of their surroundings to avoid collisions. Encourage them to use appropriate walking behaviors, such as keeping hands to themselves and respecting personal space.
- Model and reinforce positive walking behaviors according to class needs and building agreements. Provide visual cues or reminders as needed throughout the year.

Move around the school to other areas — **Walk in the Hall** — *Respectful / Be on time*

Independent

Students	Teacher
Walk slowly and purposefully	Wait for students
Quiet voice	Give directions
Walk behind person in front of you	
Give space	
Face forward	
Stay on right side of hall	

DAILY ROUTINES ◀

LESSON

DR.6 Ending the Day

UNDERSTAND (Why?)

Learning the routine for the end of the school day ensures a smooth and orderly transition from school to home. By learning the steps for packing up belongings, saying goodbye respectfully, and following dismissal procedures, students contribute to a calm and efficient end-of-day routine that promotes a positive school environment.

PREPARE (Students)

Each afternoon at the end of the school day we'll stop our activities and prepare our classroom and ourselves to go home. We're going to learn how to end our day with each other calmly and purposefully. We learn this so you know how to successfully end each day in our room and so you set yourself up for a smooth transition home.

TEACH (Explicitly)

Today I'm going to teach you our end-of-the-day routine. *(Write behaviors on I-chart while announcing them to the class.)*

At the end of the day you will follow these steps:

- Use a quiet voice
- Put materials away:
  - books
  - papers
  - pencils
  - crayons
- Pick up and tidy up:
  - scraps on floor
  - bookshelves
  - areas around the room
  - around desks
- Get coat and backpack
- Fill backpack with what needs to go home
- Stack chair
- Line up at door

Select a few students to model what it looks like and sounds like at the end of the day. When they finish modeling, read each of the behaviors on the anchor chart and ask the class if they did each behavior. Did they use a quiet voice? (Yes.) Did they put materials away? (Yes.) Did they pick up and tidy up? (Yes.) Did they get their coat and backpack? (Yes.) Did they put anything that needs to go home in their backpack? (Yes.) Did they stack their chair? (Yes.) Did they line up at the door? (Yes.) *Then, ask,* If this is what they do at the end of the day will they have a smooth transition home? (Yes.)

Then, select a few students to model the end of the day incorrectly. When they finish modeling, read each of the behaviors on the anchor chart and ask the class if they did each behavior. For example, Did they use a quiet voice? (No.) Did they put materials away? (No.) Did they pick up and tidy up? (No.) Did they get their coat and backpack? (No.) Did they put anything that needs to go home in their backpack? (No.) Did they stack their chair? (No.) Did they line up at the door? (No.) *Then, ask,* If this is what they do at the end of the day will they have a smooth transition home? (No.)

Okay, so we know these behaviors won't help us have a smooth transition home. Can you please show us the correct way to end the day? *Ask the same children to then model the correct way. When they are finished, revisit each of the behaviors again.* Did they use a quiet voice? (Yes.) Did they put materials away? (Yes.) Did they pick up and tidy up? (Yes.) Did they get their coat and backpack? (Yes.) Did they put anything that needs to go home in their backpack? (Yes.) Did they stack their chair? (Yes.) Did they line up at the door? (Yes.) *Then, ask,* If this is what they do at the end of the day will they have a smooth transition home? (Yes.)

Now we all get to show what it will looks like and sound like when we end the day with this routine. *Students practice stopping their activity and going through the end-of-day routine. When they finish, have them come to the gathering area and review as a class:*

Let's check in to see how each of us did following the end of the day routine. This check-in is only for you and will help you decide which behaviors you're doing well, and which will be your goal for the next time you line up. Please put your hand in front of your chest and indicate how proficient you were in practicing that behavior. You will hold up one finger if you found it hard to be independent with that behavior, but you're going to work on it; two fingers if you feel you did okay at being independent with that behavior, but you think you can do better; or three fingers if you were very independent with that behavior.

Point to each behavior on the chart and ask students to check in. Did you use a quiet voice? *(Pause.)* Did you put materials away? *(Pause.)* Did you pick up and tidy up? *(Pause.)* Did you get your coat and backpack? *(Pause.)* Did you put anything that needs to go home in your backpack? *(Pause.)* Did you stack your chair? *(Pause.)* Did you line up at the door? *(Pause.)* Then, ask, If this is what you do at the end of the day will you have a smooth transition home? (Yes.) Based on how you checked in, what's your goal for the next time you end the day? What would you like to work on? *Call on one or two volunteers to share their goal.*

SUPPORT
(Pivots)

- Your end-of-day routine most likely will consist of different tasks or be in a different order from what's shown here. Make the changes that work for you and are unique to your class. What stays the same is the way you introduce the routine by following the 10 Steps to Teaching and Learning Independence (page 49).

Ending the Day

Calm end to the day — *Leave class safely*

Independent

Students	Teacher
Use a quiet voice	Work with students
Working with students	
Put materials away	
Pick up and tidy up	
Get coat and backpack	
Fill backpack with necessary materials	
Stack chair	

▶ DAILY ROUTINES

LESSON

DR.7 Transitions

UNDERSTAND (Why?)

Teaching students to transition from one activity to the next helps them develop time management skills and adaptability. Additionally, smooth transitions enhance classroom efficiency, minimize disruptions, increase learning time, and maintain a positive learning atmosphere for all students.

PREPARE (Students)

There will be times when we must stop what we're doing to move to something else. We call those times transitions. When we transition, we want to do it quickly, quietly, and safely. Today I'm going to teach you what it will look like and sound like when we transition from one activity to another. The reason we practice transitions is so we can get more learning in and practice respectful behavior.

TEACH (Explicitly)

At different times throughout the day we'll need to make a transition. When it's time to transition, I'll make the quiet signal to let you know. Here's what you will do: *(Write each behavior on the I-chart as they are announced and discussed.)*

- Stop your activity right away
- Be quiet
- Look at the speaker
- Listen for directions
- Follow the directions
- Ignore distractions

You might need to change activities, clean up for recess, put art materials away, or get privacy folders out for a test. When it's time, you will quickly, quietly, and safely follow the directions I give you.

Select a student to model transitions. When the student hears the signal, they will stop the activity they are working on right away, look at the speaker, listen for directions, and follow the directions. When they finish modeling, ask When _____ heard the signal, did they stop the activity they were working on? (Yes.) Were they quiet? (Yes.) Did they look at the speaker? (Yes.) Did they listen for directions? (Yes.) Did they follow directions quickly, quietly, and safely? (Yes.) Did they ignore distractions? (Yes.) If they transition like this, will they get more learning in while being respectful? (Yes.) Let's give them a round of applause to thank them for modeling for us.

Then, select a few students to model transitions incorrectly. When they finish modeling, read each of the behaviors on the anchor chart and ask the class if they did each behavior. For example, When _____ heard the signal, did they stop the activity they were working on? (No.) Were they quiet? (No.) Did they look at the speaker? (No.) Did they listen for directions? (No.)

Did they follow directions quickly, quietly, and safely? (No.) Did they ignore distractions? (No.) If they transition like this, will they get more learning in while being respectful? (No.)

Okay, so we know these behaviors won't help us to be respectful and get more learning in. Can you please show us the correct way transition? *Ask the same children to then model the correct way. When they are finished, revisit each of the behaviors again* When _____ heard the signal, did they stop the activity they were working on? (Yes.) Were they quiet? (Yes.) Did they look at the speaker? (Yes.) Did they listen for directions? (Yes.) Did they follow directions quickly, quietly, and safely? (Yes.) Did they ignore distractions? (Yes.) If they transition like this, will they get more learning in while being respectful? (Yes.) Let's give them a round of applause to thank them for modeling for us.

Now we all get to show what it looks like and sounds like when we transition. *For this behavior we place students in various spots around the room. After giving them a few seconds to engage in conversation or a task, sound the signal and wait for students to stop, listen, and quickly, quietly, and safely follow directions.*

When they finish, have them come to the gathering area and review as a class:

Let's check in to see how each of us did with our transition. This check-in is only for you and will help you decide which behaviors you're doing well, and which will be your goal for the next time you line up. Please put your hand in front of your chest and indicate how proficient you were in practicing that behavior. You will hold up one finger if you found it hard to be independent with that behavior, but you're going to work on it; two fingers if you feel you did okay at being independent with that behavior, but you think you can do better; or three fingers if you were very independent with that behavior.

Point to each behavior on the chart and ask students to check in. When you heard the signal, did you stop the activity you were working on? *(Pause.)* Were you quiet? *(Pause.)* Did you look at the speaker? *(Pause.)* Did you listen for directions? *(Pause.)* Did you follow directions quickly, quietly, and safely? *(Pause.)* Did you ignore distractions? *(Pause.)* If you transition like this, will you get more learning in while being respectful? *(Pause.)*

Based on how you checked in, what's your goal for the next time you end the day? What would you like to work on? *Call on one or two volunteers to share their goal.*

SUPPORT (Pivots)

- Establish a consistent transition routine that students can become familiar with and practice regularly. Use rehearsal or role-playing activities to teach and reinforce the steps of the transition process, allowing students to become more independent and efficient in transitioning between activities.
- Introduce the signal that will be used to give notice of transition time. Use this signal consistently and save your voice for instruction.

Transitions

Safe · Get more learning in · Respectful

Independent

Students	Teacher
Stop right away	Give signal
Quiet	Raise hand
Look at the speaker	Stand quietly
Listen for directions	Give eye contact
Follow the directions	
Ignore distractions	

DAILY ROUTINES

LESSON

DR.8 Book Shopping

UNDERSTAND (Why?)

Knowing how to book shop helps students learn to navigate and use the resources in the classroom library effectively. Teaching book shopping encourages responsibility for choosing books, caring for library materials, and respecting shared spaces, contributing to a positive and organized learning environment.

PREPARE (Students)

Walk students to your classroom library. This is a good time to explore and explain how it's organized (by genre, author, interest, series, and so on). Explaining the setup of the classroom library will help students quickly locate books they are interested in and ensures they will be able to return them to the correct location.

Today I'm going to teach you what it looks like and sounds like when we book shop. Knowing what to do when you're looking for books in our classroom library will help you find books you want to read while still having time to be able to read.

TEACH (Explicitly)

You will choose books multiple times throughout the [week/year], which we call shopping even though you aren't really buying anything. When you shop for books, the first thing you will do is quietly pick up your book box and walk to the classroom library. (Write walk to library on anchor chart.)

Next you will pick up a book (Write pick up a book on anchor chart.) that looks interesting to you and follow I PICK to see if it's a good fit (Write Review I PICK on anchor chart). If it is, you will place it in your book box and continue to look for a few more good-fit books. If a book isn't a good fit, you will place it back where you found it and continue looking for good-fit books. (Add to anchor chart: place good-fit book in book box, place back on shelf books you aren't interested in.)

When you have found ___ to ___ books [number of books you have recommended], you will return to your spot. (Write when you have ___ books return to your spot on the anchor chart.)

Select a student to model book shopping. The student will quietly pick up their book box and walk to the classroom library, pick up a book that looks interesting, decide if it's a good fit, and then continue to look for more books or finish book shopping and return to their spot. When they finish modeling ask Did _____ quietly pick up their book box and walk to the classroom library? (Yes.) Did they pick up a book that looked interesting, decide if it was a good fit, and then continue to look for more books or finish book shopping and return to their spot? (Yes.) _____ has independently shopped for books and is ready to get back to reading. If _____ book shops like this, will they find books they want to read while still having time to be able to read? (Yes.)

Then, select a student to model book shopping incorrectly. When they finish modeling, go through the desired behaviors when book shopping, asking if they were able to follow them. For example, Did _____ quietly pick up their book box and walk to the classroom library? (No.) Did they pick up a book that looked interesting, decide if it was a good fit, and then continue to look for more books or finish book shopping and return to their spot? (No.) If _____ book shops like this, will they find books they want to read while still having time to be able to read? (No.)

Okay, so we know these behaviors won't help us to find books we want to read and give us time to read. Can you please show us the correct way transition? *Ask the same child to then model the correct way. When they are finished, revisit each of the behaviors again.* Did _____ quietly pick up their book box and walk to the classroom library? (Yes.) Did they pick up a book that looked interesting, decide if it was a good fit, and then continue to look for more books or finish book shopping and return to their spot? (Yes.) _____ has independently shopped for books and is now ready to get back to reading. If _____ book shops like this, will they find books they want to read while still having time to be able to read? (Yes.)

During the next couple of days, everyone will get the opportunity to shop for books.

SUPPORT
(Pivots)

- It helps to have an organized classroom library and provide a tour prior of the library prior to teaching students to book shop.
- Before book shopping, students should have a practice for select good-fit books. We suggest the I PICK method introduced on page 138.
- You may wish to have a student model as in the lesson example above, or you may wish to model the book shopping yourself.

Have books to read
Choose books you want

Book Shopping

Fun

Independent

Students	Teacher
Walk to library	Work with students
Pick up a book	
Review I-PICK with each book	
Place good-fit book in your book box	
Place back on shelf books you aren't interested in	
When you have 1–3 books return to your spot	
Read the whole time	

DAILY ROUTINES ◀

LESSON

DR.9 Sharing

UNDERSTAND (Why?)

Teaching students to share their learning enhances their understanding and retention of information through peer-to-peer explanation and discussion. It promotes collaboration, communication, and critical thinking skills as students engage in meaningful dialogue, exchange ideas, provide feedback to each other, and celebrate learning.

PREPARE (Students)

One way to share our learning or explain our thinking is to tell someone. When we share, or tell others, we hear, see, and think about our work. Also, listening to someone share helps us because we hear, see, and think about what was shared. Today I'm going to teach you what it will look like and sound like when we share our work with a small group or our whole class. The reason we share in this way is that it helps all of us become better readers and writers and learners, and it's fun.

TEACH (Explicitly)

You will have many opportunities to share your thinking and learning. When it's your turn to share, the first thing you will do is make sure you're ready. If you're sharing a book, have the book with you and have the part you want to share bookmarked. If you're sharing your writing, have the text with you, and be ready to read it. Every time it's your turn to share, you need to make sure you're prepared. *(Teacher writes behaviors on I-chart as they are announced to the class.)*

It's important that when you're sharing, you speak loudly and clearly so everyone can hear and understand. You can make sure you're loud and clear by sitting or standing up straight, looking at your classmates, and holding your material just below your face. You want your voice to reach the farthest person in the room.

To make the most of our precious time, you need to know what you want to share. You usually won't have time to read a whole book or piece of writing, just a paragraph or two.

Sometimes you will volunteer to share. Sometimes I'll ask you to share something I think would benefit our classmates or something to celebrate together.

Select a student to model sharing. The student will quickly and quietly choose what they want to share or follow your prompt. They will walk to the front of the gathering space (or wherever you choose) and share their reading, writing, or learning. They will speak loudly and clearly, and respond to any questions or comments. When they finish modeling, ask, Did ___ choose something to share quickly, sit up or stand up straight, share their reading, writing, or learning loudly and clearly, and respond to questions or comments? (Yes.) ____ has independently shared and is ready to listen to others.

During the next couple of days, everyone will get the opportunity to share.

SUPPORT (Pivots)

- As classroom sharing is a practice where student sharing is the focus of attention, we find they are typically successful without needing to model the incorrect behaviors.
- Allow a few students to share each day so all students have an opportunity.

▶ DAILY ROUTINES

LESSON

DR.10 Planning Template

UNDERSTAND
(Why?)

PREPARE
(Students)

TEACH
(Explicitly)

SUPPORT
(Pivots)

2.4 INDEPENDENT LEARNING

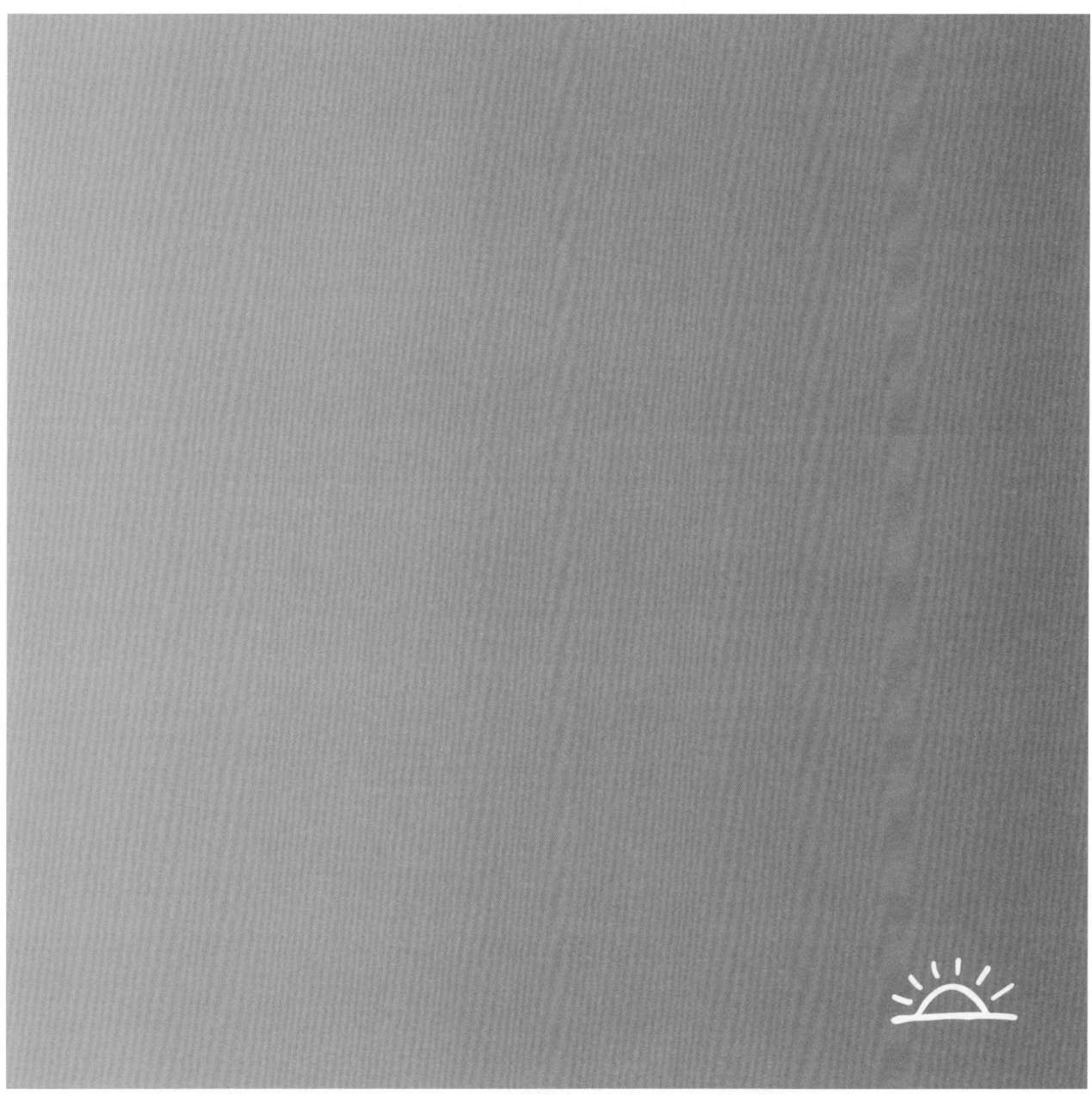

INDEPENDENT LEARNING

LESSON

IL.1 Ways to Engage with Text

UNDERSTAND (Why?)

Teaching students that there are different ways to engage with a text, such as reading the words, viewing pictures, or retelling what was read, promotes diverse learning styles, enhances comprehension, and encourages creativity in understanding the material.

PREPARE (Students)

Today I'm going to share with you three ways to engage with a text. There are many ways we can get information from books and other texts. We can view the pictures, read the words, or if we have heard a story before, we can retell the story.

TEACH (Explicitly)

The first way I'm going to show you to engage with text is by viewing the pictures. The pictures in a book are chosen carefully to support the words and learning that take place. Sometimes the pictures are drawings that depict what's taking place in a story, other times pictures are still frames, real life photographs to show an image or event, and sometimes images are graphs or diagrams that help to further explain a concept.

I'm going to show you an example of viewing the pictures with this short picture book. *Go through each page of the book sharing what thinking takes place when viewing each image.* I just showed you that one way to engage with text is to look closely at the pictures. I'm going to write that down on our chart to remind us of the three ways to engage with text. Now I'm going to show you another way, I'm going to read the words.

Engage with the same text, but this time read the words. At the end of the story, say: So, we know that one way to engage with text is to view the pictures, and now I just showed you another way and that's to read the words. I'm going to add Read the Words to our chart of ways to engage with a book. *Then tell the students:* There's a third way to enjoy a text and that's to retell a familiar story. *Use the same book and retell the story by looking at the pictures and stating what's happening.* Now I'm going to add the third way to our chart, and that's to retell a familiar story.

Class, we just went through three different ways to engage with text. When there's a text that interests you, you can view the pictures, read the words, or retell a familiar story. Now, we're all going to have a chance to practice using the books in our book box *(or the basket of books on the table or the books I have given you). After students have had an opportunity to engage with text, sound the quiet signal and revisit the anchor chart, allowing students to share how they engaged with text.*

You just had a chance to enjoy text using one of the three ways we learned about. Did you view the pictures, read the words, or retell a familiar story? Listen, turn, and talk with a partner and share one way you engaged with text.

SUPPORT (Pivots)

- It may help to model the three ways to engage with text using various texts such as picture books, nonfiction books, and graphic novels.
- Providing students a chance to practice each way gives them an opportunity to experience what it looks like, sounds like, and feels like to view the pictures, read the words, and retell a familiar text.

WAYS TO ENGAGE WITH TEXT

View the Pictures

Read the Words

Retell a Familiar Story

INDEPENDENT LEARNING ◄

LESSON

IL.2 Reading Materials

UNDERSTAND (Why?)

Teaching students to access and take care of reading materials helps develop their ability to manage resources and make independent choices, which are key skills for working autonomously. This practice also instills a sense of accountability and self-reliance, encouraging students to take initiative and responsibility.

PREPARE (Students)

We're going to take a few minutes to talk about the materials you will use during your independent work time. It's important to know where we keep them and how to take care of them, so that when it's time to work independently you can get right to work and have the materials necessary.

TEACH (Explicitly)

Sometimes when you work independently, you will be working on tasks that I have assigned. In this case, I may give your materials to you, or direct you on what's needed and where to get the needed items. Other times when you work independently you will make a choice in how you want to engage in your learning. You might choose to read or write during this time. Whichever you choose, you will need to know how to access your materials and take care of them.

Explain your organization and process for students to access, take care of, and return materials. This will look different in each classroom based on whether you have community supplies, book boxes, or individual totes. Here's an example in a classroom that uses book boxes:

On this shelf are boxes with the numbers one to twenty-six. There are twenty-six students in this class and each of you will have a number. Inside your box, you will keep the books you have chosen to read, your writing notebook, and a pencil. When it's time to work independently, you will walk to the shelf, pick up the box that has your number, and take it to the place you will work. When the signal sounds and work time is over, you will simply put your materials back in your box and place it back on the shelf. *Select a student to show what it looks like to walk to the shelf, pick up their box, and find a place to work. Then, ask the student to please put their materials away.*

We just watched as ____ walked to the shelf, selected their book box, and found a place to work with their materials. Then, when signaled, they put their materials back in their box and placed their box back on the shelf. If this is how ____ gathers their materials, uses them, and returns them, will they be independent and responsible? (Yes.) Great! This is how you will gather and return your materials each day.

SECTION 2 ☀ Independent Learning

SUPPORT (Pivots)

- Students will use I PICK to select books for their book box that they would like to read. This lesson is found on page 138.
- If students use community supplies or keep their things in a desk or other storage area, it's important to still go over the process you would like them to use in selecting their materials and returning them to their storage location.
- This process can be revisited as needed throughout the year to remind students of respectful and responsible behavior.

INDEPENDENT LEARNING ◀

LESSON

IL.3 What's Independent?

UNDERSTAND (Why?)

We teach students what it means to be independent because it empowers them to take charge of their learning, make informed decisions, and solve problems on their own.

PREPARE (Students)

Today we're going to talk about what it means to be independent. Let's all say the word "independent." Being independent in our work helps us to problem solve, build confidence, and make informed decisions. We're going to learn how to be independent because there are many times you will be asked to work independently, and it's important to know what it looks like and sounds like to be independent when working.

TEACH (Explicitly)

Being independent means you can do things on your own without always needing help from others. When you're independent it shows that you can make appropriate choices, solve problems, and take care of your responsibilities, like finishing your work or organizing your materials, all by yourself.

Let's talk about times when you already show independence. I want you all to think of a moment when you were independent, solved a problem, or completed a task on your own. Turn and talk to your partner and share that with them. *(Call on students to share. You may choose to write these on chart paper.)*

In this class, we'll have independent work time. There will be times this work will be teacher directed, meaning I'll tell you what work needs to be completed first. In this case, this work is a "must-do" and should be completed first. When you do this work independently, you will gather the materials needed, complete the work following the directions, and turn it in, all by yourself. If you have questions as you're working you can make a note so you remember to ask later, but you will work through as much as you can on your own, being independent.

Sometimes you will have time for independent work that's student directed. This means that YOU will choose how you engage in your learning during that time. You might choose to read to yourself, work on writing, or listen to reading. It's important to remember that when you're independent it means you can complete the work all by yourself. That means you will follow the steps to be successful, independently.

It's important to learn to be independent with work because it helps us to problem solve and make sense of our learning. It gives us an opportunity to apply what we have learned and practice on our own, knowing if we become stuck or have questions, we have the support of our teacher and peers when needed.

SUPPORT (Pivots)

- You may wish to have younger students write and illustrate a sentence about something they can do independently. For example: I'm independent when I _____. Older students may wish to role-play or write a story about a time they were independent. This work can then be made into a class book if desired.
- This lesson can be extended to add what to do if you get "stuck" or don't know what to do during the independent work time.

SECTION 2   Independent Learning   **197**

▶ INDEPENDENT LEARNING

Lesson

IL.4   I PICK

UNDERSTAND (Why?)

Teaching students to choose books they can read and want to read increases engagement and success.

PREPARE (Students)

Sometimes I find myself reading a book that's hard to follow or that I have lost interest in. When this happens, I often want to choose another book and sometimes it takes me a few tries to find a book that I really want to read all the way to the end. Today we're going to learn a strategy called I PICK. It's a strategy that helps us to select good-fit books, because in order to become a better reader, we need to read text that we can read successfully. Learning to choose a good-fit book will help us to be engaged readers who enjoy reading.

TEACH (Explicitly)

Today we're going to learn how to find a good-fit book from the classroom or school library, a bookstore, or anywhere else you may be looking for books. I'm going to teach you the I PICK method. This method helps us to choose books that we can read and want to read.

Using chart paper, write I PICK vertically down the side. As you introduce what each letter stands for, write the word next to the letter. This gives students a visual to refer to as they learn and practice this strategy.

The I stands for I select a book. This is when you pick up a book and look it over. The P stands for purpose. Think, why do I want to read this book? The I stands for interest. Does this text interest me? The C stands for comprehension. If you make it through purpose and interest, read a paragraph or two and ask yourself, do I understand what I'm reading? The K stands for know most of the words. When you're sampling the text, are you able to read most of the words? If the answer is yes to all of these criteria, then it's a good-fit book. If it's no to any of the above, put it down and try again. *(Teacher models this strategy with a few texts.)*

Now it's your turn to try. *Have students get their book box or hand each student a book from a pile you have selected. Have students go through I PICK and determine whether the book they have is a good-fit book or not. Have them share with someone next to them or call on a few to model for the class.*

We just learned I PICK, which is a strategy that helps us engage in the books we read so that we're successful. Be sure to use this strategy when selecting books at the library or at a bookstore.

SUPPORT (Pivots)

- As you have a few minutes here and there throughout the year, ask one or two students to select a book from their book box and share how it meets each of the categories of I PICK. This helps to hold them accountable, gives insight to the books they are choosing, revisits the I PICK strategy for the class, and can even serve as a short book talk for their peers who may hear about a book they are interested in reading.

INDEPENDENT LEARNING

LESSON

IL.5 What's Engagement?

UNDERSTAND (Why?)

Teaching students what it means to be engaged helps them understand how to participate fully in their learning, leading to better comprehension and retention of information.

PREPARE (Students)

Let's talk about the word "engagement." Being engaged means paying attention and being involved in what we're learning. It looks like raising your hand to answer questions, sharing your ideas, and really focusing on activities so you can learn and have fun at the same time.

TEACH (Explicitly)

When we're engaged, we pay attention, ask questions, and share our ideas. *Write the word "engagement" on the board and add some simple drawings or icons (like an ear for listening, a hand for raising, a speech bubble for sharing ideas).*

Being engaged looks like listening carefully when someone is speaking, actively thinking in your mind, raising your hand to answer questions, and sharing your ideas with the class. I want you to think of a time when you felt really interested and focused during a lesson or activity. What were you doing that showed you were engaged? *(Call on students to share with the group or have them all share with a partner.)* On this chart under the word "engaged" I'm going to write down some of the examples I heard you share. *On a chart write* Engaged *and under that write some of the ideas you heard.*

Now, I'm going to read you a story. As I read, I want you to listen carefully and think about the characters and what's happening. AND, I want you to think about how you're engaged. After the story, we'll revisit what we read and discuss how engaged we were. *Read a short, engaging story to the class.* When we're engaged we usually can tell what happened in the story and we know about the characters. Turn to your partner and share something about the story and the characters. *(Pause for students to share.)* Now, think about how you were engaged as we read the story. What behaviors of engagement did you use? Turn and talk to your partner and discuss how you were engaged. *(Pause for students to share.)*

Now we're going to work in small groups to make posters that show what being engaged looks like. These posters will help us remember what engagement is. You can draw pictures or write examples of engaged behavior, like listening, asking questions, and sharing ideas. *After groups finish, have each group share their poster with the class.*

Let's think about what we learned today. Think, were you able to stay engaged? What helped you pay attention and get involved? Now, I want you to think of one thing you will do to stay more engaged in your learning. It could be something like "I'll raise my hand to answer questions" or "I'll listen carefully when someone is speaking." *Pause to give students time to think. Then, have a few students share their goals with the class.* Today, we learned about being engaged. Engagement means paying attention, asking questions, and sharing your ideas. You were very focused while practicing these behaviors! We'll keep working on our engagement goals this week, and throughout the year, and we'll check in to see how we're doing. Remember, being engaged helps us learn and have more fun!

SUPPORT (Pivots)

- It may help to also explain the other two levels of engagement. When learning or completing a task, a person can be engaged (as discussed here), passive (compliant in behaviors, low or no effort given toward learning/task), or disengaged (off task, disruptive).
- Give each student a small journal where they can reflect on their engagement at the end of each day. Prompt them with questions like, "What was one way you showed you were engaged today?" or "What was something you did today that helped you stay focused?" You can also include a section for setting daily engagement goals. Reviewing these journals weekly can help students become more mindful of their engagement and identify areas for improvement.

CONTINUUM OF ENGAGEMENT

DISENGAGED	PASSIVE	ENGAGED
Disrupting Avoiding the work Off task Playing around	Compliant Low effort Lack initiative Withdrawn	Asking questions Answering questions Showing interest Investing in learning Setting goals Seeking feedback Self Assessing

Adapted and based on Amy Berry's research on teachers' perceptions of engagement (Berry & Hattie 2023)

INDEPENDENT LEARNING

LESSON
IL.6

10 Steps to Independent Learning

UNDERSTAND (Why?) — Taking the time to teach students how to work independently promotes self-reliance and critical thinking skills, enabling them to manage their tasks and solve problems without constant guidance. It gives them the tools needed to be successful.

PREPARE (Students) — We talked about what it means to be independent and engaged, and we learned how sometimes independent work will be given to you by a teacher or teacher directed, and sometimes it will be work that you choose to do, or student directed. Now we're going to learn what to do when it's time to engage in independent learning. We'll learn what it should look like and feel like when we work independently on both teacher-directed work and student-directed work.

TEACH (Explicitly) — Have an anchor chart available. At the top write "Independent Learning" and then draw a large I to separate the bottom part of the chart in two (see page 230). On one side write Students and on the other side write Teacher. As each behavior is introduced, add it to the correct space on the anchor chart.

As we learned earlier, we learn to work independently because it helps us to problem solve, build confidence, and make sense of our learning. When it's time to work independently, it's important that you get started right away. This helps us to make the most of our time and get as much learning in as possible.

The next thing you will do is stay in one spot. Find a good space to work and stay in that space the whole time. The time we have is limited and we want to get as much learning in as possible, so we get started right away and we work the whole time.

You will also work quietly. As independent means to do something on your own, all by yourself, you will work to complete your work quietly.

There are two more things you need to do when working independently. The first is to ignore distractions. This means if someone comes into the classroom or if there's a loud noise or two other classmates are talking, you're going to do your best to keep your focus on your work so they don't distract you from what you're doing. And the final thing I'm going to write on the chart is persevere. Persevere means that you keep going, even when things are hard. So, as you're working independently, you're going to really work hard to stay focused and engaged and persevere through the work so you're successful and learn as much as possible.

And while you're doing these things, I'll be working with individual students or small groups of students.

Okay. Now we're going to have a chance to see what it looks like and sounds like to work Independently. I would like _____ to go get their book box and read the first page of their book independently, while we watch. *Call on a student to model the behavior. As they are modeling, revisit the anchor chart and go through the behaviors.*

Okay, let's see how they are doing. Did _____ get started right away? (Yes.) Are they working the whole time? (Yes.) Are they working quietly? (Yes.) Are they staying in one spot? (Yes.) Are they ignoring any distractions? (Yes.) Are they persevering? (Yes.) Great! If _____ learns like this independently, will they get more learning in? (Yes.) Thank you so much for showing us what it looks like and sounds like to learn Independently.

Now I'm going to have someone show us what it doesn't look like. I would like _____ to go get their book box and show us what it doesn't look like to work independently, while we watch. *Call on a student to model the behavior. As they are modeling incorrect behaviors, revisit the anchor chart and go through the behaviors.*

Okay, let's see how they are doing. Did _____ get started right away? (No.) Are they working the whole time? (No.) Are they working quietly? (No.) Are they staying in one spot? (No.) Are they ignoring any distractions? (No.) Are they persevering? (No.) Great! If _____ learns like this independently, will they get more learning in? (No.) Thank you so much for showing us what it does NOT look like and sounds like to learn Independently. Now, as we all know you know what it should look like, would you please do it again but this time show us what it does look like and sound like to learn independently?

Now let's see how they are doing. Did _____ get started right away? (Yes.) Are they working the whole time? (Yes.) Are they working quietly? (Yes.) Are they staying in one spot? (Yes.) Are they ignoring any distractions? (Yes.) Are they persevering? (Yes.) Great! If _____ learns like this independently, will they get more learning in? (Yes.) Thank you so much for showing us what it looks like and sounds like to learn Independently.

So we just learned how to engage successfully in Independent Learning. We saw what it looks like and sounds like, and what it doesn't look like and sound like. Now I'm going to give you a chance to practice. When I call your name, you're going to go get your book box (or book you're reading) and get started right away. For this session I'm going to have you read independently. As we talked about earlier, sometimes you will be reading, other times you will be writing, and sometimes you will be completing an assignment. Today you're going to be reading. When I call your name you're going to get your book box and get started right away, work the whole time, work quietly, stay in one spot, ignore distractions, and persevere. Raise your hand if you're ready? Great!

Call students one by one and place them around the room in designated spaces or have students choose. Give them a few minutes to practice and then sound the signal to let them know it's time to return to their seat in the gathering area and review as a class:

Let's check in to see how each of us did with Independent Learning. This check-in is only for you and will help you decide which behaviors you're doing well, and which will be your goal for the next time you line up. Please put your hand in front of your chest and indicate how proficient you were in practicing that behavior. You will hold up one finger if you found it hard to be independent with that behavior, but you're going to work on it; two fingers if you feel you did okay at being independent with that behavior, but you think you can do better; or three fingers if you were very independent with that behavior.

Point to each behavior on the chart and ask students to check in. Did you get started right away? *(Pause.)* Did you work the whole time? *(Pause.)* Were you quiet? *(Pause.)* Did you stay in one spot? *(Pause.)* Did you ignore distractions? *(Pause.)* Did you persevere? *(Pause.)* If you learn independently like you just did will you get more learning in? *(Pause.)*

Based on how you checked in, what's your goal for the next time you learn independently. What would you like to work on? *Call on one or two volunteers to share their goal.*

SUPPORT (Pivots)

- Revisit behaviors listed on the anchor chart before each session of independent learning until engagement is built and students are successful.
- It can help to use an engagement graph and graph minutes to provide a visual for students.

Independent Learning
Active Listening

Respectful to Others *Fun!* *Learn more*

Students	Teacher
Get started right away	Work with students
Stay in one spot	
Work the whole time	
Work quietly	
Ignore distractions	
Persevere	

SECTION 2 — Independent Learning

▶ INDEPENDENT LEARNING

LESSON IL.7

Underline and Move On (Um ...)

UNDERSTAND (Why?)

Teaching children to underline a word they don't know how to spell and move on when writing helps maintain their writing flow and encourages continuous expression of ideas without getting stuck on spelling. This practice reduces frustration and allows writers to revisit and correct their spelling later, promoting both writing fluency and learning.

PREPARE (Students)

Today, we're going to learn a helpful strategy for when you're writing. We learn this because it will help us to keep our writing flow without getting stuck. Are you ready to learn a trick that can help you in your writing?

TEACH (Explicitly)

Here's how it works:
   Sometimes when we're writing, we come to a word that we don't know how to spell. When this happens, it can cause us to get stuck, or even forget our thoughts because we turn our focus to figuring out how to spell the word instead of what we're writing about. It makes us say "Um...." However, there's something we can do to keep writing and not lose our focus. When writing if you come to a word you don't know how to spell, it helps to say the word slowly and listen carefully for the sounds. Then, write it the best you can, underline the word, and keep writing. The trick is to underline and move on, which goes well with the "Um. . . " you're thinking when you aren't sure how to spell the word. When a word makes you think "Um. . . " then you can remember to underline and move on. When you're finished with your thought, or at the end of your writing piece, you always go back and find the correct spellings. Let me model for you.
   Write a few sentences on chart paper, modeling what happens when you come to a word they are unsure of. It might sound like this:

I'm going to write about my dinner last night. I'm going to start by sharing what we ate. Last night we had spaghetti for dinner. *(Teacher turns to chart paper to write the first sentence.)*

Last night we had spaghetti. Um . . . I'm not sure how to spell spaghetti. I'm going to say the word slowly and listen for carefully for the sounds. S-P-A-G -E-T-I. And I know I have seen the word spelled with two T's, so I'm going to write it the best I can "s-p-a-g-e-t-t-i" and I'm not sure that it's spelled right. It still makes me go "Um …" so I'm going to underline and move on.

Prepared Classroom

Last night we had spagetti. It was delicious. Um . . . I'm not sure how to spell delicious. Let me say the word slowly and listen carefully for the sounds. D-e-l-i-sh-u-s. That doesn't look right to me, so I'm going to underline it and move on.

Last night we had spagetti. It was delishus. We had garlic bread to go with it.

Okay, I could keep going and write more, but I want you to have a chance to practice our strategy of underline and move on. Or, you might want to call it the Um strategy.

Using the dry erase board in front of you (or writing notebook or piece of paper), I want you to write three sentences about what you had for dinner last night. When you're writing, if you come to a word you don't know how to spell, a word that makes you say Um . . . you're going to underline the word, and move on. *Give students a chance to practice.*

Okay, so everyone just had a chance to practice. Now I want you to turn to your elbow buddy and share your writing with them. *(Pause for students to share.)*

As you see, it really helps to have a strategy you can go to when you're writing and have to stop and think about how to spell a word. Using this strategy when we're writing will help us to keep writing and not lose focus. Then, when we go to take our writing to final copy, we can always go back and correct our spelling.

This week when you're writing during independent work, remember to use the Um strategy when you come to words you're unsure how to spell.

SUPPORT
(Pivots)

- The modeling of underline and move on will need to be done multiple times throughout the first weeks of school and even again throughout the year as students need to be reminded.
- A continuation of this lesson is how students can find the correct spellings for the words they underline.

▶ INDEPENDENT LEARNING

LESSON

IL.8 Setting Up a Writing Notebook

UNDERSTAND (Why?)

Teaching students to set up their writing notebook when working independently helps them stay organized and easily locate their work, which enhances their focus and productivity. This organization builds consistent writing habits.

PREPARE (Students)

Today, I'm excited to introduce something special that you will be using all year long—your very own writing notebook. This notebook will be a place where you can write down your thoughts, stories, and ideas whenever you have independent writing time.

TEACH (Explicitly)

Give each child their writing notebook. You have your writing notebook in front of you. It's important to keep them neat and clean so they last all year. Here are some tips: always put your notebook back in your desk or book box when you're done; don't eat or drink near your notebook; and if you want to make a change in your writing, you can erase it or gently cross it out and keep going. This is my writing notebook. I'll show you how I've set it up and how you can take care of yours too.

As you go through the steps below, model for students and give them time to complete each step following the model.

First, you will label your notebooks with your name. This helps us keep track of whose notebook is whose. Write your name on the front cover or use a label if you have one.

Each time you write in your notebook, you will open to the next available page and write the date at the top of the page. We'll start now with the first page. Open your notebook to the first page. Write today's date at the top. Now, you will have a few minutes to write a few sentences about how you're feeling today or something interesting you want to share.

Let's share some of our first entries. Would anyone like to read a sentence or two they just wrote? Sharing helps us learn from each other and get new ideas for our own writing.

Before you put your notebook away, you may wish to place a bookmark in your notebook or bend the corner page so you know where to start next time. Then, you will neatly place it back in your desk or book box so it's ready for you to use next time.

Each time you choose to write during independent work, you will use your notebook and follow these steps. I'm so excited to see all the wonderful things you will write in your notebooks this year. Remember to take care of them and use them to explore your thoughts and ideas.

SUPPORT (Pivots)

- You may wish to provide stickers, colored tabs, or decorative materials for students to personalize their notebooks.
- It could be beneficial to offer alternative tools such as larger writing lines for those who may need it or digital writing notebooks for students who benefit from technology.

▶ INDEPENDENT LEARNING

LESSON

IL.9 What to Write About

UNDERSTAND (Why?)

Teaching students to choose a topic to write about when they write independently empowers them to take ownership of their writing and explore subjects they are passionate about, which increases their engagement, motivation, and writing skills.

PREPARE (Students)

Today, we're going to learn a fun and important skill—how to choose what to write about. Picking a topic that interests you makes writing more enjoyable and helps your ideas flow better. When we know how to choose our own topics, we can write about things we care about, which makes our writing more exciting and personal.

TEACH (Explicitly)

Let's start by brainstorming some ideas together. Think about things you like to do, places you have been, people you care about, and even dreams or wishes you have. These can all be great topics for writing. Writing is more fun when it's about something you really like or something important to you. For example, I love going to the park, so I might write a story about a fun day I had at the park. I'm going to start our list with the park. What are some other ideas we could add to a list of things to write about? *Write students' ideas on the chart paper as they share.*

You're going to create a brainstorm list in the back of your writing notebook. *Have students get their writing notebook and a pencil.* Open your notebook to the last page (or back cover) and this is where you will write a list of topics you might be interested in writing about. You may use some of the ideas we brainstormed, and you may add more of your own. *Give students time to generate their lists in the back of their notebooks.*

Great! Now turn to the friend next to you and share ideas. Add any to your list you wish to add. *Give time for students to share with each other.*

We just learned how to choose a topic to write about. Remember, you can write about things you like, places you have been, people you care about, or even use our prompt list for ideas. Keep thinking about new topics throughout the year and write them down in your notebook. That way, you will always have ideas ready for when it's time to write.

SUPPORT (Pivots)

- Develop a "Topic Brainstorm Wall" in the classroom where students can post their writing ideas and get inspired by their peers.
- You may wish to have a jar filled with slips of paper containing various writing topics or prompts. When students are unsure about what to write, they can draw a slip from the jar for inspiration.

INDEPENDENT LEARNING

LESSON

IL.10 Planning Template

UNDERSTAND (Why?)

PREPARE (Students)

TEACH (Explicitly)

SUPPORT (Pivots)

2.5 COLLABORATIVE LEARNING

COLLABORATIVE LEARNING

LESSON

CL.1 Choosing a Partner

UNDERSTAND (Why?)

Teaching students to select partners helps to create a productive and harmonious working environment, which enhances their ability to accomplish tasks efficiently and learn from one another's strengths. This strategy helps students know when and how to choose partners so they can focus their energy and efforts on the learning in front of them.

PREPARE (Students)

Throughout the year there will be many times you will work with others in pairs to share, complete an assignment, read, or even to explore a new concept. There will be times your partner or groups will be chosen for you, and other times you will choose your partner. Today I'm going to share how to ask someone to be your partner in a respectful way.

TEACH (Explicitly)

There are certain qualities you will look for when choosing a partner, and in turn, you will want to display these qualities for others. Respectful partners are kind, good listeners, willing to help, and thoughtful of others' ideas.

When asking someone to be your partner, you will make eye contact, walk to them and ask, "Will you please be my partner?" *(Say the question in a way so the inflection of your voice goes up at the end of the question.)* Did you notice that my voice went up at the end of the question? This is done on purpose because it's inviting and engaging. Listen to the difference when I ask the question and my inflection goes down. "Will you please be my partner?" And now listen when it goes up. "Will you please be my partner?" It sounds different. When your inflection goes upward it's inviting. That's what we want to do when inviting others to be our partner. Repeat after me, "Will you please be my partner?" (Pause for students to repeat.)

Now I'm going to ask _____ and _____ to model this for us. Watch how they make eye contact, walk to each other and say, "Will you please be my partner?" and respond, "Yes, thank you." *After the demonstration, discuss what went well.* Ask the class, "What did you notice about how they chose each other as partners? What made their interaction respectful?"

Have students practice choosing a partner using the method modeled. Encourage them to use eye contact, polite language, and appropriate voice inflection. Walk around the room to provide support and positive reinforcement. After a few minutes, bring the class back together and ask for volunteers to share their experiences. Discuss any challenges and highlight successful interactions.

How did it feel to choose your partner respectfully? Why do you think it's important to be kind and polite when choosing a partner? When you have an opportunity to choose a partner, it's helpful to remember the steps to take so that you're respectful and kind.

SUPPORT (Pivots)

- You may wish to use any of the ideas for selecting partners on the following page.
- Revisit the qualities of a good partner frequently so students remember the characteristics that help to make them an effective partner.

7 Ideas for Having Students Choose Partners

1. **Random Selection with a Deck of Cards:**
   Create pairs from a deck of cards (two kings, two queens, two jokers, etc.). Have students select a card and find their partner. This method ensures randomness and can add an element of fun and excitement.

2. **Interest-Based Pairing:**
   Create a survey or a list of interests and have students choose a topic they are passionate about. Pair students with similar interests together. This method helps in forming connections based on common interests, which can enhance collaboration and engagement.

3. **A Quick Way to Form Pairs, Number Matching:**
   Assign numbers to students randomly. Then, call out pairs of numbers that will be partners. For example, number one pairs with number two, number three with number four, and so on. This method is quick and ensures a random pairing each time.

4. **Colored Stickers to Speed Up Partner Selection:**
   Place different colored stickers on students' desks or shirts. Students must find a partner with the same color sticker. This visual method is simple and effective for younger students, helping them quickly find their partners.

5. **Can't Decide Who to Pick? Use Criteria Cards:**
   Create partner selection cards that have different criteria on them (i.e., choose someone you haven't worked with yet, or choose someone who is a good listener). Students can draw a card to guide their partner selection.

6. **An Icebreaker Uses Puzzle Pieces:**
   Create simple two-piece puzzles (e.g., animal pictures cut in half). Hand out one piece to each student and have them find the person with the matching piece. This activity can be both fun and a good icebreaker.

7. **Add a Compliment:**
   Ask students to choose their partner and then give them a compliment. This method not only helps in forming partnerships but also fosters a positive classroom environment and encourages kindness and respect among students.

COLLABORATIVE LEARNING ◄

LESSON

CL.2 Voice Level

UNDERSTAND (Why?)

When students understand how to regulate their voice level it ensures ideas will be heard, which enhances communication, teamwork, and learning.

PREPARE (Students)

Today, we're going to learn about different voice levels and how to use them. It's important to know when to use a quiet voice, a conversational voice, and a loud voice so we can communicate well and respect each other.

TEACH (Explicitly)

Let's look at our voice level chart. *Hold up the Voice Level Chart with visual aids.*

First, we have the whisper voice. Can everyone see the picture of the person whispering? A whisper voice is very quiet, like this *(Demonstrate a whisper voice.)*. We use a whisper level when we need to be very quiet, like during silent reading time or when someone is speaking and we don't want to interrupt. Let's practice our whisper level. Everyone say, "Would you help me?" in a whisper level." *(Students practice whispering "Would you help me?")*

Great! Now, let's talk about the conversational-level voice. This is how we talk when we're inside, working with our partners, or speaking during class. It sounds like this *(Demonstrate a conversational speaking level.)*. Let's all use our conversational-level voice to say, "Would you help me?" *(Students practice using their normal speaking voice.)*

Finally, we have the loud level. This is for when we're outside or need to get someone's attention quickly, like on the playground or in an emergency. It sounds like this *(Demonstrate a loud-level voice.)*. We don't use our loud-level inside because it can be disruptive. Let's try our loud-level together, just once, and say, "Would you help me?" *(Students practice using their loud-level voice.)*

Excellent! Now, think when might we need to use our whisper-level voice? *(Call on student.)* How about our conversational-level voice? *(Call on student.)* And when is it okay to use our loud-level voice? *(Call on student.)*

By using the appropriate voice level, we can make sure everyone can hear and understand us, and we can create a positive classroom for learning. Remember to look at our chart if you ever forget which voice level to use.

SUPPORT (Pivots)

- When teaching voice levels to young students, it's important to use age-appropriate language and examples. Younger children may benefit from visual aids, gestures, and relatable scenarios that help to make the lesson more concrete. For example, you might use pictures of different settings (library, classroom, playground) to show where different voice levels are appropriate.

- Consistent reinforcement of voice-level expectations is important for helping students internalize the concept. Consider creating and displaying a voice-level chart in the classroom that children can refer to throughout the day. Frequently remind students of the appropriate voice level for different activities. Incorporate regular practice and gentle reminders to help students develop the habit of adjusting their voice levels appropriately based on the context.

VOICE LEVELS

 WHISPER

 CONVERSATIONAL

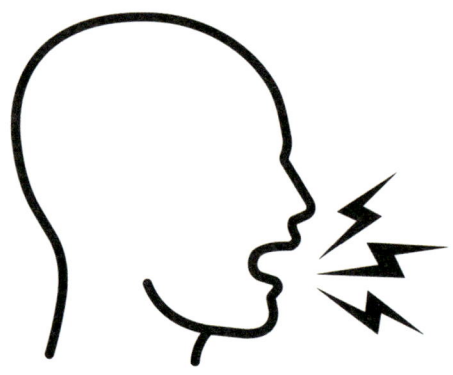 LOUD

COLLABORATIVE LEARNING ◀

LESSON

CL.3   Take Turns

UNDERSTAND (Why?)

When students understand how to take turns, it minimizes disruptions and creates a focused, cooperative atmosphere, so students complete tasks more effectively and learn from each other in a structured way.

PREPARE (Students)

Today, we're going to learn how to take turns when working with a partner. Taking turns is important because it makes sure everyone gets a chance to participate, share their ideas, and be included.

TEACH (Explicitly)

Let me explain what it looks like and sounds like to take turns. When you're working with a partner and they are talking, you need to listen carefully to what your partner is saying. Listening means you're quiet and looking at your partner while they are talking, which shows respect and helps you understand their ideas. It looks like this. *(Demonstrate what this looks like with a student.)*

Then, when it's your turn to talk, you wait until your partner is finished speaking. You can take turns by saying, "Now it's your turn," or "Now I'll share my idea." This way, you know when to speak and when to listen. *(Model this with a student volunteer.)*

Let's practice! I'm going to say something, and then I'll ask _____ to take their turn. Remember, listen first, then take your turn. "I think we should use the blue crayon for the sky. What do you think, _____?" *(Student practices responding.)*

Great! Did everyone see how _____ waited until I finished talking before sharing their idea? That's how we take turns. Now, I want everyone to practice with their partner. Remember to listen first, then take your turn. *(Students practice in pairs.)*

Taking turns helps us work together and makes sure everyone's ideas are heard. Keep practicing this when you work with your partner, and soon it will become a habit.

SUPPORT (Pivots)

- Recognize and respect the diverse cultural backgrounds of your students. In some cultures, communication styles and norms about taking turns and interrupting may differ. Be mindful of these differences and explain the concept in a way that's inclusive and respectful of all students. Providing examples from various cultures can help make the lesson more relatable and ensure all students feel included and understood.
- You may find it helps to use a talking stick, which is a stick that gets passed back and forth between partners as they share. The partner holding the stick is the one who is speaking. Using a talking stick helps students internalize the behavior of taking turns so they apply it not only in the classroom but also in other social interactions. This scaffold teaches the concept of sharing a conversation and can be removed once students demonstrate understanding.

▶ COLLABORATIVE LEARNING

LESSON

CL.4 Check for Understanding

UNDERSTAND (Why?)

Teaching students to check for understanding as they work together helps to ensure they are on the same page and can move forward effectively with their tasks. This practice helps to clarify any misunderstandings, preventing potential errors, and enhances the overall quality of their work.

PREPARE (Students)

Today, we're going to learn about something very important to do when working with a partner. We're going to learn how to check if our partner understands what we're talking about. It's called Check for Understanding. We learn this because when we check for understanding, we make sure that our partner knows what we're saying. This helps us learn better together.

TEACH (Explicitly)

Check for Understanding means you explain something to your partner, and then your partner explains it back to you in their own words. They might say, "I just heard you say . . . " If they can share the most important parts of what was said, it means they understand. Let me show you how it works.

First, I'll explain something simple. For example, "To make a peanut butter and jelly sandwich, you need two slices of bread, peanut butter, and jelly. You spread the peanut butter on one slice and the jelly on the other, then put them together." Now, I need a volunteer to check for understanding. *(Student raises hand and shares the most important parts of what was said.)*

You explained it back in a way that shows me you understood what I was saying. If you had trouble remembering what was said or needed help, you could have asked, "Would you please repeat what you said?" so that you could listen again and share your understanding. However, in this case you were able to remember and share without difficulty.

Now you're going to turn to a partner, and I want one of you to share what you did last night and the other is going to check for understanding. *(Students share with partner and practice Check for Understanding.)*

I heard lots of great examples of Check for Understanding, and I even heard a few students ask their partner to please repeat what they had said. Using the strategy of checking for understanding and asking someone repeat the information if we missed it the first time is a great way to make sure we understand and learn together.

SUPPORT (Pivots)

- Teach students to use kind and encouraging language. Emphasize the importance of being patient and supportive when their partner doesn't understand something right away.
- Young students need straightforward guidance to understand and apply new concepts. Clear instructions help them grasp the steps involved in Checking for Understanding without feeling overwhelmed.

COLLABORATIVE LEARNING ◀

LESSON

CL.5 Think: What's My Purpose?

UNDERSTAND (Why?)

Thinking about the purpose of a learning task provides a sense of direction and understanding. Knowing and setting the purpose increases motivation and helps students to focus their efforts and prioritize their actions, and leads to more effective and meaningful work. When learners are clear about their objectives, they are able to monitor their progress and adjust as needed, enhancing their problem-solving and critical thinking skills.

PREPARE (Students)

Today, we're going to learn how to think about our purpose when we're learning. Purpose is why we do something. When we know our purpose, it helps us stay focused, work hard, and learn.

TEACH (Explicitly)

Imagine you're running a race. The purpose, or goal of running a race is to reach the finish line. You know what you need to do to be successful, right? Learning is the same way! When we know why we're learning something, it helps us know what to do and how to get better.

Let's think about some of the things we learn in school. For example, when we practice reading, our purpose might be to understand a story or learn new words. When we do math, our purpose might be to solve problems or figure out how many things we have. Knowing our purpose helps us know what we're trying to achieve.

I'm going to give you some examples, and I want you to tell me the purpose. Ready? Why do we practice writing our letters? (To get better at writing.) Exactly! And why do we do science experiments? (To learn how things work.) Yes! Now, I want you to think about your purpose when you're learning. Here's what you can do: before you start a task, ask yourself, "Why am I doing this?" and "What do I want to learn or achieve?" This will help you focus and know when you have accomplished what you decided.

Let's practice together. Everyone, take out one of your good-fit books. Today, our purpose for reading is to understand the story. Think about this purpose while you read. We know one way we can check if we understand the story is to ask questions about what's happening in the story. Asking questions helps us stay focused on our purpose. Now, let's start reading and remember to think about our purpose. (Students start reading. The teacher walks around, offering support and reminding students to think about their purpose.)

Alright, everyone, let's come back together. How did thinking about your purpose help you while you were reading? (It helped us remember to pay attention to the story.) That's wonderful! Remember, thinking about our purpose helps us learn and stay focused. Let's keep practicing this every day. Before we start any task, let's always ask ourselves, "What's my purpose?" and "What do I want to learn?"

- Incorporate regular check-ins where students are reminded to think about their purpose before starting tasks. This could be a routine question asked before beginning any activity: "What's our purpose for this task?"
- Incorporate visual aids such as pictures, charts, or props to illustrate the idea of purpose. Visuals can help young students grasp abstract concepts more concretely.

COLLABORATIVE LEARNING

LESSON

CL.6 What To Do When Finished

UNDERSTAND (Why?)

Teaching students what to do when they finish a teacher-directed/must-do task helps maintain a productive and effective learning environment. It helps students develop independent and collaborative learning habits and prevents off-task behavior, ensuring that classroom time is used effectively. Having a clear plan for what to do next encourages continuous learning and personal responsibility.

PREPARE (Students)

Today, we're going to talk about what to do when you finish teacher-directed or "must-do" work. Having a plan for what to do next helps us use time wisely and keep learning.

TEACH (Explicitly)

When you finish with a "must-do" learning assignment or task, it's important to know what to do next. I'm going to share your options for what to do when you finish what you're working on. I'll title this chart "Next Steps" because it provides options or "may-do" tasks for next steps when you finish what you're working on. *(Write these on chart paper for students to refer to later.)*

1. You will make sure all teacher-directed/must-do work is complete. This is any work that was given to you by the teacher. You always do the work the teacher has given you first. Then, when that work is completed, you may move to student-directed work, or may-do work. It's important to remember if you're engaged in independent learning you will choose a learning task you will do independently, and if you're in collaborative learning you will choose a learning task you will do with a partner.

2. If you're engaged in independent learning you might choose:
   - Independent Reading—Read from a self-selected, good-fit book.
   - Independent Writing—Write in your writing notebook about a self-selected topic or one from the topic jar.
   - Listen to Reading/Technology—Use a device (tablet/Chromebook) to engage with an audiobook or an approved app or website.

   If you're engaged in collaborative learning you might choose:
   - Read to Someone—Read a text with a partner.
   - Write with Someone—Create a story or writing piece with a partner.

We have many ideas for what to do when we finish your must-do work. Now we're going to practice together. I'm going to give you a short task, and when you finish, I want you to choose one of the "Next Steps" to do quietly.

SECTION 2 — Collaborative Learning

Students complete a short task such as read a short story on the board or complete a few math problems. Then walk around, observing and offering guidance if needed as they choose their next activity. Sound the quiet signal after students have had a chance to practice.

Please put your things away and join us in the gathering area. *(Pause.)* I saw some of you reading, some writing, and some working on tablets. Remember, any time you finish teacher-directed work, you can always look at our "Next Steps" chart to remind you of the options. This helps us all use time wisely and keep learning.

SUPPORT (Pivots)

- Create a "Next Steps" chart or poster with clear, simple options that students can easily refer to. Include both words and pictures to accommodate different reading levels.
- Include a mix of activities such as the ones mentioned above. Ensure there are options for both individual learning and collaborative learning and that all options lead to progress toward learning goals and objectives.

COLLABORATIVE LEARNING

LESSON

CL.7 Planning Template

UNDERSTAND
(Why?)

PREPARE
(Students)

TEACH
(Explicitly)

SUPPORT
(Pivots)

2.6 CONFERRING

CONFERRING

LESSON

C.1 Engagement Conference

UNDERSTAND (Why?)

An engagement conference takes place to help students learn, practice, and build learning behaviors that will help them to be successful during whole-group lessons, as well as independent and collaborative learning time. It's designed to help students identify and understand what's keeping them from being successful, while setting small, attainable goals to help them grow stamina and gain independence. As the class is building engagement with independent and collaborative learning, the teacher pays attention to student engagement behaviors, taking note of who could benefit from more guidance.

PREPARE (Students)

I want to take a few minutes to revisit a behavior of engagement that I think could really help you to focus and learn more. I'll share this behavior and then we'll practice it and set a goal for you to work on it independently.

TEACH (Explicitly)

An engagement conference helps students with any behaviors that effect their engagement. The following is an example. Each engagement conference will sound different based on the individual child's needs.

> **Teacher:** I'm going to talk to you for a moment about staying in one spot during our work time. I've noticed you have been moving around a lot, and one of our behaviors is to stay in one spot so we can be engaged. Can you tell me what makes you want to move around?
>
> **Student:** I just get bored sitting in one place, and sometimes I want to see what my friends are doing.
>
> **Teacher:** I understand. It's natural to feel like moving around sometimes. When you stay in one spot, it helps you focus better and get your work done more quickly. Let's think of some ways to make it easier for you to stay in your spot. Maybe we can set up a little area with everything you need right there. How does that sound?
>
> **Student:** Okay.
>
> **Teacher:** How about we make a plan: you will stay in your spot while you're completing your "must-do" work, and when you finish then you may choose your "may-do" work like reading a book or working on one of our games on the tablet. All of the things you need are right here within reach. Does that sound like a good plan?
>
> **Student:** Yes, I like that.
>
> **Teacher:** Great! Let's try it today. I'll check in with you later to see how it's going. Remember, staying in one spot helps you do your best work, and I'm here to help you with that. If you need anything or feel like moving, just let me know, and we can find a solution together.
>
> **Student:** Okay, I'll try my best.
>
> **Teacher:** I know you can do it. I'll meet back with you at the end of the day today to see how you did.

By having this kind of conversation, the teacher can address the student's specific needs and concerns while reinforcing the importance of staying in one spot. This approach also allows for collaborative problem solving and sets clear expectations and strategies to support the student's engagement behavior.

SUPPORT (Pivots)

- Plan for actionable follow-up steps after the conference to ensure that discussions and agreements translate into tangible actions. This may include creating action plans, setting deadlines for specific tasks, or scheduling follow-up meetings to monitor progress and make necessary adjustments.

CONFERRING

LESSON

C.2 Informative Quick Check

UNDERSTAND (Why?)

Informative Quick Checks are used to help teachers and students familiarize with the practice of conferring. It provides essential information that can guide future instructional decisions, allows for brief interactions with students, and initiates the process of writing down student progress. They are a quick check in to see what a child is working on and are an indicator of pace or engagement with their work.

PREPARE (Students)

Hello! I want to spend just a minute with you to find out what you're doing and how it's going. I'm going to take a few quick notes and then I'll leave you to continue working.

TEACH (Explicitly)

An Informative Quick Check works to familiarize students with having a conversation about their learning while at the same time informing the teacher of small pieces of information that inform instruction and help with progress monitoring. The following is an example. Each Quick Check will sound different based on the individual child's work and responses.

Teacher: I noticed you're working on your writing assignment. Can you tell me a bit about what you're writing?
Student: I'm writing a story about a pirate adventure. My main character is Captain Blackbeard.
Teacher: That sounds exciting! Can you show me what you have written so far?
Student: Sure, here it is. I'm at the part where Captain Blackbeard finds a hidden treasure map.
Teacher: I see. Your story has an interesting beginning. How do you feel about writing this story? Is it challenging, just right, or a bit easy for you?
Student: It's kind of hard, especially thinking of what happens next.
Teacher: Thinking of new ideas can be tough. What strategies are you using to help you come up with the next part of your story?
Student: I've been brainstorming ideas in my notebook and thinking what might happen.
Teacher: That's a great strategy. Brainstorming can really help. How about the pacing? Do you feel you're making good progress with your writing?
Student: I think so. I try to write a little bit each day, so I don't get behind.
Teacher: That's a helpful habit. I'll check in with you later to see how your story is developing. Keep up the great work!

SUPPORT (Pivots)

- Quick Checks provide great information that can be used in goal setting and instructional conferences later. Take note and schedule a conference if there's a concern that needs attention.

▶ CONFERRING

LESSON

C.3 Planning Template

UNDERSTAND (Why?)

PREPARE (Students)

TEACH (Explicitly)

SUPPORT (Pivots)

2.7 BRIEF AND EFFECTIVE LESSONS

BRIEF AND EFFECTIVE LESSONS ◀

LESSON

BL.1 Brain Break Review

UNDERSTAND (Why?)

Students are taught how to engage in brain breaks in lesson DR.2 (page 171). They help students participate effectively when they are used as a class, and when used independently. By learning specific techniques, students develop habits for maintaining focus and managing stress, which are essential skills for both academic success and personal well-being. This lesson is a review, and helps students remember the purpose of a brain break so they are effective.

PREPARE (Students)

Hey class! Today, we're going to learn about brain breaks. These are special little breaks we take to help our brains take a moment to remember what was taught and stay fresh and focused. Just like our bodies need rest after playing, our brains need rest after thinking hard. Brain breaks are fun activities that help us feel calm and ready to learn more.

TEACH (Explicitly)

Now that we know why brain breaks are important, let's learn how to do one. We're going to start with a simple brain break called Balloon Breathing. Imagine you have a big balloon in your favorite color. First, sit up straight and put your hands on your belly. We're going to pretend to blow up our balloon with our breath.

Take a deep breath in through your nose, filling up your belly like you're filling up a big balloon. Feel your belly get bigger. Now, slowly breathe out through your mouth, and imagine you're letting the air out of the balloon. Feel your belly get smaller.

Let's do this together three times. Ready? Breathe in and fill up your balloon . . . and breathe out, letting the air out. *Inhale . . . exhale . . . .*

Great! Show me thumbs up if that made you feel a little more calm. Balloon Breathing is a great way to calm down and focus whenever you need a break. You can use it anytime you feel worried, tired, or just need a moment to relax.

Brain breaks can also be more active. When we move our bodies, it helps our brains get more oxygen and wakes us up! Let's try "jumping jacks" for thirty seconds. Ready? Go! *(Wait thirty seconds.)* Stop! How do you feel now? Do you feel more awake and ready to learn?

Remember, you can use brain breaks anytime you start to feel tired or distracted. It could be deep breathing, stretching, or even a quick dance party. It's a great way to help your brain stay strong and ready for anything.

SUPPORT (Pivots)

- Be sure the brain break activities you choose are suitable for the students' age and developmental level. Younger students might benefit from simple, quick activities like deep breathing or easy stretches, while older students might enjoy more complex or physically engaging activities.
- Integrate brain breaks into the daily routine consistently. Establishing a regular pattern helps students anticipate and look forward to these breaks, making them a natural and expected part of the learning process. This consistency also helps students recognize the benefits and importance of taking brain breaks.

▶ BRIEF AND EFFECTIVE LESSONS

LESSON

BL.2 Hook

UNDERSTAND (Why?)

When you want a learner to continue to gain new information and you have reached the optimal lesson length, it's important to provide a "brain break" that allows students to process what they have already learned.

PREPARE (Students)

Once you have taught students the purpose of a brain break and how to engage in them, use them throughout the year as needed. A "hook" brain break is similar, only it's a break given in the middle of a lesson and relates to the content. We don't prepare students for a "hook" brain break, we simply interject it in the middle of a lesson as needed. See the example below.

TEACH (Explicitly)

Today, we have been learning about animals and their habitats. We're going to take a quick brain break called a "hook," which is a time for us to refresh our brains while continuing to learn. I'll start by sharing that one of my favorite animals is the panda. Pandas live in cool, misty mountains in China, and they love to munch on bamboo all day long. Isn't that interesting?

Now, I want you to turn to a friend and tell them about your favorite animal and where it lives. Maybe it's a tiger in the jungle, a whale in the ocean, or even a bird in a tree. You have two minutes to share with each other. Ready? Go! *Students share their stories with each other.*

So fun! I enjoyed hearing you share your favorite animals. Now that our brains are refreshed and we have learned something new, let's get back to our lesson and continue learning about animals and their habitats.

SUPPORT (Pivots)

- Be sure the "hook" brain break is directly related to the lesson content. The activity or story should tie into the current topic, reinforcing key concepts and making the learning experience more cohesive and engaging for students.
- Choose hooks that actively involve students and engage their emotions, curiosity, or physical movement. This could be through sharing personal stories, fun facts, discussions, or interactive activities that make the content more memorable and enjoyable.

BRIEF AND EFFECTIVE LESSONS ◀

LESSON

BL.3 Active Listening

UNDERSTAND (Why?)

Active listening skills are essential for whole-group lessons because they help students remain engaged, follow instructions accurately, and contribute meaningfully to discussions. By teaching these skills, students learn to respect each other's perspectives, creating a positive and collaborative learning environment.

PREPARE (Students)

Throughout the year there will be many times you come to the gathering area for whole-class lessons, or you participate in a small group lesson, or you work collaboratively with a partner. In all of these circumstances, it's important to be an active listener. When you're an active listener, it shows respect for others and allows you to learn and remember more information.

TEACH (Explicitly)

We're part of whole-group lessons and small-group lessons and partner work for many reasons. We gain information, learn new things, and have fun. A lot of the time it is so we can work and learn together and have thoughtful discussions. Whatever the reason, it's important to be active listeners when someone is talking so we can get the most out of it and it's respectful.

Using an anchor chart, list the expected active listening behaviors.

When listening to someone speak, it's important to make eye contact, sit quietly, keep your hands and body to yourself, focus your listening on what the speaker is saying, and ignore distractions.
   Select a student to demonstrate active listening by modeling appropriate behaviors while you share with them a short story about your day. When finished, reflect on student behaviors. Ask the class, Did ___ sit or stand quietly? Did they make eye contact? Did they keep their hands and body to themselves? Did they focus on what was being said? Did they ignore distractions? If this is how you actively listen, is it respectful to the speaker? (Yes.) Do you have a better chance to understanding what's said to you? (Yes.)
   Have students practice active listening behaviors as a whole class. Now we're going to practice as a class. When I tell you to begin, you're going to turn to your partner. One of you will tell a short story about something that has happened during your day. The other partner will practice being an active listener. Remember, the listener sits or stands quietly, making eye contact with the speaker, keeping their hands and body to themself, focusing on what the speaker is saying, and working to ignore distractions. You will have one minute. Go ahead and get started. *Give students one minute to practice. Then sound the signal and have them switch roles.*

When finished, ask students to self-reflect on their behaviors as you review the I-chart.

Okay, now I want you to think about yourself during that practice session. Show me thumbs up for yes and thumbs sideways if it's something you want to work on. Did you sit or stand quietly? Did you make eye contact? Did you keep your hands and body to yourself? Did you focus on what was being said? Did you ignore distractions? If this is how you actively listen, is it respectful to the speaker? (Yes.) Do you have a better chance to understanding what's being said? (Yes.)

Way to go! You will be a part of many lessons and partner work throughout the year, often many times in one day. When someone is speaking or the teacher is teaching, it's important to make sure to follow these behaviors so you can understand what's being said.

SUPPORT (Pivots)

- Provide clear examples of active listening behaviors and opportunities for students to practice these skills. Role-playing activities, listening exercises, and structured discussions can help reinforce and refine active listening techniques.
- Offer specific feedback on students' listening skills, highlighting areas of improvement, and recognizing instances of effective listening. Positive reinforcement can encourage students to continue using active listening strategies in various learning contexts.

BRIEF AND EFFECTIVE LESSONS

LESSON

BL.4 Planning Template

UNDERSTAND (Why?)

PREPARE (Students)

TEACH (Explicitly)

SUPPORT (Pivots)

2.8 PROGRESS MONITORING & ACCOUNTABILITY

PROGRESS MONITORING & ACCOUNTABILITY

LESSON

PM.1 Goal Setting

UNDERSTAND (Why?)

Knowing how to set goals helps students understand what they are working toward and allows for clear progress tracking.

PREPARE (Students)

Today, we're going to talk about goals. A goal is something you want to achieve or get better at. For example, you might have a goal to learn to ride a bike or to read a certain number of books, or to work on a specific strategy that will help you in reading, writing, or math.

TEACH (Explicitly)

Purposeful goals have five characteristics. *Write each characteristic on an anchor chart as they are introduced.*

Purposeful goals are Clear: The goal will be easy to understand. For example, instead of saying you want to read "more" books, be clear and specific and say "I want to read three new books."

Purposeful goals are Measurable: You will be able to see how you're doing. You could measure the above goal by being able to count how many books you read.

They are also Achievable: The goal will be something you can actually do. Is reading three new books something that's doable? Yes. So this goal is achievable.

A purposeful goal is Important: The goal will matter to you. We know that the more we read the better we get at reading, and reading is important to help us learn more, so this goal would be important because we want to be better at reading and it helps us learn more.

And finally, a purposeful goal should be Timed: The goal will have a time frame. In the example of reading books, we can make it timed by stating how long we think it should take us to read three new books. For example, I'll read three new books in one month.

Hand out goal form. (See page 243.)

Now you're going to think about something you want to get better at in school. Maybe you want to get better at math or reading. Think about what you would like to get better at, and you're going to make a goal for that. Using the form given to you, you're going to set a goal that's clear, measurable, achievable, important, and has a time frame. I'll give you a few minutes to work, and then we'll share a few.

Have students share their goals with a partner or the class.

We'll revisit our goals from time to time as a class, and when I meet with you in small groups or individually, we'll also talk about your goals and your progress toward achieving them. Today, we learned how to set purposeful goals. These goals help us know what we want to achieve and how we can do it. I'm excited to see you reach your goals!

SUPPORT
(Pivots)

- For younger students, goals should be simple and concrete. Use clear and simple language and provide concrete examples that they can easily understand. Visual aids and hands-on activities can also help make the goal-setting process more engaging and comprehensible.
- Help students identify realistic and achievable goals, offer feedback, and model how to break down large goals into smaller, manageable steps. Regular check-ins and encouragement help students stay motivated and on track.

Name: _____

My purposeful goal is

	YES
Clear—The goal is easy to understand.	☐
Measurable—I will be able to see how I am doing.	☐
Achievable—It is something I can do.	☐
Important—The goal matters to me.	☐
Timed—The goal has a timeframe.	☐

Name: _____

My purposeful goal is

	YES
Clear—The goal is easy to understand.	☐
Measurable—I will be able to see how I am doing.	☐
Achievable—It is something I can do.	☐
Important—The goal matters to me.	☐
Timed—The goal has a timeframe.	☐

▶ PROGRESS MONITORING & ACCOUNTABILITY

LESSON

PM.2 Self-Assessment Skills

UNDERSTAND (Why?)

Teaching students' self-assessment skills encourages critical reflection and goal setting and improves metacognitive abilities. Through self-assessment, students take responsibility for their progress, and teachers provide personalized support based on individual needs.

PREPARE (Students)

Today, we're going to talk about how to self-assess. This means how to check your own work and understand how you're doing. We're going to learn to do this with a checklist, a rubric, and a reflective journal.

TEACH (Explicitly)

First, we have a checklist. A checklist is a list of all the steps or items we need to complete a task. For example, if we're writing a story, our checklist might include "Did I write a beginning, middle, and end?" or "Did I check my spelling and punctuation?" *Show an example of a checklist, page 245.* When we finish our work, we can go through each item on the list and check it off. This helps us make sure we haven't forgotten anything important.

Next, we have a rubric. A rubric is like a scoring guide that tells us exactly what we need to do to achieve different levels of performance. For example, for our story, a rubric might show that to get a top score, we need to have clear and detailed descriptions, correct grammar, and a strong plot. *Show an example of a rubric, page 246.* We can use the rubric to compare our work to the criteria and see where we stand. This helps us understand what we did well and what we might need to improve.

Finally, we have a reflective journal. This is where we can write down our thoughts about our work after we finish it. We can reflect on questions like "What did I do well?" "What was challenging?" and "What will I do differently next time?" *Show an example of a journal entry, page 247.* Writing in a reflective journal helps us think deeply about our learning process and recognize our progress over time.

I just shared how to self-assess and think about how you're doing in your work. We learned three ways to do this. We can use a checklist, a rubric, or a reflective journal. All of these will help us get better at what we do.

SUPPORT (Pivots)

- Demonstrate how to fill out a checklist, evaluate work using a rubric, and write reflective journal entries. Scaffold the process by starting with simpler tasks and gradually increasing complexity as students gain confidence in self-assessment.
- Use student age and engagement to determine whether you will need to teach this in one, two, or three lessons.
- Offer alternative formats for checklists, rubrics, and reflective journals, such as visual aids, audio recordings, or simplified versions, to ensure all students can effectively engage in self-assessment.

Story Writing Checklist

Title: _____
Name: _____
Date: _____

1. Story Elements:
   ☐ I have a clear beginning.
   ☐ I have a detailed middle.
   ☐ I have a strong ending.

2. Characters:
   ☐ My characters are well described.
   ☐ My characters have clear goals or problems.

3. Setting:
   ☐ I described where and when the story takes place.
   ☐ The setting helps create the mood of the story.

4. Plot:
   ☐ The events in my story are in a logical order.
   ☐ There's a clear problem or conflict.
   ☐ There's a resolution to the problem or conflict.

5. Language and Style:
   ☐ I used descriptive words and details.
   ☐ My sentences are clear and varied.

6. Grammar and Mechanics:
   ☐ I checked my spelling.
   ☐ I used correct punctuation.
   ☐ My sentences start with capital letters and end with proper punctuation.

7. Revision:
   ☐ I read my story out loud to check for flow and clarity.
   ☐ I made changes to improve my story after reviewing it.

Story Writing Rubric

Title: _____
Name: _____
Date: _____

Criteria	4—Exceeding	3—Meeting	2—Approaching	1—Beginning
Beginning	Engaging and clear introduction of setting and characters	Clear introduction of setting and characters	Basic introduction of setting and characters	Little or no introduction of setting and characters
Middle	Detailed and well-developed plot with logical events	Developed plot with mostly logical events	Basic plot with some logical events	Underdeveloped plot with few or no logical events
Ending	Strong and satisfying resolution	Clear resolution	Basic resolution	Weak or no resolution
Characters	Well-developed, interesting characters	Developed characters with some depth	Basic characters with limited development	Underdeveloped characters with little to no depth
Setting	Vivid and detailed description of setting	Clear description of setting	Basic description of setting	Little or no description of setting
Conflict/Resolution	Clear, engaging conflict and resolution	Clear conflict and resolution	Basic conflict and resolution	Weak or no conflict and resolution
Language/Style	Highly descriptive language and varied sentence structure	Descriptive language with some varied sentence structure	Basic language with little variation in sentence structure	Simple or repetitive language and sentence structure
Grammar/Mechanics	No errors in spelling, punctuation, or grammar	Few errors in spelling, punctuation, or grammar	Some errors in spelling, punctuation, or grammar	Many errors in spelling, punctuation, or grammar

Reflective Journal Entry

Title: _____
Name: _____
Date: _____

1. **What did I do well in my story?**
   - I think I did a great job describing the setting. I used lots of details to make it vivid and interesting.
   - My characters have clear goals and personalities, which made them feel real to me.

2. **What was challenging for me?**
   - It was challenging to keep the plot events in a logical order. I had to revise my story several times to make sure everything made sense.
   - I found it hard to come up with a strong ending that resolved the conflict in a satisfying way.

3. **What will I do differently next time?**
   - Next time, I'll plan my plot more carefully before I start writing. I'll make an outline to help keep my events in order.
   - I'll also spend more time brainstorming different possible endings before choosing the best one.

4. **Additional Thoughts:**
   - I really enjoyed creating my characters and imagining how they would react in different situations.
   - I learned that revising is an important part of writing. My story got much better after I made changes based on my self-assessment.

▶ PROGRESS MONITORING & ACCOUNTABILITY

LESSON

PM.3 Understanding Feedback

UNDERSTAND (Why?)

When students learn how to understand feedback it helps them identify areas of strength and areas for improvement in their work.

PREPARE (Students)

We're going to talk about feedback. Feedback helps us learn and get better. It's like getting advice or tips to improve.

TEACH (Explicitly)

Imagine you're playing soccer, and your coach gives you feedback after a game. Your coach says, "I noticed you had consistent effort in passing the ball to your teammate." That's positive feedback. Or they might say, "Try to keep your eyes on the ball next time." That's feedback to help you improve.

Think about being in school. When you turn in your math homework, I might give you feedback to help you learn. For example, if you got all the addition problems correct, I might say, "Your addition skills are really improving." That's positive feedback. If you made a mistake, I might say, "Check your subtraction signs and see what answers you get." That's feedback to help you fix mistakes and learn.

When we get feedback, we can use it to make our work better. Let's look at some examples of feedback and think about how we can use it in our work.

Example 1: Your story has a strong beginning and end. The middle could use more details.
Based on this feedback, what could be done to improve the work? *(Give students a chance to turn and talk or think.)* Yes, the person receiving the feedback could add descriptive language and more information to the middle of the story so the reader is more engaged and has a better understanding
Let's look at another example.

Example 2: You answered most of the math problems correctly. Double-check your multiplication facts for accuracy.
Based on this feedback, what could be done to improve the work? *(Give students a chance to turn and talk or think.)* Yes, the person receiving the feedback could practice multiplication tables and review any facts that were incorrect to ensure accuracy in future math assignments.

It's important to remember feedback is a tool to help us improve and learn how much we know. We learn and grow when we use feedback to make our work the best it can be.

SUPPORT
(Pivots)

Here are six prompts or questions to encourage thoughtful reflection and discussion about feedback:

1. What did you find most helpful or valuable about the feedback you received?
2. How can you use the feedback to improve your work or performance?
3. Did the feedback help you better understand your strengths or areas for growth?
4. What additional information or examples would you like to receive in feedback to enhance your learning?
5. How do you plan to implement the feedback in future tasks or assignments to achieve better results?
6. How might I support you in the way I give feedback?

▶ PROGRESS MONITORING & ACCOUNTABILITY

LESSON

PM.4 Planning Template

UNDERSTAND
(Why?)

PREPARE
(Students)

TEACH
(Explicitly)

SUPPORT
(Pivots)

SO NOW WHAT?

This book shares eight proven, highly effective practices that help teachers create engaging classrooms where students thrive. We've included practical teacher tips to use all year long, and specific lessons to build a well-prepared classroom where both teaching and learning flourish. The best part? These strategies work in any classroom and with any curriculum.

So, what's next? How do you fit this information into your unique curriculum and schedule? (Hint: You don't have to "fit" it in, it integrates seamlessly.)

Teachers often find themselves in one of two situations: either they have a very structured schedule with a scripted curriculum and little flexibility (we will call this teacher Pat), or they have a flexible schedule with standards or outcomes defined, many resources, and instructional autonomy. (We will refer to this teacher as Lois). The good news is the practices and lessons in this book are designed to work in both scenarios, and any scenario in between.

Let us show you:

Pat's Classroom:

Meet Pat. Pat has been teaching for three years and works in a district with a highly structured curriculum. His day is meticulously planned, with detailed lesson scripts that ensure consistency and alignment across the team. This structured approach ensures that all students receive the same high-quality instruction and helps streamline the teaching process for Pat and his colleagues.

Pat's biggest challenges are behavior and engagement. While following the structured lessons, he recognizes that sometimes the mandatory lessons don't meet the interest and needs of his students, causing them to disengage quickly and leading to more off task behavior. Finding creative ways to enhance these lessons can build a more dynamic and attentive classroom environment.

Upon reading *Prepared Classroom*, Pat was thrilled to find practices that could help his students become self-regulated learners. However, he had one big question: "With a tightly structured schedule, when do I best integrate these practices?" (Fair question, Pat, fair question.)

Pat shared his schedule:

- Morning Work (required work students must complete each morning)
- Morning Meeting (scripted curriculum)

- Number Corner (scripted curriculum)
- Online Math Program (required)
- Math lesson (scripted curriculum)
- Math work time (teacher-directed work from curriculum)
- Lunch
- Writing (scripted curriculum)
- Shared reading (scripted curriculum)
- Specials (PE/Art/Music)
- Phonics (scripted curriculum)
- Intervention time
- Read aloud (scripted curriculum)
- Reading mini lesson (scripted curriculum)
- Small groups and independent work time (scripted curriculum)
- Science (scripted curriculum)

As you see, there was little time in Pat's day for anything that wasn't scripted. We shared with him that because *Prepared Classroom* is full of evidence-based teaching practices, it can be used effectively all throughout his day.

The components focusing on relationship, environment, and daily routines are integrated throughout the year, with an emphasis at the beginning of the year when introducing expectations and procedures. Every teacher must introduce routines and expectations at the beginning of the year, and the lessons in these sections of *Prepared Classroom* provide an explicit way to do this.

The practices and lessons in the independent and collaborative learning components teach the expectations and procedures students follow when they work independently or collaboratively. Many of these are taught at the beginning of the year, and once learned and practiced, they become part of the students' muscle memory, freeing up their cognitive load to focus on their learning.

Regardless off curriculum design, every classroom must prioritize cultivating relationships and building a successful learning environment, along with a clear way to communicate expectations. *Prepared Classroom* offers a systematic way to ensure all students (and the teacher) are on the same page.

What about the components of conferring, brief focus lessons, and progress monitoring/accountability? HOW do those fit in with scripted curriculum?

It's important to remember that *Prepared Classroom* is not a curriculum. It doesn't dictate WHAT you should confer about, teach in your lessons, or monitor. Instead, it's a guide on HOW to confer, teach, and monitor progress. Pat will undoubtedly have one-on-one conversations with students about their literacy, math, and science learning, and when he does, this guide will help him start those conversations and keep track of that information.

And, without a doubt, as the classroom teacher Pat will teach lessons during the year. Some will be whole group and others will be small group, with most of these lessons being scripted. The Brief Focus Lesson section of *Prepared Classroom* shares effective ways to make these lessons more impactful. By incorporating brain breaks between shorter lessons, brief hooks in the middle of longer lessons, and teaching students to be active listeners, student engagement increases, leading to improved learning outcomes.

Finally, progress monitoring and accountability are integral parts of teaching and learning. In a scripted program, these elements may or may not be provided. *Prepared Classroom* doesn't change that; instead, it offers lessons to teach students to set goals, self-assess, and understand feedback, making the progress monitoring and accountability within the provided curriculum more effective.

Prepared Classroom isn't just another tool in Pat's teaching toolbox; it's the key to unlocking his potential as an educator. With its focus on evidence-based practices, seamless integration into any curriculum, and systematic approach to building relationships and fostering independent learning, *Prepared Classroom* is more than a guide—it's a game-changer. So, as Pat navigates through his scripted lessons and one-on-one conferences, he can rest assured that *Prepared Classroom* has his back, helping him create a dynamic and engaging learning environment where every student can thrive.

Yay for Pat! He just leveled up his teaching!

Okay, so now what about Lois? Remember Lois who has a flexible schedule and instructional autonomy? Let's take a glimpse into her room and how *Prepared Classroom* can help her.

Lois's Classroom:

Meet Lois. She's been teaching for 25 years and works in a district that embraces an adaptive approach to teaching and learning. While there's a required curriculum with specific grade-level outcomes, Lois has the autonomy to design her own lessons and schedules based on what her students need. Her district provides the flexibility to use a variety of resources, and without a strict pacing guide, each classroom hums with unique activities.

Lois's biggest challenge? Deciding what to teach and when. With so many resources at her fingertips, it can be difficult to determine what will have the greatest impact on her students' learning. Additionally, while she's working with small groups, keeping the rest of the class engaged in effective learning can be tricky.

Like Pat, Lois found a lot to love in *Prepared Classroom*. She was excited about the practices designed to help her students become self-regulated learners. But she had a pressing question: "What is the rest of the class doing when I meet with small groups? And how do I decide what to teach and when?"

Here's a peek at Lois's schedule:

- Morning Work (students choose to read or write)
- Morning Meeting (standards/student need)
- Calendar (standards/student need)

- Online Math Program (required)
- Reading Block (standards/student need)
- Lunch
- Science (standards/student need)
- Specials (PE/Art/Music)
- Math Block (standards/student need)
- Intervention time (standards/student need)
- Read aloud (standards/student need)
- Writing (standards/student need)

Lois's schedule is a world apart from Pat's, but *Prepared Classroom* fits perfectly into her classroom too. Let's break it down:

Just like in Pat's scenario, the components focusing on relationships, environment, and daily routines are essential throughout the year. With the practices and lessons from *Prepared Classroom*, Lois will build strong relationships and establish daily routines right from the start. This allows her to focus on planning her curriculum and beginning-of-year assessments instead of focusing on how to teach routine behaviors.

The *Prepared Classroom* components of independent and collaborative learning provide instruction and practice on what it means to be engaged in both styles of learning. This ensures that when Lois's students are working independently or in groups, they have the skills to be successful.

That leaves us with the components of conferring, brief focus lessons, and progress monitoring/accountability. Remember, *Prepared Classroom* isn't a curriculum—it's a guide on how to confer, teach, and monitor progress. It's not the WHAT, but the HOW. For Lois, this means that once her students are practicing engaged behaviors in independent and collaborative learning, she can seamlessly start using the conferring practices to learn more about each student.

The practice of Brief Focus Lessons will be a game changer for Lois, offering a consistent structure for creating effective lessons. She will use the progress monitoring and accountability practices along with conferring to set goals and plan strategically. The supporting lessons in Section 2 will help her students maximize the instruction Lois provides. By learning in short, focused chunks with brain breaks or hooks, understanding engagement, and knowing how to self-assess and interpret feedback, the students in Lois's classroom will become active agents in their own learning.

Prepared Classroom provides Lois with the perfect framework to tackle her unique challenges and leverage her flexibility. With its evidence-based practices, Lois can seamlessly integrate relationship building, the three spaces of environment, and daily routines right from the start, freeing her to focus on curriculum planning and assessments. The independent and collaborative learning components give her students the skills they need to succeed, whether working alone or in groups. And while *Prepared Classroom* doesn't dictate what to teach, it offers invaluable guidance on how to confer, teach brief focus lessons, and monitor progress. This ensures Lois can effectively plan her lessons and keep her students engaged in a flexible and resource-rich environment. With these tools, Lois can transform her classroom into a dynamic and supportive learning space where every student thrives.

Three cheers for Lois! She just raised the bar of her teaching practice!

So what about you? Are you a Pat or a Lois? Or does your teaching scenario fall somewhere in between? Don't worry—your plan for *Prepared Classroom* doesn't change much! The key is to understand the purpose behind each practice and why it's effective. Then, you can start integrating these practices and lessons into your daily teaching routine.

At the start of the school year, you'll spend a significant amount of time with this book. Think of it as your trusty go-to resource that you revisit each year before school starts, ensuring your plans are ready for day one and beyond. By frontloading expectations and giving students ample time to practice engagement behaviors in the early days and weeks, you'll see a noticeable increase in on-task behaviors and a decrease in off-task behaviors. And you too will level up your teaching!

Three cheers for you!

Okay, it's time to take a deep breath and gather your enthusiasm. Then, with renewed determination, say those familiar words once more: "Ready…set…go!" Your students are waiting, and your journey as an extraordinary teacher continues.

ACKNOWLEDGEMENTS

A huge shoutout to all the amazing teachers who have thrown open their classroom doors, shared their stories, and collaborated with us over the years. Your openness, dedication, and camaraderie have been truly inspiring. You've shown us what it means to be true colleagues and friends in this wonderful world of education. Here's to the countless laughs, brainstorming sessions, and shared cups of coffee that have made this journey unforgettable. Thank you for being the heart and soul of this book!

To the remarkable early career teachers who've offered us feedback: Samantha, Reilly, Niki, Megan, Olivia, Chloe, Nick, and Taryn. Your conversations, suggestions, and insights have been invaluable. Thank you for your fresh perspectives and enthusiasm. We're so grateful for your contributions and can't wait to see the incredible impact you'll have in your classrooms!

A sincere thank you to all the educators, authors, and researchers whose work has inspired and influenced us, shaping the very essence of this book. With a special nod to Regie Routman for the encouragement and support from beginning to end. These contributions have not only enriched our understanding but also played a pivotal role in shaping the final product you hold in your hands. We stand on the shoulders of giants, and we are immensely grateful for your dedication to education and the insights you have shared with the world.

To the incredible Team at Teach Daily! This book is a true collaboration of our amazing crew—Doug, Dusty, Madeline, Emily, and Kelli. From the brilliant artwork and design, to the thoughtful content choices, to connecting with teachers around the globe and getting this book into their hands, we've got the best team ever. We are beyond grateful for each of you and all that you do. Thank you for making this journey so fun and fulfilling!

A big high-five to our amazing editor, Terry Thompson, and the fantastic team at Routledge! Your keen eyes, brilliant insights, and unwavering support have been invaluable. Thank you for believing in our vision and helping us turn it into reality. We couldn't have done it without you, and we're so grateful for your partnership.

A heartfelt thank you to our supportive families—you've given us the time we needed, listened to countless versions of our work, helped us choose the perfect words, and provided the purpose behind our passion. To Gail's family: Doug, Jolie, Brad, Emily, Madeline, Chris, Hadley, Hollis, Reggie, Quincy, and Marlee. To Ali's family: Carl, Samantha, Nathan, Dusty, and The Sunshines. Thank you all for being our biggest cheerleaders and for your endless support and love. This book wouldn't be the same without you!

And, of course, we are so very thankful for each other and the dynamic duo we've become. From the crack-of-dawn brainstorming sessions to the burning-the-midnight-oil edits, it's been a journey of laughs, challenges, and triumphs. Together, we've woven our passions, creativity, and expertise into every page, crafting something we're truly proud of. Here's to many more adventures and collaborations ahead!

REFERENCES

Allen, P. 2009. *Conferring: The Keystone of Reader's Workshop*. 1st ed. New York: Routledge.

Anderson, C. 2000. *How's It Going?: A Practical Guide to Conferring with Student Writers*. Portsmouth, NH: Heinemann.

Argyropulo-Palmer, A. 2022, May 9. "Exploring the Evidence Base: The Role of Routines in Creating an Effective Learning Environment." *Chartered College of Teaching*. https://my.chartered.college.

Baddeley, A. 2012. "Working Memory: Theories, Models, and Controversies." *Annual Review of Psychology* 63: 1–29.

Barron, L., and P. Kinney. 2021. *We Belong: 50 Strategies to Create Community and Revolutionize Classroom Management*. Alexandria, VA: Association for Supervision and Curriculum Development (ASCD).

Berger, R. 2003. *An Ethic of Excellence: Building a Culture of Craftsmanship with Students*. Portsmouth, NH: Heinemann.

Berger, R., D. Strasser, and L. Woodfin. 2021. *Management in the Active Classroom*. New York, NY: EL Education.

Berry, A., and J. Hattie. 2023. *Reimagining Student Engagement: From Disrupting to Driving*. Thousand Oaks, CA: Corwin Press.

Boushey, G., and A. Behne. 2020. *The Cafe Book: Engaging All Students in Daily Literacy Assessment and Instruction*. (2nd ed.). Portland, ME. Stenhouse Publishers.

Boushey, G., and J. Moser. 2014. *The Daily 5: Fostering Literacy Independence in the Elementary Grades*. (2nd ed.). Portland, ME. Stenhouse Publishers.

Brown, L., M. Jones, and R. Smith. 2023. "The Impact of Classroom Physical Space on Learning Environment: A Review of Current Research. *Journal of Educational Psychology* 47(2): 123–140.

Brulles, D., and K. L. Brown. 2018. *A Teacher's Guide to Flexible Grouping and Collaborative Learning: Form, Manage, Assess, and Differentiate in Groups*. Minneapolis, MN: Free Spirit Publishing.

Burkins, L., and F. Sibberson. 2023. *Classroom Design for Student Agency*. Champaign, IL: National Council of Teachers of English.

Cambourne, B. 2020. *Made For Learning: How the Conditions of Learning Guide Teaching Decisions*. Katonah, NY: Richard C. Owen Publishers.

Carrington, J. 2019. *Kids These Days: A Game Plan for (Re)connecting with Those We Teach, Lead, & Love*. Altona, Manitoba: FriesenPress.

Cassetta, G., and B. Sawyer. 2015. *Classroom Management Matters: The Social-Emotional Learning Approach Children Deserve*. Portsmouth, NH: Heinemann.

Cornelius-White, J. 2007. "Learner-Centered Teacher-Student Relationships are Effective: A Meta-Analysis." *Review of Educational Research* 77(1): 113–143.

Corwin Press, Inc. Visible Learning Meta^X. June, 2023. https://www.visiblelearningmetax.com.

Cowan, N. 2001. "The Magical Number 4 in Short-Term Memory: A Reconsideration of Mental Storage Capacity." *Behavioral and Brain Sciences* 24(1): 87–114.

Crouch, D., and B. Cambourne. 2020. *Made For Learning: How the Conditions of Learning Guide Teaching Decisions*. Katonah, NY: Richard C. Owen Publishers.

Davis, M., and A. Chan. 2015. "How the Digital Age is Shaping the Way We Learn." *Journal of Educational Technology* 12(3): 24–30.

Denton, P., and R. Kriete. 2000. *The First Six Weeks of School*. Turner Falls, MA: Center for Responsive Schools.

Dueck, M. 2021. *Giving Students a Say—Smarter Assessment Practices to Empower and Engage*. Alexandria, VA: Association for Supervision and Curriculum Development (ASCD).

Duffy, G. G. 2014. *Explaining Reading: A Resource for explicit Teaching of the Common Core Standards*. New York, NY: Guilford Publications.

Duncan, S., J. Martin, and S. Haughey. 2018. *Through a Child's Eyes: How Classroom Design Inspires Learning and Wonder*. Lewisville, NC: Gryphon House.

Durlak, J. A., R. P. Weissberg, A. B. Dymnicki, R. D. Taylor, and K. B. Schellinger. 2010. "The Impact of Enhancing Students' Social and Emotional Learning: A Meta-Analysis of School-Based Universal Interventions." *Child Development* 82(1): 405–432.

Ebbinghaus, H. 1964. *Memory: A Contribution to Experimental Psychology*. Garden City, NY: Dover.

Ed Trust and MDRC. 2023, August 9. The Importance of Strong Relationships Between Teachers & Students—A Strategy to Solve Unfinished Learning. The Education Trust. https://edtrust.org/resource/the-importance-of-strong-relationships/.

Eisenberg, N., T. L. Spinrad, and A. Knafo-Noam. 2015. "Prosocial development." *Handbook of Child Psychology and Developmental Science* 3(1): 1–48.

Evanshen, P., and J. Faulk. 2019. *Room to Learn: Elementary Classrooms Designed for Interactive Explorations*. Lewisville, NC: Gryphon House.

Fisher, D., and N. Frey. 2021. *Better Learning through Structured Teaching: A Framework for the Gradual Release of Responsibility*. 3rd ed. Alexandria, VA: Association for Supervision and Curriculum Development (ASCD).

Fisher, D., N. Frey, S. Ortega, and J. Hattie. (2020). *Teaching Students to Drive Their Learning: A Playbook on Engagement and Self-Regulation, K-12*. Bloomington, IN: Solution Tree.

Forbes, H. T. 2020. *Classroom 180: A Framework for Creating, Sustaining, and Assessing the Trauma-Informed Classroom*. Boulder, CO: Beyond Consequences Institute, LLC.

Fuchs, D., and L. S. Fuchs. 2006. "Introduction to response to intervention: What, why, and how valid is it?" *Reading Research Quarterly* 41(1): 93–99.

Grinder, M. 2007. *Envoy: Your Personal Guide to Classroom Management*. Battle Ground, WA: Michael Grinder & Associates.

Hafen, C. A., B. K. Hamre, and R. C. Pianta. 2012. "Building Science, Policy, and Practice Partnerships to Support Social and Emotional Development in PreK-12 Classrooms." *Infants & Young Children* 25(1): 35–59.

Hamilton, D. J., Lasky, B. A., & Roberts, S. K. (2009). Instructional strategies to facilitate the inclusion of students with disabilities in general education classrooms. *Education and Training in Developmental Disabilities*, 44(4), 516-530.

Hattie, J. 2009. *Visible Learning: A Synthesis of Over 800 Meta-Analyses Relating to Achievement*. New York: Routledge.

Hattie, J. (2023). *Visible Learning: The Sequel: A Synthesis of Over 2,100 Meta-Analyses Relating to Achievement* (1st ed.). New York: Routledge.

Henderson, M., and M. Corry. 2021. "The Role of Conferring in Developing Metacognitive Skills in Students." *Journal of Educational Research and Practice* 11(3): 45–61.

Hess, K. 2018. *A Local Assessment Toolkit to Promote Deeper Learning: Transforming Research into Practice*. Thousand Oaks, CA: Corwin Press.

Hmelo-Silver, C. E. 2004. "Problem-Based Learning: What and How Do Students Learn?" *Educational Psychology Review* 16(3): 235–266. https://doi.org/10.1023/B:EDPR.0000034022.16470.f3.

Howard, M. 2012. *Good to Great Teaching: Focusing on the Literacy Work that Matters*. Portsmouth, NH: Heinemann.

James-Ward, C., D. Fisher, N. Frey, and D. Lapp. 2016. *Using Data to Focus Instructional Improvement*. Alexandria, VA: Association for Supervision and Curriculum Development (ASCD).

Jensen, E. 2008. *Brain-Based Learning: The New Paradigm of Teaching*. Thousand Oaks, CA: Corwin Press.

Johnson, D., and R. Johnson. 1999. "Making Cooperative Learning Work." *Theory into Practice* 38: 67–73. DOI: 10.1080/00405849909543834.

Johnson, D. W., and R. T. Johnson. 2009. "An Educational Psychology Success Story: Social Interdependence Theory and Cooperative Learning." *Educational Researcher* 38(5): 365–379.

Johnson, R., H. Smith, and L. Williams. 2022. "The Impact of Visual Space in Classroom Environments on Learning Outcomes." *Journal of Educational Psychology* 49(3): 325–342.

Johnston, P. (2024). *Choice Words: How Our Language Affects Children's Learning*. New York: Routledge.

Johnston, V. 2016. "Successful Read-Alouds in Today's Classroom." *Kappa Delta Pi Record* 52(1): 39–42. https://doi.org/10.1080/00228958.2016.1123051.

Jones, S. M., and S. M. Bouffard. 2012. "Social and Emotional Learning in Schools: From Programs to Strategies." *Social Policy Report*, 26(4), 1–31.

Jones, V., and L. Jones. 2017. *Comprehensive Classroom Management: Creating Communities of Support and Solving Problems*. 11th ed. Upper Saddle River, New Jersey: Pearson.

Kagan, S. 2009. *Kagan Cooperative Learning*. San Clemente, CA: Kagan Publishing.

Kanold, T. D. 2017. *Heart!: Fully Forming Your Professional Life as a Teacher and Leader*. Bloomington, IN: Solution Tree.

Kelemanik, G., Lucenta, A., & Janssen Creighton, S. (2016). *Routines for reasoning: Fostering the mathematical practices in all students*. Heinemann.

Kirschner, P. A., J. Sweller, and R. E. Clark. 2006. "Why Minimal Guidance during Instruction Does Not Work: An Analysis of the Failure of Constructivist, Discovery, Problem-Based, Experiential, and Inquiry-Based Teaching." *Educational Psychologist* 41(2): 75–86.

Kriete, R., and C. Davis. 2014. *The Morning Meeting Book*. 3rd ed. Turners Falls, MA: Center for Responsive Schools.

Lemov, D. 2015. *Teach Like a Champion 2.0: 62 Techniques That Put Students on the Path to College*. Hoboken, NJ: Jossey-Bass.

Lerner, R. M., Lerner, J. V., Bowers, E. P., & Geldhof, G. J. (2019). Positive youth development, thriving, and civic engagement: A relational developmental systems model. In J. E. Lansford & P. Banati (Eds.), *Handbook of adolescent development research and its impact on global policy* (pp. 24–52). Oxford University Press. https://doi.org/10.1093/oxfordhb/9780190847128.013.2

Lester L., and D. Cross. 2015. "The Relationship between School Climate and Mental and Emotional Wellbeing over the Transition from Primary to Secondary School." *Psychology of Well-being* 5(1): 9. DOI: 10.1186/s13612-015-0037-8.

Li, X., C. Bergin, and A. A. Olsen. 2022. "Positive Teacher-Student Relationships May Lead to Better Teaching." *Learning and Instruction* 80: 101581.

Mayer, R. E., and R. Moreno. 2003. "Nine Ways to Reduce Cognitive Load in Multimedia Learning." *Educational Psychologist* 38(1): 43–52. https://doi.org/10.1207/S15326985EP3801_6.

Medina, J. 2014. *Brain Rules: 12 Principles for Surviving and Thriving at Work, Home, and School*. Seattle, WA: Pear Press.

Moss, C. M., and S. M. Brookhart. 2019. *Advancing Formative Assessment in Every Classroom: A Guide for Instructional Leaders*. Alexandria, VA: Association for Supervision and Curriculum Development (ASCD).

Muhammad, G. 2020. *Cultivating Genius: An Equity Framework for Culturally and Historically Responsive Literacy*. New York, NY: Scholastic.

Nordengren, C. 2022. *Step into Student Goal Setting: A Path to Growth, Motivation, and Agency*. Thousand Oaks, CA: SAGE Publications.

Norris, J. 2006. *Classroom Routines That Really Work for Pre-K and Kindergarten*. New York, NY: Scholastic Inc.

O'Donnell Wicklund Pigozzi and Peterson Architects Inc, VS Furniture, and Bruce Mau Design. 2010. *The Third Teacher: 79 Ways You Can Use Design to Transform Teaching & Learning*. 1st ed. New York, NY: Abrams.

Olson, K. 2014. *The Invisible Classroom: Relationships, Neuroscience & Mindfulness in School*. New York, NY: W. W. Norton & Company.

Parker, P. 2018. *The Art of Gathering: How We Meet and Why It Matters*. New York, NY: Riverhead Books.

Perry, T., S. Zemelman, and K. Smith. 2022. *Teaching for Racial Equity: Becoming Interculturally Competent in the Classroom*. Portland, ME: Stenhouse Publishers.

Pianta, R. C., B. K. Hamre, and J. P. Allen. 2012. "Teacher-Student Relationships and Engagement: Conceptualizing, Measuring, and Improving the Capacity of Classroom Interactions." In *Handbook of Research on Student Engagement*, edited by S. L. Christenson, A. L. Reschly, and C. Wylie, 365–386. Berlin, Germany: Springer.

Rimm-Kaufman, S. E., and C. S. Hulleman. 2015. "Social and Emotional Learning in elementary School Settings: Identifying Mechanisms That Matter." *Handbook of Social and Emotional Learning: Research and Practice* 3(1): 292–307.

Rimm-Kaufman, S. E., and R. C. Pianta. 2000. "An Ecological Perspective on the Transition to Kindergarten: A Theoretical Framework to Guide Empirical Research." *Journal of Applied Developmental Psychology* 21(5): 491–511.

Robinson, K. A., and E. A. Patall. 2013. "The Role of Autonomy in Promoting Academic Motivation and Performance." *Educational Psychology Review* 25(4): 497–528.

Roehlkepartain, E. C., K. Pekel, A. K. Syvertsen, J. Sethi, T. K. Sullivan, and P. C. Scales. 2017. *Relationships First: Creating Connections that Help Young People Thrive*. Minneapolis, MN: Search Institute.

Reeves, D. B. 2004. *Accountability in Action: A Blueprint for Learning Organizations*. Bloomington, IN: Solution Tree.

Routman, R. 2024. *The Heart-Centered Teacher.* New York, NY: Routledge

Salmons, J. 2019. *Learning to Collaborate, Collaborating to Learn: Engaging Students in the Classroom and Online*. 1st ed. Sterling, Virginia: Stylus Publishing, LLC.

Schimmer, T. 2017. *Redefining Student Accountability: A Proactive Approach to Teaching Behavior Outside the Gradebook (Your Guide to Improving Student Learning by Teaching and Nurturing Positive Student Behavior)*. Alexandria, VA: Association for Supervision and Curriculum Development (ASCD).

Schmidt, P. R., and W. Ma. 2006. *50 Literacy Strategies for Culturally Responsive Teaching, K-8*. Thousand Oaks, CA: Corwin Press.

Schunk, D. H., and B. J. Zimmerman. 2007. "Influencing Children's Self-Efficacy and Self-Regulation of Reading and Writing through Modeling." *Reading and Writing Quarterly* 23: 7–25.

Serravallo, J. 2015. *The Reading Strategies Book: Your Everything Guide to Developing Skilled Readers*. Portsmouth, NH: Heinemann.

Slavin, R. E. 2014. "Cooperative Learning and Academic Achievement: Why Does Groupwork Work?" *Anales de Psicología* 30(3): 785–791.

Smith, J., A. Johnson, and K. Thompson. 2023. "The Impact of Classroom Environment on Teaching and Learning: A Comprehensive Review." *Journal of Educational Psychology* 45(3): 237–256.

Sousa, D. A. (2011). *How the brain learns* (4th ed.). Corwin Press.

Smith, T., et al. 2019. "Teacher Stress and its Influence on Student Wellbeing: A Longitudinal Study." *Educational Psychology* 45(2): 241–256.

Spencer, J., and A. J. Juliani. 2017. *Empower: What Happens When Students Own Their Learning*. San Diego, CA: Dave Burgess Consulting, Inc.

Stanton, J. D., A. J. Sebesta, and J. Dunlosky. 2021. "Fostering Metacognition to Support Student Learning and Performance." *CBE Life Sciences Education* 20(2): fe3. DOI: 10.1187/cbe.20-12-0289.

Stecker, P. M., E. S. Lembke, and A. Foegen. 2008. "Using progress-monitoring data to improve instructional decision making." *Preventing School Failure: Alternative Education for Children and Youth*, 52: 48–58.

Sullo, B. 2009. *The Motivated Student: Unlocking the Enthusiasm for Learning*. Alexandria, VA: Association for Supervision and Curriculum Development (ASCD).

Sweller, J. 1988. "Cognitive Load during Problem Solving: Effects on Learning." *Cognitive Science* 12(2): 257–285. https://doi.org/10.1207/s15516709cog1202_4.

van den Berg, Y. H. M., E. Segers, and A. H. N. Cillessen. 2016. "Considerations for classroom seating arrangements and the role of teacher characteristics and beliefs." *Social Psychology of Education* 19(4): 749–772.

Vansteenkiste, M., R. M. Ryan, and B. Soenens. 2020. "Basic Psychological Need Theory: Advancements, Critical Themes, and Future Directions." *Motivation and Emotion* 44: 1–31. https://doi.org/10.1007/s11031-019-09818-1.

Vygotsky, L. S. 1978. *Mind in Society: The Development of Higher Psychological Processes*. Cambridge, MA: Harvard University Press.

Wang, M. C., G. D. Haertel, and H. J. Walberg. 1990. "What Influences Learning? A Content Analysis of Review Literature." *The Journal of Educational Research* 84(1): 30–43.

Wayman, J. C., V. Cho, J. B. Jimerson, and D. D. Spikes. 2012. "District-Wide Effects on Data Use in the Classroom." *Education Policy Analysis Archives* 20: 25. DOI: 10.14507/epaa.v20n25.2012.

Whitaker, T. 2020. *What Great Teachers Do Differently: Nineteen Things that Matter Most*. Boca Raton, FL: CRC Press.

Wiliam, D. 2017. *Embedded Formative Assessment (Strategies for Classroom Formative Assessment That Drives Student Engagement and Learning) (New Art and Science of Teaching)*. 2nd ed. Bloomington, IN: Solution Tree.

Wiliam, D., D. Fisher, and N. Frey. 2024. *Student Assessment: Better Evidence, Better Decisions, Better Learning*. Thousand Oaks, CA: Corwin Press.

Williams, K. 2022. *Ruthless Equity: Disrupt the Status Quo and Ensure Learning for All Students*. Bloomington, IN: Solution Tree.

Willis, J. 2006. *Research-Based Strategies to Ignite Student Learning: Insights from a Neurologist and Classroom Teacher*. Alexandria, VA: Association for Supervision and Curriculum Development (ASCD).

Wong, H. K., and R. T. Wong. 2009. *The First Days of School: How to Be an Effective Teacher*. Mountain View, California: Harry K. Wong Publications.

Zimmerman, B. J., and A. Kitsantas. 2014. "Comparing Students' Self-Discipline and Self-Regulation Measures and Their Prediction of Academic Achievement." *Contemporary Educational Psychology* 39(2): 145–155.

Zimmerman, B. J., and A. R. Moylan. 2009. "Self-Regulation: Where Metacognition and Motivation Intersect. In *Handbook of Metacognition in Education*, edited by D. J. Hacker, J. Dunlosky, and A. C. Graesser, 299–315. New York: Routledge.

Zwiers, J., and M. Crawford. 2020. *Culturally Responsive Teaching: A Guide for Educators*. New York, NY: Teachers College Press.

INDEX

academic settings 65
academic success 7, 31, 41–42, 54, 72, 79, 105, 233
acceptance, and positive relationships 8
accountability, and collaborative learning 72
active listening 235–236
active listening skills 73, 235
Allen, J. P. 79
Alma and How She Got Her Name (Martinez-Neal) 119
Always Anjali (Sheth) 119
Anderson, C. 79
anxiety 30, 32, 41
assessment: emotional 34; formative 80, 106, 108, 135; physical 33; visual 33
authentic application 32, 72–74
autonomy 32, 34, 53, 54, 72, 73
autonomy-supportive: strategies 53–54; teaching practices 53

Baddeley, A. 95
Berger, R. 79
body language 8, 12, 32
book review 59
book shopping 187–188
The Boy Who Tried to Shrink His Name (Parappukkaran) 119
brain: cognitive processing capabilities 96; -compatible teaching practices 96; natural attention span 96
brain break review 233
brain breaks 171–173, 233
brain research 96
Brain Rules: 12 Principles for Surviving and Thriving at Work, Home, and School (Medina) 98
brief and effective lessons 93–102, 231–237; active listening 235–236; brain break review 233; brain break *vs.* hook 98; brief focus lessons 102; four stages of 99; "hook" brain break 234; lesson length 98; one to two learning targets 98; planning template 237; prepare 99; setting (whole group/small group/individual) 99–101; support 99; teach 99; understand 99
brief focus lessons 102
Brookhart, S. M. 106

CAFE Menu 164
Calvin (Ford) 119
Campbell, Nicola I. 119
caregivers, communicate with 108
Chan, A. 96
choice 32, 72; collaborative learning 72
classroom library 38
classroom management 41, 44
classroom read-aloud sessions 123
classroom tour 160, 161
cognitive load theory 95, 101
cognitive processing capabilities 96
cognitive psychology 95
cognitive toolkit 66
collaborative learning 63–76, 211–223; accountability 72; authentic application 73–74; check for understanding 218; choice 72; choosing a partner 213–214; collaborative story writing 68–70; intrinsic motivation 73; jigsaw activity 67; planning template 223; student-directed work 72; take turns 217; thinking about the purpose 219–220; think-pair-share 68; voice level 215–216; what to do when finished 221–222
collaborative story writing 68–70
comfort 8, 27, 29, 30–31
communication 13, 27, 32, 65, 73, 123, 125, 132; with caregivers 108; respectful 145–149
community 7–8, 12, 65, 121, 123, 125, 127, 129, 145, 191
conference notes 23
conferences 13, 72, 79, 84–85, 107
conferring 77–91, 225–230; conferring notebook 82–83; engagement conference 84–85, 227–228; with feedback 72; Informative Quick Checks 85–87, 229; learning goals 84; performance goals 84; planning template 230; tangible learning aids 84
conferring form 20
conferring notebook 82–83
conferring notes 88
conflict resolution 65
consistent reinforcement 215
content, and morning message 130
Corry, M. 80

263

Cowan, N. 95
Crawford, M. 80
critical thinking skills 30, 53, 66, 189, 201, 219
current events, and morning message 130

daily routines 39–49, 167–190; book shopping 187–188; brain breaks 171–173; daily routine of lining up 176–177; ending the day 181–183; getting explicit 45; making learning visible 45; morning routines 174–175; planning template 190; quiet signal 169–170; routines to teach 44; sharing 189; state in positive, not negative 45; teaching and learning independence 45–49; transitions 184–186; walk in the hall 178–180
data-driven decision making 105
data-driven insights 106
Davis, M. 96
dependability 8; positive relationships 8
Dueck, M. 106
Durlak, J. A. 41

Ebbinghaus, H. 96
educational neuroscience 95
effective teaching and learning 105, 107
emotional assessment 34
emotional space 27–28, 31–33
encouraging words 73
engagement 199–200, 203
engagement conference 84–85, 227–228
environment 25–49, 143–165; CAFE Menu 164; classroom library, building 38; classroom tour 161; emotional assessment 34; emotional space 31–33; flexible seating 155; gathering area 156–158; physical assessment 33; physical space 29–31; planning template 165; respectful communication 145–149; S.P.A.C.E. 152–154; stress management 150–151; stress reduction 36; visual assessment 33; visual space 31; Word Collector 159–160
exit slips 135–137

facial expressions 32
feedback 73, 79, 105, 106; progress monitoring and accountability 108, 248–249; understanding 248–249
Fisher, D. 105
flexible seating 30–31, 155; arrangements 27; defined 155; options 28
"flip a card" behavior system 42
Foegen, A. 105
Ford, J. R. 119
Ford, Vanessa 119
forgetting curve 96
formative assessment 80, 106, 108, 135
Frey, N. 105
Fuchs, D. 105
Fuchs, L. S. 105

gathering area 44, 132, 156–158
gestures 32

goal setting 241–243
green chair 28
group conferring notes 89

Haertel, G. D. 42
Hamre, B. K. 79
Hattie, John 3, 14, 95
Henderson, M. 80
Hmelo-Silver, C. E. 54
honesty 8; positive relationships 8
"hook" brain break 234

incorporate visual materials 74
independent learning 51–61, 71–75, 191–209; 10 steps to 201–203; accountability 72; authentic application 73–74; choice 72; engagement 199–200; independent, meaning of 197; intrinsic motivation 73; I PICK strategy 198; peer book review 55; planning template 209; reading logs 56–58; reading materials 195–196; reading response 55, 61; student-directed work 72; underline and move on 204–205; ways to engage with text 193–194; writing about 208; writing notebook 206–207
individualized attention 73
Informative Quick-Checks 13, 72, 85–87, 229
inquiry-based tasks 74
interactive activities 96
interactive elements: morning message 130
interpersonal relationships 66
intrinsic motivation 53, 66, 72–73; encouraging words 73; feedback 73; goals/purpose 73; individualized attention 73
I PICK Book Talks 138–139
I PICK strategy 198
"I Wish My Teacher Knew" activity 140

Jensen, E. 96
jigsaw activity 67
Johnson, D. 66
Johnson, R. 66
Jones, L. 41
Jones, V. 41

kindness 8, 12; positive relationships 8
Kirschner, P. A. 95
Kitsantas, A. 53

leadership 65
learning: collaborative (see collaborative learning); independent (see independent learning); making visible 45; reinforcement in 73; short-term motivation in 73
learning concepts 31
learning experiences 27, 32; collaborative 53; enhancement 41; independent 53; novelty and variety in 96
learning goals 79, 84, 105; vs. performance goals 84
Lembke, E. S. 105

Lerner, R. M. 42
lesson length 98
listening 73; active 235–236
longterm engagement 73

Martinez-Neal, Juana 119
math concepts, and morning message 130
Medina, John 95, 98
metacognitive skills 53, 80
"Me Too"! (fun and interactive game) 127–128
morning message 129–130
morning routines 174–175
Moss, C. M. 106
Moylan, A. R. 54
multimedia presentations 74, 96

The Name Jar (Yangsook Choi) 119
name pronunciation 119–120
natural attention span 96
nonverbal communication 32

off-task behavior 221, 225
organizational habits 41

Parappukkaran, Sandhya 119
Patall, E. A. 41
peer book review 55
peer-to-peer explanation 189
performance goals 84, 108; *vs.* learning goals 84
perspective 8, 30, 34, 54, 65, 66, 106; positive relationships 8
phone & email sign-up 18
physical assessment 33
physical space 29–31
Pianta, R. C. 41, 79
pivots 109
planning template 141, 165, 190, 209, 223, 230, 237, 250
positive affirmations 121–122; morning message 130
positive reinforcement 213, 236
positive relationships: acceptance 8; dependability 8; honesty 8; kindness 8; perspective 8
posture 32, 153
primacy/recency in memory formation supports 96
print-rich environment 161
problem-solving abilities 53, 65
problem-solving activities 74
problem-solving skills 53, 66
problem-solving strategies 54
progress monitoring and accountability 103–111, 239–250; communicate with caregivers 108; feedback 108; formative assessments 108; goal setting 241–243; pivots 108; planning template 250; regularly review data 108; self-assessment skills 244–247; self-efficacy 108; setting clear learning objectives 108; student information 108; tools 72; touchpoints 108–109; understanding feedback 248–249

quiet signal 169–170

read-aloud behaviors 123–124
reading logs 56–58
reading materials 195–196
reading response 55, 61
real-world applications 96
real-world contexts 54
real-world settings 65
reinforcement: consistent 215; in learning 73; positive 213, 236; visual 164
relationships 7–24; be available 12; conferring form 20; confidence 10; conversation 13; invitation to lunch 12; kindness 12; learning their names 10–11; making phone calls 11; meeting students at the door 13; phone & email sign-up 18; school welcome 10; school welcome checklist 17; sending welcome note and/or picture 10; sharing smile 11; showcasing student work 11–12; talk and connect 12
respectful communication 145–149
Rimm-Kaufman, S. E. 41
Robinson, K. A. 41
Roosevelt, Theodore 7
routines to teach 44
Ryan, R. M. 53

schedule considerations, and morning message 130
school welcome checklist 17
Schunk, D. H. 106
seasonal themes, and morning message 130
self-assessment skills 244–247
self-directed learning 54, 84
self-discipline 53
self-efficacy 106, 108
self-evaluation 106
self-improvement 80
self-reflection 79
self-regulated learning 53–54
self-regulation skills 54
self-reliance 201
sentence structure, and morning message 130
sharing 189
Sheth, Sheetal 119
Shin-Chi's Canoe (Campbell) 119
short-term motivation 73
Slavin, R. E. 66
social skills 65
Soenens, B. 53
Sousa, D. A. 95
space: emotional 31–33; physical 29–31; visual 31
S.P.A.C.E. 152–154
speaking 73
Stecker, P. M. 105
stress: levels 32, 41; management 150–151
stress management techniques 150
stress reduction 36
structured approach 41–42

student-directed work 72
students: -centered learning environment 79; -directed work 72, 74; metacognitive skills 80; -teacher relationships 13; unique learning needs and challenges 79
Sweller, J. 95

tangible learning aids 84
teacher-directed work 74
teachers: -directed work 72; -student interactions 80; -student relationships 31, 79
teaching and learning independence 45–49
teaching brief and effective lessons 95
teach read-aloud behaviors 123–124
teamwork 31, 65, 171, 209, 215
think-pair-share 68
Thompkins-Bigelow, Jamilah 119
time management skills 41, 47, 184
transitions 184–186
"True, True, False" game 131
Turn, Listen, and Talk strategy 125–126

Vansteenkiste, M. 53
viewing 72, 73, 74
visual aids 27, 30–31, 45, 84
visual assessment 33

visually representing 72, 73, 74
visual reinforcement 164
visual space 27, 31
vocabulary, and morning message 130
Vygotsky, L. S. 65

Walberg, H. J. 42
walking in the hall 44, 176
wall space 162–163
Wang, M. C. 42
well-defined learning spaces 27
well-organized displays 31
well-stocked classroom library 30
whole-group lessons 227, 235
Willis, J. 96
Word Collector 31, 84, 159–160
"Would You Rather" game 132–134
writing notebook 206–207
writing skills 68, 159, 208

Yangsook Choi 119
Your Name is a Song (Thompkins-Bigelow) 119

Zimmerman, B. J. 53, 54, 106
Zwiers, J. 80